CW01500280

Sex, Drugs, Enlightenment:

Noble Secrets from an
Orthodox Buddhist ex-Monk

By Alex Walking

Walking Publications LLC
Lewes, Delaware

Legal Disclaimer:

Pre-existing psychological and physical conditions may render any experimentation with certain meditation and yoga techniques direly consequential. Under no circumstances whatsoever should any part of this book be construed as an endorsement of activities where the law prohibits them, no matter how a statement is expressed. Due diligence is everyone's personal responsibility. In light of all of the above statements, all liability is disclaimed.

Copyright 2017 by Walking Publications LLC

This book remains the copyrighted property of the publisher, and may not be reproduced, copied and distributed for commercial or non-commercial purposes. Thank you for your support.

ISBN: 978-0-692-88102-6

With the deepest of gratitude I dedicate this book to four persons:

My loving wife and Tantric Shaman

My teacher of Samadhi

My teacher of Vipassana

And my teacher of Red Tantra

The last three have left this world.

The first two of those are named herein.

Their contributions are priceless and beyond measure.

Contents

INTRODUCTION

Namo Tassa Bhagavato Arahato Samma Sam Buddhasa
"Homage to Him, the Worthy One without defilements,
perfectly self-enlightened."

This book will be condemned by many. No vows of secrecy bind me. Exposing as much as I do will bring reproach from different quarters.

The most damning will be those who believe they understand the teaching of the historical figure honoured above in the Pali language, a dialect of which he spoke daily. Now he's usually known by the Sanskrit rendering 'Siddhartha Gautama (the) Buddha', although his friends may have called him 'Sid'. He was big on open hearts and critical thinking. May all dogmas evaporate.

Commonly accepted comic-book-grade fantasies aside, this son of an elected provincial governor on a short minor arm of the Indochinese trade route,[1] Siddattha of the Gotama clan (Pali rendering), is widely regarded as the greatest genius to walk the face of our Earth in recorded times. Immediately before his death, he said, "I've taught the nature and laws of the universe without any idea of inner and outer teachings. I don't have the closed fist of the teacher who holds things back."[2]

Almost all of those who read this will never have personal access to an accomplished meditation teacher. I've written this for them as well as for those that do. You never know who might have only a little dust on their eyes. May it help a lot of people become more balanced, present, and effective – for the good of us all.

---

[1] *The Historical Buddha,* H.W. Schumann, English translation by M.O'C. Walshe, 1989, pp. 5, 6, 17. Motilal Banarsidass Publishers, India, 2004

[2] Digha Nikaya 16, 2.25

I'm going to stick with plain English as much as possible although I don't know what exactly that is nowadays. I intend to bring you to the threshold of your mind, then give you a nudge. From there, you can draw on your other resources to better understand and work with the nature of reality.

Scholars always spell Pali with pronunciation marks (diacritics) developed in a system of Italian phonetics around 150 years ago. These are left out where I've used words in this language. Some words in Pali and Sanskrit are left capitalised, as is traditional.

British grammar and spelling were a conscious choice, but my colloquialisms rule. I chose American punctuation for dialogue because I prefer the way it looks. In the short glossary, there are some words I treat unconventionally.

Of the 129 footnotes, forty-two refer to the Pali canon of Theravada Buddhism and twenty more to the Visuddhimagga, one of its two chief commentaries. I have zero tolerance for "The Buddha said…" or did, or taught, without authentication.

Part autobiography, part textbook, I waste no time in getting a bit technical in places. It then speeds up because the groundwork's in place. Six chapters of fast-paced storytelling start with Chapter 5. My prescription for more satisfying living begins in Chapter 12. Personal history zigzags through all of it.

Every part is designed to be an appetiser for deeper understanding. My aim is for this nutritious buffet to be complete as an introduction to interwoven topics. Just a little knowledge is a dangerous thing…

Integral to fully comprehending the chapters are the last sections of the book called 'Theory and Practice'. They're not just a pile of appendices. These sections all start with what pages they refer from for ease of navigation and cohesive reading.

Advance Warning: Theory and Practice sections C, D, and E contain definite spoilers for Vipassana meditation practitioners. Traditionally, these derail ultimate success, but this book wouldn't be complete as a definitive work without them. In this new paradigm of the Information Age, anything less than full disclosure isn't fair to you. There are warnings where they start. If you read them, consider yourself to be a consenting adult.

Although first in the title, the sex comes after a lot of juicy education. That allows it to be in context. Think of this arrangement as indispensable foreplay for your peak pleasure.

I'm fortunate to have a memory for detail. Although I sometimes paraphrase conversations, I've tried to avoid doing so. I invoke artistic licence in relating them as well-remembered as possible.

'Alex Walking' is a pen name. I deeply value my privacy. To that end, I've omitted many details that would allow me to be traceable.

Suffice it to say my life has been satisfying and unhomogenised. Who I am is inconsequential. The autobiographical part of this book is only to let you know how I attained the knowledge it contains.

I don't care if you even find me to be a sympathetic character. The manuscript had an editor midstream. He flipped that I wanted to finish this introduction with 'May all beings be happy... and please stay out of my face.' Most of his advice was invaluable.

What I do care about is that you find something in this book that helps you in a meaningful way. Here you have a manual woven from noble truths. I don't need to be the loved hero of the story. I hope to empower you in your world to make sense of it all. I want you to manifest your full potential.

In northern Thailand, there's a traditional blessing that I was taught to use as a monk while out gathering alms food in the rural villages if a person wanted one. I'd like to leave you with it as you turn the page:

"May you have happiness more and more. May you have Nibbana, *then* every wish as well."

Chapter 1

Put This in Your Pipe...

"Just by definition, all culture is borrowed."

Bhikkhu Sumedha - a Swiss monk, once a famous 'jet-set' artist, who lived in a cave in the jungled hills of Sri Lanka. Brahmi script over the doorway identified it as a Buddhist site for around 2,000 years.

Her face was only a foot from mine as we lay on her living room rug in each other's arms. We were mildly high on a little pot.

"Watch this," she said.

Two moments later, I was standing ten feet away, adrenal glands squirting and heart pumping. Somehow I'd sprung straight up and back. "Whoa!" I screamed, panting.

In the moment in between, my new lover's face had suddenly and completely morphed into a bizarre beast.

"What did you see?" she asked.

"Your head became twice its size! A completely different creature with these big simian nostrils! Its face had leathery, wrinkled skin so black it was almost blue the way the light in the room reflected off it."

I breathed deeply to calm the pounding in my chest, waiting for the racing to slow. Swallowing hard before continuing, I tried not to sound so freaked.

"Your hair turned into this coarse, tawny-coloured fur with bushy eyebrows the same colour. Your - its - eyes were huge! With big red irises and big black pupils! And it was right here, just staring at me, deadpan!"

"Oh goody!" she said, clapping her hands. "Yamantaka, the yak-headed god. That's what you were supposed to see. I've been doing his mantra daily for three years."

I'd just come face to face with a Tibetan Buddhist tantric deity.

A week and a half later I ran into her ex on the street. He grew the best indoor pot I'd ever smoked. That was no small feat as I was already well versed in the world of cannabis, both international and domestic. I'd enjoyed his at least a dozen times by that point, so my opinion about its quality wasn't based only on an isolated circumstance. My new lover told me it was because he meditated daily with his plants.

We'd met several weeks before when I'd participated in a Tibetan *tsok* ('feast offering', a type of ceremony that includes invocation) in English to another deity, Vajrayogini. Their small group performed this ritual once a month on the traditional day of the moon for such. We smoked some of his herb during a break in the proceedings.

Vajrayogini, the 'Diamond Yogini' (a yogini is a female practitioner of yoga) is also called the 'Red Dakini'. She rules over a semi-wrathful, sexually superior form of finer-frequency beings. These are the *Dakinis* (Sanskrit: 'sky dancers'), a category of *Devas*, ('the shining ones'). 'Uber-sexy Angels' doesn't quite cut it as a translation for *Dakinis*, but it starts to give you the idea. They can also be Hellions in a snit.

Vajrayogini is the archetype or 'embodied sentient primordial force' of this semi-wrathful class. As such, she is potentially quite volatile. Never underestimate her in that. She's not always wrathful, just when she wants to be. Other times, when it suits her, this goddess is the most seductive, irresistible enchantress that you could ever imagine but didn't know enough to.

In Tibetan Tantra, 'The Shining Diamond Who Bestows Sacred Union' is the awakened female sexual access to the matrix of existence. It is she who grants the sexual initiation to the deserving yogi.

I told this quiet and intriguing grower about the shift I'd seen in his ex. He looked both ways before answering to make sure we were alone. Lowering his voice anyway, he responded.

"Last month [his girlfriend] and I went to [a town nearby] for a Yamantaka *tsok*. It was in English as well. By the time it came to the offerings, the guy who was leading it had completely morphed. You'd swear it was Yamantaka pacing back and forth at the front, speaking in the guy's voice." He chuckled, continuing, "It was the most complete case of transmogrification I've ever seen. It was really impressive."

That was over twenty-six years ago. To this day, according to Google, there's nothing written anywhere about shape-shifting being part of Tibetan Buddhism except in a practice they call 'dream yoga'. It's part of their traditionally confidential ceremonies, which are now long published, but is considered to be metaphorical, merely a personal visualisation in meditation. An authentic piece of esoteric knowledge, it's a secret hidden in plain view. Only the initiated can see it for what it is.

At that time, it astounded me that Westerners had absorbed this exotic ancient practice from the Himalayas of becoming the deity to the extent that I could witness the evidence of the mental training in one of them. I'd just arrived in their area. Because of my history, and what was considered to be a sign from the universe by my lover-to-be, I was invited into their small group to share their secret practices.

Usually, in the Tibetan tradition, a person has first to complete a preliminary practice of 100,000 full-length prostrations before being admitted to such a *tsok*. They say this purifies a person's intentions before being initiated into a 'power practice'. A full-length prostration begins in a standing position with palms pressed together in front of the chest in a 'prayer salute'. Then one sinks to the ground or floor, stretching out completely prone, before rising back up into standing, palms again pressed together in salutation.

Forgoing this and being permitted to participate was the perfect complement to my education in Asia. Up to that point, I'd spent half of my adult life over there benefitting from special attention in two extremely important inner sanctums of Theravadin Buddhism.

Confronted with the yak-headed god that night confirmed something for me; I was part of a cultural shift in Western society, the outcome of which no one could predict. I was in that large wave of Westerners who in the 1970s and '80s started exploring India, Southeast Asia, and South America. Some hit the 'Hippie Trail', as it became known early on, filled with curiosity and lofty spiritual aspirations. Others were just looking for a better way to get high or all three combined.

My situation was a little different as my teenage years were unique. At least, they were compared to most everyone I knew. At nineteen, I went to Peru with an introduction merely looking for cocaine business connections. My new housemate in Lima hollowed and filled Samsonite fibreglass suitcases for a living.

I took with me the three-piece suit that I'd bought the year before for a Lebanese Mafia introduction. They needed someone to set up an importation company, walk into a Customs house where a signature was already supposed to be in place, and claim a shipment of 'tractor parts' from Lebanon. The gig fell through due to no fault of mine.

It was all a natural progression of years free of parental supervision. I found my father dead in bed when I was nine. I never knew he was terminally ill. My loving mother died when I was sixteen. Many dinners in between she graced me with stories of what a great man he was in an attempt to provide me with a role model. Both fell to cancers.

My father was diagnosed with Hodgkin's lymphoma when I was ten months old and given two years to live. I remember him as a very busy, successful man who kept large gardens. Whenever I had a question, he'd put everything down, and ask me questions back until I arrived at the answer. I believe this was his way of teaching me how to figure things out for myself as he never knew when he wasn't going to be there.

Suburban story:

When I was thirteen, I was hanging out at a local strip mall one slow Tuesday night, when an older teenage girl approached me. She said there was a youth meeting going on at the church across the road where they were playing guitars, singing, and serving refreshments. I thought she looked kind of cool, so I rode my bike over to check it out.

There weren't just teenagers there but adults as well. Not only was this happy bunch singing and clapping but they were working themselves up into an ecstatic state. Some were babbling away in strings of incomprehensible syllables, then passing out, falling to the floor. The others would rush over and place their hands on them, praying out loud.

Raised in a small, white Anglo-Saxon Protestant church in which my parents were a central couple, I'd never seen anything like it. It was certainly a more interesting study than the strip mall. With my mother's permission, I went back the next week.

As I impartially watched, the emotions in the group start to peak. I felt a light-headed buzzing begin. Suddenly an irrepressible urge, I can only compare to vomiting but without any nausea, burst up through my torso, then out of my mouth as a babble of sounds. As I continued to wretch unknown syllables from my diaphragm, some of the group jumped over and laid their hands on me.

"He's been saved! He's been saved by the blood of the lamb!" they exclaimed.

They were quite excited, but I wasn't. I just couldn't stop dry-heaving these utterances. I listened to their explanation of these being a "gift of the Spirit" called "tongues" and how they were ancient languages. Fascinated, I went to their meetings and attended their Bible studies for about a year examining their beliefs.

Each person with this 'gift' seemed to have a different language that remained constant. Including my own which had unusual glottal drops and pronunciations unknown in English. I identified various recurring prose-like passages.

They were all good-hearted people in this church, but their cosmological explanations didn't hold up under my scrutiny. Eventually, I drifted away. The ability to drop into this 'language' lingered just below the surface until I was seventeen, hitchhiking through my country and camping. At any time, I could bring it to the forefront but always without any of the emotional access I'd witnessed in the others.

Back in my home city, I plunged into wholesaling pot while my girlfriend explored dancing topless, lunchtime at a bar. This new and intense world grabbed my attention, and the ability to shift soundtracks disappeared without me giving it much thought. Now this story takes a pause. Its conclusion occurs in Chapter 5.

Several months after my mother died, I had a waking 'dream' like no other I'd had before. Her face appeared more vividly in hyper-focus than real life allows for. She was smiling and radiantly beautiful.

I gasped, and as I pulled back, I saw glaring white light surrounded her. Suspended behind my mother in that light were a handful of women and men at what I understood to be a respectful distance. All were smiling at me. I knew they were reassuring me not to be afraid.

"Alex," she said in a loving, musical tone, "I know you feel guilty that you didn't visit me more in the hospital all those months I was in there. Don't be. I understand how hard it was for you to see me like that."

It had been an ugly nightmare. The doctors took her off of the chemo when they saw she was too weak to continue, saying that the compassionate thing to do was just to let her go. When she started to recover, they decided she was strong enough to have it again.

On the third round of taking her off of the poison, her recovering, and them putting her back on it, she finally succumbed. Watching this torture repeated for almost a year was hell on me. By the middle of the second round, I could only bear to visit once a week.

My mother continued, "I want you to know I'm happy now. I'm with friends. I'm not in pain anymore. I just wanted to say goodbye. I love you."

With that, she disappeared, and I woke up. By the vividness, I knew it was a real visitation and not just an ordinary dream. I was beyond thrilled; I was electrified. This would be my first experience involving a brilliant white light without a physical source.

My high school years were in that brief window in the mid-seventies when they dared to teach us conceptual grasp through critical thinking. Those were liberal years in the field of government-sanctioned Education, before the great homogenising that followed. My teachers told me over and over I could be anything I wanted to be, do anything I wanted to do. I listened. I realised that I didn't want to be anything they wanted me to be.

At fourteen, I started having regular sex. It turned psychedelic at sixteen. I learned about tequila and 'three-ways' while I was supposed to be at school. By eighteen; I was living with age-appropriate girls. A couple of Femme Fatales have played their roles as well. Some hearts need to be broken open.

By twenty-two, I was bored with living in the fast lane of dealing serious amounts of herb in an urban existence of bodyguard-chauffeurs, stash apartments, restaurants, and night clubs. The year I was eighteen, I sold close to one tonne of imported pot alone, not counting the hashes or oils. I had no misconceptions about being a 'big dealer' though. Big dealers use forklifts.

It was with great relief that never majorly busted I left for Sri Lanka, vowing never to deal again. I went looking for legal business opportunities and to dry out.

Without looking for anything 'spiritual,' my path crossed some very special persons in the world of Theravada Buddhism (pronounced 'terra-VAH-dah'). They changed my direction radically. This led to six years of living in Asia over a spread of seven in the mid-eighties.

From initially scuba diving for months around Sri Lanka, I travelled overland through India up to Nepal to trek in the Himalayas. Later, I enjoyed living in caves and jungle practising meditation. That took me well off of the beaten track in India, Sri Lanka, and Thailand.

At one point, I had the bright idea to go to the Archeological Survey of India in Madras looking for a list of abandoned Jain cave temples. The glory of India is in its past, and they know exactly where everything is. The Jains were dreadlocked, hardcore, naked ascetics whose founder was an older contemporary of the Buddha. They declined in numbers partly because their leaders had a penchant for starving themselves to death, and then persecution from other religious groups. They enjoyed royal patronage in tandem with the Buddhists for over a thousand years.

Some of these caves had carved beds in their rock floors like embedded full-length polished gravestones, complete with oval-shaped polished stone pillows. They were well over 2,000 years old. I was looking for 'power spots' to camp in and meditate. I did find some incredible ones. It was a journey out of time.

Later on, as a fully ordained monk of the orthodox Theravadin forest tradition in northern Thailand, I stayed in an isolated jungle cave near a waterfall from time to time. I visited others, but they quickly became Thai tourist attractions, and too busy for practical use. Due to the destruction of habitat, actual forest monks are now an almost extinct species. Hopefully, that's only almost.

As a monk, I also returned to my favourite ancient cave temple by a beautiful waterfall high in the hills on the remote backside of Sri Lanka. Brahmi script carved in the rock over its door identified it as the abode of a monk renowned in an ancient text for his mastery of supernormal powers. In this fairy tale setting of unspoiled jungle, I came to the painful realisation that my productive time in robes was over.

This period was incomparably formative due to a lot of comprehensive instruction in two types of meditation. One was Samadhi, originally a Pali and Sanskrit word for what I define as 'accessing the matrix of existence'. The other was Vipassana, originally a Pali word, which I define as 'discorporating the matrix of existence', as in, the opposite of incorporating.

I need to get technical about what these two forms of meditation are for the next two pages. This book is not only intended to be entertaining, but I wish to empower you, dear reader, as well. Understanding the difference between these two types of meditation will open the rest of this book for you, perhaps your existence as well.

Being fully empowered as an Individual comes from experiencing the results of each type. Towards that end, I detail both of these forms of meditation in the 'Theory and Practice' section. They're also in the glossary for reference.

Samadhi usually translates into English as 'serenity', 'tranquillity' or 'concentration'. Samadhi is known throughout the world, viewed through the lens of local cultures in their religious teachings. From the blissful, mystic states of Christian nuns to the shamanic practices of the Balinese Hindu group I was initiated into years later, all fall into this category. Science tells us everything is made up of frequencies, like signals on radio waves. Full absorptions in Samadhi are like changing the station on the radio to another frequency.

A person can teach themselves Samadhi to the first level of absorption, if they have to, as it's working with an increase in generated phenomena as the sign of progress. The 'sign born of perception' arises in many ways. For some, it may be light, for others sound, a tactile sensation or all three, plus taste or smell combined.

Vipassana, which means 'inward vision', and is usually translated as 'insight meditation', is unique to Buddhism. Most practitioners just find their lives go more smoothly for practising it.

Relatively few develop it to the point of full absorption which apparently changes a person's makeup and destiny irrevocably. My teacher liked to say the first sign of progress in it is that your friends become nicer people. It's considered impossible to take it to full culmination by yourself as the signs of progress in it are elusively mundane to the uninitiated.

It uses a different set of objects of awareness than Samadhi as the purpose of the practice is different. Instead of developing concentration for absorbing into one finer frequency, to the exclusion of coarser frequencies, a person develops mindfulness which is an inclusive form of focus. Mindfulness sorts through the current impressions that flow through the sense doors moment to moment which create our everyday mundane coarse frequency of many working parts.

In the Vipassana method I learned, one focuses on the abdomen rising and falling with one's breathing or the feet during slow-motion walking. These are impossible to build a frequency with because they're moving. As the mind naturally sifts through the mental and physical impressions that pop up, a person sees their reference points for self-identity. The opportunity arises to lose the ones that aren't profitable.

Completely developed, fully concentrated absorption into that object-in-motion drops a person's awareness in between the cycles per second, so to speak, of the coarse frequency they're already in. Then a person has an experience of no frequencies at all. This is like finding the on/off switch on the radio instead of tuning into a different station.

Those 'cycles per second' of coarse-frequency mundane awareness are composed of compulsively incessant moment-to-moment definitions and momentary subjective reactions to them. These are what shape our perception of reality. Stepping outside of them confers an understanding of what they are.

Letting go of clutching at the personal reference points in those moment-to-moment definitions can be traumatic. We even cling to our sources of suffering as they also give us our identities. Everyone's enlightenments, great and small, are preceded by a great deal of trauma. As a result, Vipassana is called 'the method without tears of joy' or 'straight up the mountain'.

Whom my teachers were in both of these forms of meditation starts in Chapter 4.

For now, suffice it to say that in Asia I had these forms of mental training thrust upon me by adepts in them which blew my world not apart but right open. As they were tailor-made for me in my cultural set, they worked.

By 'they worked', I mean they climaxed with the experience of Nibbana being thrown into my system at a toe-in-the-door level of understanding. An accredited master in the world's oldest orthodox lineage of Buddhist monks did that through the path of Vipassana.

I prefer to use the word 'Nibbana', originally from Pali, as I've just heard too many woolly thinkers pontificate using the Sanskrit-originated word 'Nirvana', all of them ambiguously. The Pali term is always quite specific. I like to define Nibbana as the 'here and now free of definition', or as the 'unformed',[1] as my teacher of Samadhi liked. It's the awareness of no frequencies at all. Understanding Nibbana at four progressively deeper levels confers enlightenment from barely to fully.

That monk taught me how to repeat the experience which is essential for becoming fully enlightened. I was objectively tested for it over and over by his lineage's secret methods to make sure there was no mistake. Because of it, I emerged, apparently, irrevocably a different sort of human being. Theory and Practice C, D, and E explain how this happens and what it means.

Returning to the West, I played it prudently, for once in my life. I opted for a position as a silent observer rather than claiming the ability to lead the charge for some, although that would have

---

[1] *The Life of the Buddha* by Bhikkhu Nanamoli, *asankhata* as synonym for Nibbana, p. 223 (cited under Sources, p. 367, for Udana 8:1-3, 'utterances on Nibbana'), p. 256 (cited under Sources, p. 365, for Samyutta Nikaya 43:1-44, 'epithets of Nibbana'). Buddhist Publication Society, Kandy, Sri Lanka, 2015. Bhikkhu Nanamoli (alternate rendering 'Nyanamoli') is my favourite Pali translator.

been an easy fit with my history. I really just preferred not to be bothered about my strong personality traits by anybody.

That monk mentor had said many times in public lectures, "If you want to save the world, it's best first to save it from yourself." I only wanted to save myself from a lot of scrutiny. My appreciation of life best lived as a covert operation was well ingrained.

As did that small group of Tibetan Buddhists with some morph-savvy practitioners prefer secrecy in that seemingly ordinary setting of front lawns and flush toilets where, much to my surprise, I discovered Alice through the looking glass. Beneath the veil of mixed suburban and rural properties, an exotic Asian ascetics' practice of mental training in cloistered circumstances had taken root among lay people with kids. Some had never left the West.

They were completely unorthodox couples, but they wouldn't attract attention on the street in their neighbourhood. They were the survivors of counterculture gone underground to avoid detection.

They knew well the value of LSD and MDMA (pure 'Ecstasy' or 'Molly'), and other entheogens[2] for their sexual practices. My lover in the group introduced me to MDMA. Ritual always accompanied its use.

I participated in more Vajrayogini *tsoks* with their group for a while. I sought out no Western Buddhists during my five years out of Asia up to that point or after. I see nothing to be gained for me by association, nor wish to be involved in a confrontation. A situation that would be a probability if I opened my mouth, looked more knowledgeable than or contradicted someone with a vested interest in being right.

So besides expecting a more peaceful existence while I continued at a more pedestrian rate to work out my 'nothing personal' glitches, I figured that the universe would marvel me in unimaginable ways if I remained a private figure with my process of

---

[2] 'Substances that generate the divine within'.
http://dictionary.reference.com/browse/entheogen

maturation. I was right about that. I knew my experiences were real, and so, some bigger understanding would naturally grow from the planted sprout. Only time would tell what it would grow into with such different soil to grow in.

Flashback to around 2500 years ago (historians still debate over exact dates): five hundred men, some of whom had been with the Buddha for forty-five years, held a council three months after his death. In this council, they committed to memory in verse form part of his teaching with the stories of how it came to be. Other memorizations followed.

Somehow, they incorporated a mnemonic device to seal their work hermetically. The word 'mnemonic' today means any helpful technique or strategy to remember something. Back then, a mnemonic device was a type of lock to protect a work from tampering.

How a true mnemonic device works is still unknown, but that it does is irrefutable. Each syllable acts as a key for the next. If one syllable is forgotten, the rest of the entire piece can't be accessed until it's corrected. There is no chance to 'hum along to the melody' and pick it up later. Anyone who has learned to chant a work devised like this has had this experience.

This form of true mnemonics is found only in the Pali texts of the Theravadin Buddhists and the oldest Hindu texts in Sanskrit. Pali and Sanskrit were sister languages, having the same Aryan roots.

Mnemonically sealing their work ensured the purity of vast blocks of material. The First Council's intention was to preserve the Buddha's teaching in its original cultural context, then to send it forward in time in such a way that it couldn't be easily corrupted. All that would be necessary for any future generation would be to add their culture and stir at the other end.

Think of dehydrating yoghurt cells for a journey of unknown duration to which milk can be added later. Incubating it with just the exact right conditions again brings it to fresh life, creating living nutrition for physical assimilation. But instead of indefinitely suspending the shelf life of physical food, this was done for mental nutrition.

The Buddha said to learn his teaching in your local tongue.[3] His monks memorised it in theirs. *Pali*, their word for 'text', is our name for that everyday language of the ancient kingdom of Magadha where they lived, now the borderland between India and Nepal. *Theravada* is what nineteenth century C.E. scholars called the lineage from those monks at that First Council. Although a Pali word, its first known use was in 1882.[4] It means 'doctrine of the elders'.

Their repetition of stanzas with little variation, done for the purpose of memorization, renders those texts extremely dull and boring by today's standards. Think of reading computer code, or should I say, "Think computer code."

Now people want juicier titillation, and they want it fast. But it had to be dry as dust with an unbreakable code. That's the only form in which it could travel so far through so many very different cultures so well, waiting for fresh life in each one.

Fast forward to here and now, where many places a pizza can make it to your door quicker than an ambulance. Some experts say it takes around one hundred and fifty years for Buddhism to enculture wherever it goes. We're at that tipping point now in the West. On Wikipedia (since we are talking about our Information Age) anyone can see that there are 535 million Buddhists in the world the last time someone counted.[5] More probably, depending on the extent of syncretism and the reliability of numbers from China.

---

[3] Cullavagga V. 33 1=Vin. II, 139, "Anujanamibhikkhave sakaya niruttiya buddhavacanam pariyapunitum." In 1882, Rhys Davids and Hermann Oldenberg translated this passage as "I allow you, oh brethren, to learn the words of the Buddha each in his own dialect." *The Book of the Discipline* (Vinaya-Pitaka), Vol. 5: Cullavagga (Classic Reprint), I. B. Horner, Forgotten Books, London, UK, 2015
[4] https://www.merriam-webster.com/dictionary/Theravada
[5] *An Introduction to Buddhism: Teachings, History and Practices* (2nd ed.) by Peter Harvey, p. 5. Cambridge University Press, UK, 2013

'Syncretism' is defined as '[T]he combining of different, often contradictory beliefs, while blending practices of various schools of thought' (also from Wikipedia). Conservatively without that, there's at the very least then 8% of us humans living today who feel their beliefs are in line enough with what this celibate ascetic taught that they embrace the label of being his follower. Few even know any details of his life or teaching.

For example, that he wandered just around an area roughly only 370 miles by 185 miles in his eighty-year lifetime[6]. Most Buddhists don't even know when that was. I'm impressed that he did it all barefoot.

In my bathroom, instead of a yellow rubber ducky, for years now I've had a squeaky rubber toy of a smiling, shaven-headed monk in yellow robes, sitting cross-legged, holding a cell phone and a cup of coffee. I consider it a potential cultural artefact if there ever was one. The package suggested buying two, so you could squeeze them to make them chant together.

CDs with names like 'Buddha Bar' and 'Buddha Lounge' abound. Legal cannabis dispensaries sell a "Blue Buddha" strain of bud. Obese caricatures of him adorn Chinese restaurant menus. I recently saw a statuette of such a caricature on all fours the size of a small watermelon. He was covered in hot pink velveteen, laughing his guts out. I had to grin.

Last week I saw a woman wearing a T-shirt with a photo of a stone Buddha statue on it. Superimposed on top was a timeless profundity: 'Let that shit go'. Holy colloquial Buddhism, Batman! Everyone in our cultural soup knows the word 'Buddha', but that's often where the knowledge ends.

As for that ancient, esoteric science of human development called 'Tantra'? Often associated with Buddhism, it developed over the last two millennia. It includes sexual practices for personal

---

[6] *The Historical Buddha* by H.W. Schumann, English translation by M.O'C. Walshe, 1989, p. 231 (reference: 600 kilometres x 300 kilometres). Motilal Banarsidass Publishers, India, 2004

empowerment. Traditionally, its practitioners considered the sexual act to be inviolably sacred. In recent decades, the word is popularly a euphuism for escort services in newspapers and on the internet.

There's been much borrowing of the term throughout these millennia for it to be debased into just meaning sexual fast food in our culture. But it doesn't. Underneath the disposable, lurid wrappings where people rarely peek, ancient wisdom blooms fresh in the hearts of some women and men. Its power and clarity nourish those that use sex and drugs to morph into interpreted archetypal forms. They incorporate such for their personal betterment and thereby society's enrichment. Their donation of love ennobles our world.

Chapter 2

Grabbing the Greased Piglet: Defining Tantra

It was a sunny afternoon in the subtropics with the sound of waves crashing in the background when I saw her for the first time. We were alone. Beautiful and smiling, gracefully floating up a wide, spiral staircase towards me, she was enveloped in light like nothing I'd ever seen before. Reaching me, I saw the resolution of her face and the space surrounding it was more refined than anywhere else in the room.

I kept my observations to myself. Her reputation preceded her through a new lover of mine who said she was her "teacher of polyamorous Tantra." I wanted us to meet.

I wasn't disappointed. In my mid-thirties, I was surprised by the exalted class of this exquisite human accomplishment in her fifties. Thanks to science, health care knowledge, and the wise attention of some women, we now have a new archetype on the planet: The Sexy Crone. But then, it's an old tantric maxim that it's always the crone who initiates the yogi.

In our contemporary case, we both consumed MDMA for the occasion. I'd been introduced to this entheogen for ritual sex years before and was intimately familiar with its benefits as was she. But this was different for me. As different, I imagine, as flying an airplane is to flying a spaceship.

We spent many hours alone together before our relationship turned sexual. At one point during that time, I said to her, "Okay, if you're a *Tantrika*, define Tantra for me. This usually throws off the New Agers."

After thinking about it for a moment, she replied, "Whatever comes up you stay with it and work it through to completion."

I laughed. "You know," I said, "that might be the only definition both the East and the West could agree on."

That said, it's best to put Tantra into context with the big picture beginning with a thumbnail sketch of the term meaty enough for the experts in the hallowed Halls of Academia to chew on and find fault with. This book is intended to hold up under the scrutiny of every Buddhologist, whether if they want it to or not.

For those of you who may or may not 'practice Tantra', here's an acceptable definition of the subject for the next time someone asks you. The twenty-one-word version comes at the end of the chapter.

The oldest definition of the Sanskrit word *Tantra* is 'device for weaving' from 1700 BCE. In India, around 500 CE, it came to mean the spiritual science of working with the forces which underlie reality, both to understand and to modify it. *Tantrikas* relate to the world as a great symbolic interplay of archetypes and anthropomorphized forces of nature thought of as deities.

Archetypes are prototypes or the 'primordial images' (Jung)[1] which make up human awareness. In the first chapter, I defined them as embodied sentient primordial forces. Think of them as the implicate order of the patterning of mental objects behind explicit expressions in reality (Plato, Bohm)[2]. Or even as the noumena behind the phenomena of our world (Kant)[3].

---

[1] "There is a thinking in primordial images, in symbols which are older than the historical man, which are inborn in him from the earliest times, eternally living, outlasting all generations, [that] still make up the groundwork of the human psyche. It is only possible to live the fullest life when we are in harmony with these symbols; wisdom is a return to them." 'The Stages of Life', published in *Modern Man in Search of a Soul*, C.G Jung, p. 115. New York, 1933

[2] *Republic*, Allegory of the Cave, Plato, 514a-520a, first published in 380 BCE; *Wholeness and the Implicate Order*, David Bohm, Routledge, London, 1980. Comparisons of their ideas are common, such as in *An Introduction to the Collected Works of C. G. Jung: Psyche as Spirit*, Clifford Mayes, p.93, Rowman and Littlefield, London, 2016; and *Ordaining Reality in Brief: The Shortcut to Your*

Since the early twentieth century, some biologists speak of 'morphogenic resonance', and 'morphogenetic fields' reinforced by repetition of occurrence but consider their nature to be obscure (Sheldrake)[4]. The *Alaya Vinnana* (Pali), the 'storehouse consciousness', is in Theravadin thought the blueprint for moment-to-moment awareness. None of these ideas or observations are new.

Carl Jung hit the nail on the head when he wrote, "Not for a moment dare we succumb to the illusion that an archetype can be finally explained and disposed of. Even the best attempts at explanation are only more or less successful translations into another metaphorical language."[5]

The body is the supreme temple of transformation where all of these sentient primordial forces converge. Different meditations, yogas, and rituals achieve a deep communion with these forces through a conscious weaving of these strands of our nature to become a superior being. The idea isn't just to worship deities; the goal is to become extensions of them incarnate, by isolating and cultivating these sentient primordial energies into existing form. From there, dogmas become fractal constructions based on cultural adaptations of what those deities are.

The surprising thing is, those ever-transforming practices have a power-bestowing vitality by tapping into something enduringly primal underneath them. Jung also put it well when he wrote, "Every archetype is capable of endless development and differentiation."[6]

Future, Joseph E. Donlan, p. 149. Universal Publishers, Boca Raton, 2009

[3] Noumena are "things in themselves" while phenomena are the things that appear to us. *Critique of Pure Reason*, Immanuel Kant, Cambridge University Press, 1998

[4] *A New Science of Life*, Rupert Sheldrake, Stone Hill Foundation Publishing Pvt. Limited, 1981

[5] *The Archetypes and the Collective Unconscious*, C.G.Jung, translated by R.F.C. Hull, Princeton University Press, 1968

[6] *Psychology and Alchemy*, C.G. Jung, translated by R.F.C. Hull, Princeton University Press, 1968

Before putting Tantra into context, you need to know there are just four ways to get to Nibbana for understanding the big picture:

1) Vipassana preceded by Samadhi.

2) Bare Vipassana. Alternatively, it's called 'Samadhi preceded by Vipassana'. That's because at the moment of penetration there's fully concentrated absorption into the chosen object of awareness which is in motion. Access to supramundane absorption (Nibbana) only requires momentary concentration, *khanika-Samadhi* in Pali.

3) Samadhi coupled with Vipassana.

4) The Zen koan.

Theory and Practice A, 'Grasping the Big Picture', explains the rich dynamics involved in the four processes listed above.

Buddhist Tantra is a term only associated with Tibetan Buddhism, which became established approximately 1200 years after the Buddha's death. It's exotically embroidered. Tibetan adherents pray to multi-armed gods and goddesses, multiple eternal Buddhas and eternal Bodhisattvas (Beings who are destined to become Buddhas, as in, eternally not yet there but will be sometime. Is this their cosmological version of a Zen koan?).

Tibetan Buddhists vow to become a Buddha in a next life and to forgo the experience of Nibbana while working for all others to get there before them. Insistence on this vow is mandatory if one wishes to learn the rest of their teachings. They say it eliminates self-interest.

Tibetan Tantra is Himalayan shamanism with a thin veneer of Buddhist vocabulary. One can't always expect sense when comparing its definitions to the original ones. It's an incredibly powerful form of mental training, as the story that opens Chapter 1 shows, although most practitioners never achieve such an ability.

Tantra is the Tibetan Buddhists' 'magician's path'. The practice of becoming the deity is a stage in a form of Samadhi. They then take this ability to concentrate and change the primary object of awareness to the concept of 'emptiness', *Sunyata* in Sanskrit. *Sunyata* becomes their working object of awareness to access Nibbana. This is Vipassana preceded by Samadhi.

In their *Vajrayana*, (Sanskrit: 'diamond vehicle'), some of their lineages teach that when the yogi is ready, the final step required to push him into the experience entails intercourse with a woman, ideally skilled in the arts of love. They refer to the woman as an 'action seal', or an 'action *mudra*' (Sanskrit), sometimes only using this euphuism as a form of code in their texts. They say it's impossible to attain full enlightenment in one lifetime without one.

Common are the images of their different male deities sitting with female consorts mounting them. Likewise, dancing face to face, each with one bent leg raised while in sexual union.

So, picture this exotic scenario from a bygone age: the Tibetan monk aspirant has been walled into a cave for the traditional period of three years, three months, three weeks, and three days, and fed through a hole in the wall. He's equipped with instruction in different yogas, visualisations of deities, and their cosmological order.

Upon completion of this period, if he lives and is still sane, he's cleaned up, and they sit a woman on top of him in copulation. The monk, whom one can assume has been a virgin up to this point, must not, *absolutely must not*, ejaculate. That'll raise his vibratory rate on all levels! If he can remember his instructions in the heat of the moment, hang on (don't forget, she's supposed to be skilled), make it through her transformation into Vajrayogini still hanging on, and finally see past this to it all being empty, he attains Nibbana. This is Samadhi coupled with Vipassana.

There's a traditional story that before Vajrayogini gives the sexual initiation to the yogi, he must show that he deserves it. He has to prove that if he spills his seed he can suck it all back up. Stories are sometimes just that, but it certainly reinforces their seriousness about not losing it.

Incidentally, this is nowhere near 'the Middle Path' taught by the Buddha between self-mortifying asceticism and sensual indulgence but is the Tibetans' own extreme cultural adaptation. They're different people, whose society evolved under different conditions up in the high Himalayas. We can expect this form of training died out there after Chinese occupation. I hear that time-honoured sexual practices live on in Bhutan.

Active sexuality in a spiritual practice is known as Red Tantra. White Tantra is a celibate practice involving other archetypes as well. Vajrayana practitioners, celibate or not, of both sexes visualise transforming into both female and male deities as a white practice.

I define spiritual as 'refining thoughts and feelings'. If that seems 'soulless' to you, you're right! *For a better understanding of that subject, please read the start of Theory and Practice E, 'Inner Sanctum Secrets of Vipassana'.*

When taken to the extent I'll explain next, embracing sexual intimacy as a spiritually transformative practice qualifies as Samadhi. This validates it as a part of the formulas 'Vipassana preceded by Samadhi' and 'Samadhi coupled with Vipassana' for attaining Nibbana (*as explained in Theory and Practice A*).

Working skillfully with sensual pleasure empowers the inherent divinities in our nature towards the end of achieving liberation from suffering. Energy builds, vibrational rates rise, and focus reaches a higher frequency. As such it's a useful stage, a power practice, the same as the Tibetan practice of becoming the deity.

Of course, my date with an archetypal sexual deity is going to be very different than a Tibetan's. If you put an electric guitar in a modern boy's hands, you don't get Baroque harpsichord music. The 'music of the spheres' is an ever-transforming soundtrack, as is sexual expression respectfully undertaken an ever-transforming act of worship.

From my explorations, I've found female practitioners can have experiences of Samadhi in sexual rituals in two ways. In one, they enter a full absorption in which they're unaware of their immediate surroundings. Instead, they have an experience of communion with that purified archetypal force of the primordial sexual frequency. It can be complete with instructional conversation with the deity, visions, and other auditory perceptions. The subjective length of this participation to the woman far exceeds the time of it objectively in this frequency.

In the moments of the shift (access to the absorption), along with staccato visual images for starters, there's a 'magnetic invitation' coupled with the certainty that the acceptance of it is beneficial. This shift often includes a light that the woman 'becomes' before emerging into the other frequency. Gratitude always accompanies this, along with a sense of donating love to an archetypal pool of such. A receptive state of mind is the forerunner, which is simple in a state of orgasmic bliss.

In another manner of experience, the archetypal sexual force manifests with a radical shift of physical features. Visually, this type of shift is always into a glowing, purified sexually attractive form. There's an old saying that all women are beautiful while they're making love.

 This expression approaches the fact that such divinity is inherent in women. Here, though, we're talking about the difference in shine between a sequin and a laser-lit diamond. Their features become more classically symmetrical which is how we judge physical beauty.

The skin of the woman, and the air immediately surrounding her, take on an ultraviolet-red glow part way between lava-orange and pink. It's easiest to see this energy field in indirect candlelight. It can be seen to a lesser extent in the access state to full absorption, and more entirely in full absorption itself.

This glow is the colour brought to life of Vajrayogini in the paintings (*thankas*) that Tibetan practitioners use as a visualisation aid for her. Great Truths get spoken in clear, ringing musical tones. There is no doubt for the man that he's in the presence of divinity.

Almost always signalling both of these types of Samadhi absorption in the woman are full-body orgasms complete with massive ejaculations of up to a half litre (two cups) or more of clear fluid, often repeatedly. After there's proficiency in shifting, such ejaculations are still usually but not necessarily present.

Female ejaculation is not a myth. It's a signpost of connection, both inner and outer, for a woman. For some, it's natural, while for others, it's a learned response. A woman who has established this connection inside of herself is said to be 'sexually awakened'. That doesn't necessarily mean spiritually attuned, but physically attuned as a prerequisite in this case. Not all orgasmic ejaculations are a sign of accessing concentrative absorption.

The coarsest level of this connection occurs through physical stimulation. Finer levels include directing the attention while sitting untouched in meditation, up to just the hearing of a Great Truth spoken triggering the ejaculation. This level of orgasm reaches the realm of female sexual response as an oracle.

As my teacher of Red Tantra put it, "Women just awaken to the secrets of love, men need to train."

This builds on another old saying that for women, first, sex is considered a relationship, and second, it's an act, while for men, first, it's an act, and second, it's a relationship.

She also said, "It's easier for a sexually unawakened woman to reach such frequencies with a sexually trained man than it is for a sexually awakened woman to get there with an untrained man. Of course, an awakened woman with a trained man is the ideal combination."

One of the most accessible archetypes for a modern man to align with is that of the Noble Magician. It empowers him with the capacity to imagine, decide, and create. The act of identification with being a Noble Magician places a man in the centre of events as the instigator of phenomena and a sovereign entity. It enables him to create his own effective rituals as 'the one who knows' with just basic guidelines. Tantric rituals are simply concerted positive efforts to direct your will upon a part of your environment or reaction to it that you'd like to change.

The Noble Magician is one of the most accessible archetypes because of the high value our culture places on the ethically empowered individual as an ideal. It's in our group consciousness as an admirable quality. It's one of the first initiations (empowering rituals) the Tibetans perform in their system of mental training.

The Balinese, a small and ethically cohesive society, name their children One, Two, Three, and Four. Number five is named One again, etc. Their group consciousness is very different as a result. In group rituals, they fall into particular Samadhi trances according to their cultural interpretation of primal forces as easily as you or I can fall off of a chair.

In the sexual ritual, the male Tantrica can easily reach the point of access in momentary concentration repeatedly when having reached an energetic expansion beyond the physical urge to ejaculate. A corresponding radical shift of features also takes place in this state of access.

His skin and the air immediately surrounding him glow. The glow may be the same colour as the transformed woman. That depends on how much of her energy he knows how to absorb and wishes to run in this fashion.

Or it can be an ultraviolet cerulean[7] blue. This tone of blue corresponds with the traditional colour of male sexual archetypal beings in Tibetan Tantra (*Dakas*) and Hindu Tantra.

The practised man's glow can also be white with rolling undertones of red. This shade of white with red corresponds with the depicted colour of the mystical yogi Padmasambhava, the tantric noble magician who founded Tibetan Buddhism.

Whichever of these three colours his energy field lights up with; the practitioner is aware of the illumination. Staccato images flash on the periphery of his awareness in this state of access. An immense intake of spiritual information happens.

---

[7] 'Sky blue'. In this particular usage, it's the colour of a clear sky on a summer morning immediately before dawn.

In full absorption, the perception of one's surroundings can disappear. The ability to reach full absorption takes more training than just reaching the access state does. The man must abdicate self-interest to get there because, as the instigating magician, he is more responsible for keeping the event on track for both of them. Such is the nature of yin and yang. It's also the nature of appropriately worshipping the goddess.

The major sign of approaching both access and an absorption state for both sexes is the incredible, palpable increase of energy in the body. Just the sensual deliciousness of the expanding sexual energy is enough to work with integrating into their balanced dance. For integration, the couple needs to keep their increasing vibrational rates building in harmony. Focussing on energetically connecting their torsos, and remembering to smile, maintains a calm, blissful centre to the cyclone.

Prudent use of entheogens can facilitate these shifts. In a sexually unawakened woman, they can bypass the ejaculatory response or initiate it. In an awakened woman, they enhance it manyfold. In a man who is still in training, they can assist him in expanding past the urge to ejaculate. The danger in their usage is real, including death. Indiscriminate use is a basis for madness.

Red Tantra, the fully coupled path between human 'becomings', has many benefits in contemporary society – for a price, of course. For those willing to pay the price, Chapter 15 is for you. Remember: you pay, and you pay, and you pay.

For a brief treatment on Hindu Tantra, please read Theory and Practice B, 'Hindu Tantra and Assumptions'.

Defining Tantra in twenty-one words could be stated like this: Mundanely, it is mastering the comings and goings between interactive frequencies. Supramundanely, it is preparatory purification according to the human blueprint.

As such, Tantra is the art of living itself. It's the management of all we say and do to coordinate our passions with our intentions so that they correspond with the desired forces of the universe. It's recognising within ourselves those resonant qualities that are important. Then, it's striking a focussed chord of mindfulness with those desired forces to sort our identifications into alignment so that every part of daily living supports our becoming.

Chapter 3

The New Age Piglets:
Know Your Animal

Tantra now is popularly considered in many Western cultures to be simply a guide for hotter sex. Instruction is readily available. Distortion is guaranteed: this is the comic book section of the spiritual library. I've called it that ever since a guru bragged to me upon introduction about how many hundreds of pounds he could lift with his penis.

Sex at any level gives most participants a more viscerally real experience than society's religions. So, all increase in its quality is taken as a confirmation of progress to the pilgrims on this path. The unscrupulously clever use this to their full advantage in manipulating others for their own ends. Buyer beware.

A soundbite definition, popular with practitioners of New Age Tantra, is 'Tantra is the Path of Intimacy'. 'New Age' is a contemporary marketing term for ancient esoterica repackaged for the modern consumer in the current astrological Age of Aquarius. New Age Tantra's main thrust is the promise of longer sexual staying ability for men with more frequent powerful orgasms for women. It's also birthed therapeutic gynaecology into our world. Okay, that all makes for an exciting start!

If the spiritual part of being a couple – the refinement of thoughts and feelings through sharing experiences – is only undertaken as the path of intimacy, then one must remember something. As well as requiring polarity and passion, above all else, it's then by necessity also a path of infinite patience. It's quite true that the reward of patience *is* patience. It's both a path as well as a destination. Once you've found it stay with it, you're already on track. Then it doesn't matter if you run or walk, as long as you don't wobble.

Polyamorous Tantra is a subcategory of New Age Tantra. 'Polyamorous' means 'loving many'. It has gotten a lot of press, becoming the catch-all concept surrounding tantric practitioners for numerous people today. After all, we like our pigeonholing headlines lurid and scandalous. Considering its racy fame, let's examine it a little for more perspective.

Like many theories, polyamorous Tantra looks good on paper but put into action the pitfalls tend to outweigh the benefits. Often, it's just the preferred explanation for simply enjoying sex with multiple partners, free of a sense of responsibility for fostering attachment in others. Use of entheogens is rampant and not always useful.

It's distinctly different than being in a committed triad, which I call a 'duogamy'. I've known duogamies that worked for many years involving considerate, intelligent persons. It takes courage to think outside of the box and is necessary in some circumstances.

Polyamory tends to be a short-term practice, although I've also heard "it saved our relationship." For how long is the question. From my non-omniscient observations, what happens is that a person who finally meets someone who's an accomplished lover wants only to be with him or her, and expresses a desire for monogamy.

After all, if you sexually connect deeper with someone than you ever have before, the natural assumption is that it's the same for the other person. The other person doesn't necessarily feel that way, but hey, he or she likes having sex with you. And thus, the game on the merry-go-round plays out with predictably unprofitable emotions and manipulations.

I arrived at this conclusion about polyamory through personal experience and after years of watching major and minor players in the game. I knew an illustrious teaching couple who emotionally beat the crap out of each other as they broke up with the maturity level of high schoolers. Unfortunately, it's easier to get dragged down to a less noble level of relating than to rise to a profitable one. A couple, even those who claim to be in an open relationship, never just splits: they always rip apart.

The Buddha never spoke in terms of good and bad actions, only what is profitable and not profitable.[1]

I've reduced this lofty aspiration of loving many profitably at the same time to a simple mathematical equation:

1 person + 1 lover = emotional processing

1 person + 2 lovers = emotional processing squared

1 person + 3 lovers = emotional processing cubed

Ad infinitum

Adding more persons means that as the emotional processing multiplies exponentially, time and ability to build energy can be expected to diminish exponentially as well. This is why it's usually a short-term practice. Unless, of course, becoming an accomplished manipulator *is* your idea of profitable as, from what I've seen, at least for men with a multiplicity of women, it becomes a requisite for survival. Often, that's initially unintentionally so. Also from what I've seen, all Masters of Ceremonies ultimately go down in flames.

There'll always be tales of happy, closed groups of couples who are well-educated and relatively affluent. Perhaps, all I can say is that knowing any is beyond my personal experience. Up close, I expect my mathematical formula holds true, but then, it serves me to keep an open mind. I'd be happy to be wrong.

If they're drinking alcohol, I doubt any refinement of thoughts and feelings is going on.

In all forms of Buddhist Tantra, it's safe to say that reaching the final goal is through transcending all tendencies to attach. Attachments to pleasure, to power, even clinging to the notion of there being a self that isn't just more compounded phenomena; they all have to drop. Noble intentions, which will be tested, are

---

[1] Bhikkhu Nanamoli's translations of the Pali words *kusala* and *akusala*.

critical for the final success of the practitioner, which is never assured.

One really silly guru-king of New Age Tantra, a well-practiced and adept manipulator, sat on the bedroom rug with us, chatting. He leaned back against the wall, gave his head a little toss, and parted his lips with a tiny, self-satisfied sneer. For my benefit, he was going to enlighten me with a great tantric truth, as if I'd never heard it before. It's an entry-level warning in the world of sacred sexuality, usually learned at the same stage of development.

"The path of Tantra is littered with the bodies of saints and yogis," he intoned as if he himself had passed through the Valley of Death unscathed.

"No," I replied flatly. "'Would-be' saints and yogis. Get it?"

As my meditation teacher in Sri Lanka was fond of saying, in the tradition of all of the greats, "The path is wide at the bottom and as thin as a razor's edge at the top."

Chapter 4

What Will and Won't
Be Here Now

There's an old saying that when it's truth versus credentials, credentials usually win.

First, I must say that I wouldn't expect an endorsement for this book from the teachers I name. They lived out their lives as celibates in the Theravadin tradition. But then, I didn't write it for them.

None the less, to support with credibility the truths I'm presenting, I will tell of my two primary teachers of Buddhism in Asia, and my time with them in the next chapters.

The most incredible Mrs. Helen Wilder was my teacher of Samadhi in Sri Lanka from 1982 to 1984. The last time I saw her was in 1986 when I returned there from Thailand as a monk. In 1987, she became the Theravadin equivalent of a nun at that time, a woman with ten training precepts and yellow robes. Only monks had the right to wear saffron. In Thailand that was under penalty of law.

The fully ordained order of nuns died out among the southern school of migrated Buddhism nine centuries ago. It was reinstated amongst contention from some fundamentalist quarters on December 8, 1996, at Sarnath, India.[1] Helen supported the movement's ideals, but it was never her fight. Her work with Buddhist Publication Society was her community service.

Upon entering the robes, Helen's name changed to Ayya Nyanasiri.[2] I wrote her letters sporadically which she always

---

[1] http://www.buddhanet.net/nunorder.htm

answered promptly, the last being in 1996. She passed away in 2004 in Sri Lanka.

We met in 1981 after a tiny Muslim astrologer named Rafi sat behind me on an evening bus climbing the narrow, winding road to Kandy from the capital city of Colombo. He pestered me relentlessly until I agreed to meet his recently widowed American friend. Upon meeting her, I learned her American husband, Bob, had died upright, meditating, a few months earlier.

Helen, who had little money, had been gifted accommodation in a guesthouse by the owner who respected them both immensely. Later, the woman's sister gave her a house to use on the same property for a couple of years. More private, it overlooked a beautiful terrace of rice paddies next to the jungle.

I was immediately impressed with Helen's agile intellect, buoyant mood, and how totally present she was in our conversation. She taught English and Philosophy at Cornell University for many years. More than twenty years older than me, Helen was in her mid-forties, tall, slender, and always wore her long brown hair in a thick braid.

She had just become the personal secretary (her term) of the Mahathera Nyanaponika, an old German Buddhist monk. Besides being the founder and editor of Buddhist Publication Society (BPS), he was the world's most respected living Western-born Theravadin scholar and Pali translator.

I must stress that my time with Helen was in between her having lost her husband and her formal entrance into the 'solo path' with its traditional vows.

Many times, I would ask her, "How can I ever pay you back for all of this?"

Helen's answer was always the same and the first time I heard this expression, "You can't. All you can do is pay it forward."

This book is part of my attempt to do just that.

---

[2] *Ayya* – Pali for 'sister'

My teacher of Vipassana was Bhikkhu Anavilo, formerly George Bickell. He was known as Phra George[3] to all, including those of us who called him "The Dragon." In 1984, under unusual circumstances I'll explain later, I landed on his doorstep unaware it was the meditation section of Wat Mahadhatu. It was the temple which at that time was to Thai Buddhism what the Vatican is to Catholic government. I immediately went into retreat under his direction.

Phra George roped me into staying and practising meditation with him. I extended my planned three days in Bangkok indefinitely to do so. He figured I was ripe for Nibbana and that we'd become friends, which we did. He was a Londoner in his late fifties, truly brilliant, and difficult to describe, as many truly brilliant, charismatic individuals are. I soon found out that he turned away nine out of ten foreigners who wished to study with him. I eventually learned that his official title translated as "the teacher for foreigners under the auspices of the teacher of meditation for all of Thailand."

I spent the next seventeen months in Thailand. A good portion of it was in retreat benefitting from his guidance before going back to Sri Lanka where I left the robes. I returned to Thailand during the next two years to continue practising Vipassana under his direction.

In 1988, George left the Order himself. Within weeks, he was sponsored by a friend of mine to lead a meditation retreat at my rural mountain home in the West. In 1994, I spent seven weeks in retreat with him in Austria where a couple of Viennese doctors had brought him to establish a small centre when he left the monkhood. George passed away in 2004.

It was through Phra George's example that I learned what is the complete selflessness of the dedicated teacher.

Both he and Helen expected I'd be a bridge between East and West for Buddhism. They poured a lot of attention into me towards that end. George would write me letters with lines in them like

---

[3] *Phra* – Thai for 'monk'. Hard 'P', breathy 'h'.

'May I remind you that the Buddha founded a teaching order and not a hermetic one'.

I didn't answer him for a while after that. Neither he nor Helen had a preconceived notion of what form such bridging would take.

Once, Helen relayed a conversation to me which she had with the Nyanaponika that day during their one morning per week work period. They discussed how the English wanted Buddhism with God, and the Americans wanted it with sex. They didn't see how either was possible.

English society and its colonial offspring that felt driven to worship 'God' have long since passed. As well, every Westerner for the last fifty years knows that sex is successfully separable from procreation. These changes begat a Golden Age of Promiscuity throughout the economically privileged First World, characterised by a hitherto unknown appetite for exploration coupled with a social acceptance for such.

By now, media and the internet have had lots of time to synthesise information on all aspects of this impersonal biological drive of ours. They inject it deeply into everyone's awareness at an unprecedented level of influence. The resultant impact of this influence on our culture today was partially anticipated by Helen and George. It couldn't be fully anticipated by anyone before our current global milieu flowered into intergenerational existence.

So, let's work with it. Enter the ancient concept of divine sex as the vehicle for spiritual evolvement. Now complete it with a toolkit, drivers' manual, and condensed road map for contemporary travellers.

My late teacher of Red Tantra died unexpectedly within a year of the others. I will continue to honour a pact not to disclose her story, marvellous as it is.

I will say this: those that knew her at even the most superficial level considered her to be a role model for women. Fully ejaculatory while making love, she had the amazing ability to morph spectacularly into the archetypal sexual goddess, 'She Whose Name

Cannot be Spoken by Human Tongue'. This brilliant lady considered such access to be every woman's birthright which they've been denied through the subjugation of their sexual energy.

She would retain in her features some of the shift afterwards. A gorgeous diamond, she looked nothing like she did in pictures of her youth. As a mature woman, after a prolonged period of debilitating sickness, she awakened her sexual energy. Her lips naturally filled out to supermodel proportions. Even her receded gums regenerated which is considered a medical impossibility.

She was adroit in her navigation of the realms and her ability to articulate the experience. That made her, for me, the indispensable Initiatress into the secrets of sexual connection, a gift from the universe profoundly loved and respected.

It is my honour that she deeply loved me for what turned out to be her last nine years. I hope to do justice to her understanding of sensual access by indicating the right ennobling direction for women to awaken sexually, and for men to wish to help them do so. That would be a legacy she would have wanted.

As for me, all I'd like to say is I have a career in relieving the suffering of others. I do my best to do it gracefully. My professional skills stem from my successes in meditation. They place me at the forefront of my field. My occupation challenges me both mentally and physically while demanding I always be mindfully present. It deepens my understanding of the human condition and my empathy for others.

I like my way of life. It's satisfying to earn a living by reducing some of the sufferings in the world, no matter how small a contribution that may be. It entails great responsibility and trust. My work makes me feel beneficially effective in my environment which is so important for a human being.

It has nothing to do with sex or drugs. It's 'right livelihood' by any Buddhist's definition.

Chapter 5

Master of Samadhi in Sri Lanka

It was the spring of 1982. I'd just returned to Sri Lanka after nine months of travelling up through India into Nepal, then back down. It was a pleasant evening temperature in the hill town of Kandy; a short-sleeved shirt with long trousers was enough.

Helen and I were alone for dinner in the lush garden of the Queen's Hotel. The Queen's had been the centre of British High Command for the Indian Ocean during World War Two, and not much had changed in it. The waiters still wore white *sarongs* (a rectangular cloth for wrapping the lower body) with white jackets. They padded around quietly in bare feet. They just no longer sported the traditional white gloves of their contemporary counterparts whom I'd encountered further up in tea country.

As usual, the two of us were talking a mile a minute. I'd looked forward to this first visit of my return for a while. Helen always opened my mind and fired my imagination.

"You're always talking about energy!" I exclaimed to her. "What is this 'energy'?"

"Close your eyes," she replied.

She lightly placed three fingers on my right forearm. Suddenly, what felt like 2,000 volts of electricity without any jolt travelled up my arm, exploding in my head in a blinding white flash. I sat completely still, shocked by the intensity of it. She removed her hand from my arm a few seconds later.

I kept my eyes closed for about ten more seconds, then opened them, blinking a few times. I turned my head to face her.

Helen was gazing down to one side at the garden behind my chair. She didn't even glance up, her features set in a demurring look.

Very quietly and lightly in a matter-of-fact voice, she answered my question, "That's energy."

Later, over dessert, I said, "I want to learn more about meditation."

"There's a ten-day insight meditation course being given by a Burmese teacher named Goenka starting tomorrow at the University. It's free; you donate what you want to at the end. It's a residential course; you stay in the dorms. There's no talking for the duration of it. If you're interested, it'll give you some practice sitting, and when you get out, I'll sit with you once."

"That's too good an offer to pass up. I'll do it."

When we met the year before, we instantly became friends. She also liked to smoke a joint which I thought was pretty cool for an ex-professor. From our first meeting, having a toke was a regular part of our routine. Our conversations would fly. Her incredible intelligence never dulled and her spectrum of knowledge was fascinating.

Straight off the bus and ten minutes into my first visit with Helen she told me she was a Buddhist. Never one to pass up an opportunity to show attitude, I replied, "Oh yeah? Buddhism? If there's anything to it, you can give it to me in twenty-one words or less, just like the contests on the back of cereal boxes."

She laughed, and then went on to explain that absolutely everything being impermanent is a central tenet of the Buddha's teaching. I agreed. Then, that life is inseparable from suffering. I agreed to that as well. Lastly, she said that because everything is impermanent and inseparable from suffering, it means there's no self or soul in any of it.

"No self? Wait a minute. This *is* different," I replied. "Tell me more."

During that visit with Helen, I spied an unusual book in her packed bookcase. The 890 pages bound inside of a cream-coloured, grainy-textured hardcover with gold lettering on the spine looked thoroughly soaked in severe orthodoxy. The title read *Visuddhimagga* with *The Path of Purification* underneath. I had to ask about it.

"Oh, that! That'll even teach you how to fly," she replied in a lighthearted, whimsical tone. Her playfulness with it was in stark contrast to the book's solemn appearance.

I surprised myself with the thought, "That would be the book to spend a year in a cave with." I never expected that it would accompany me through caves and jungles in southern India and Lanka, the monkhood in Thailand, and beyond. I even packed it along for over a year while riding a bicycle and camping Down Under. The weight was always worth it.

Over the course of my four months in Sri Lanka in 1981, I passed through Kandy usually every two weeks. I was scuba diving up and down the east coast, and Immigration in the capital didn't like me much so I could only get two-week visas at a time. I didn't take it personally; they didn't seem to like any young foreigners. I was just part of the stream of travellers who didn't want to change a ridiculous amount of money to show them, and then have to carry it around. Besides, we didn't have the good taste to wear wrinkle-free polyester or grease their palms. They didn't veil their resentment in the least.

So I'd take the train from the east coast, disembark in Kandy and go to Helen's with some freshly baked goods in hand. We'd make super-strong 'Nescoffee', as the Lankans called it, which was better than the island's ground stuff. We'd load our cups with powdered full-cream milk. Then I'd roll a joint of the local, always-mild pot. We thoroughly enjoyed each other's company while high and the comfortable dynamic of flowing from one topic to another.

Sometimes, I'd stay in the adjoining guest house for a night. Other times, I'd just take her out to dinner, and then get on a late bus down to Colombo. This same routine would often take place on the return journey. Our visits made crisscrossing the island a pleasure for me that first season.

A revelation the first morning of the ten-day retreat at Peradeniya University floored me. Goenka announced that while we were meditating, he was going to intone a free-form version of the Pali chanting that Theravadin monks do in temples every morning. As soon as he started, I immediately recognised it as the language that came out of me at thirteen and stayed just below the surface until I was seventeen. Being a silent retreat, I got to sit there and examine it for the next nine days as he repeated it daily. The unusual glottal drops and pronunciations, some of the recurring passages, they were all there.

After the retreat, I returned to see Helen and reported in. I told her about recognising Pali. I asked her about one recurring passage, "Buddhung saranung gotchowme, damhung saranung gotchowme, sanghung saranung gotchowme."

Smiling, she answered, "I go to the Buddha for refuge. I go to the teaching for refuge. I go to the community that practices the teaching for refuge."

She told me this was a standard chant learned by every child in the Theravadin world for thousands of years. I later learned it was the original ordination oath that the Buddha sanctioned to be used by his first monks in admitting others to the newly formed Order.[1]

After chatting a bit more, Helen said, "So let's smoke a joint and go sit. We'll see what you learned while you were there."

We went into her meditation room, sat on cushions on the floor, and faced each other. She asked, "So what would you like to do?" meaning, what experience would I like to have.

Having just returned from India, one image kept lingering in my mind even though it hadn't ever been a part of our conversation as I recalled. I'd heard it somehow meant the death of the ego. This image was Shiva, the solar lord of yoga, dancing, natty dreads flying. His arms are aloft with one foot swinging in a high arc, and the other on the back of a small, prone, pygmy-like figure whose eyes are wide with surprise.

---

[1] Mahavagga 1.12.3-4, Vinaya Pitaka

The Hindus say Shiva dancing makes the universe go 'round, and that ganja is sacred to him. I'd seen some beautiful bronze statues of him in this pose. They always intrigued me.

"I want to do the dance of Shiva."

"Oh, that! That's easy!" she replied, settling herself into half-lotus. Cued to do the same, I followed suit.

"So, what did they teach you?" she asked.

"First, it was watching the breath at the nose."

"Okay then, do it."

I closed my eyes and proceeded to pay attention to the air passing in and out of the tips of my nostrils. After about only twenty seconds Helen interrupted me, impatience in her voice, "Okay, you can't do that. What else did they teach you?"

"On the fourth day, we started rolling the awareness around the body."

"Okay, try that."

Again I closed my eyes. I started focussing on feeling my body bit by bit in a moving flow of attention based in the breath from one part to another in the pattern I'd practised. About ten seconds into it, she said encouragingly, "Ahh, this you can do! Keep going."

All of a sudden, I felt a perfectly round ball of energy grow to the size of a melon down in the centre of my pelvis. It rose like a bubble through my middle to my chest, and then disappeared. It was more solid than my body, arching my torso as it passed through. My eyes popped open in surprise. Helen just looked at me.

I closed them once more. Again the same thing happened, but this time, I saw it inside of me like a clear bubble of light. I flashed on how I had no idea how I was seeing this. Again my whole body arched as it passed through as if it was more solid than my form. It happened quickly.

Keeping my eyes closed, it manifested once more, but now the ball of light started travelling up and bounce back down, faster and faster. Simultaneously, a slightly smaller ball of a different energy appeared at the base of my pelvis, glowing opaquely. My body undulated as the bouncing one squeezed through my torso. I had no control over it. All this was happening fast.

At this point, I realised the ball of energy was trying to bounce lower down to where the luminous ball of different energy had emerged but was blocked by an unseen partition at the exact level where I'd had tremendous back pain since I was fifteen. The orthopaedic surgeon who pinned my broken hip at fourteen wanted to put me in a full-length brace for ten years to outgrow the serious problem. I nixed that option as ridiculous and am fortunate I did. At that time, though, I suffered horribly.

In the next instant, the bouncing ball of energy changed shape. Suddenly, it grew a long tail, becoming exactly like a massive spermatozoon. Along with this change, its sentience became evident. My shock was extreme.

The next movement wasn't a bounce, but the autonomous move of a living creature as it veered down to the right. It started to drill through the block in my vertebrae that was the centre of my pain. It retreated up a bit and plunged again, the tail whipping back and forth, intent on penetration. I knew I had no control over this thing that wasn't me but was in me with a mind and a mission of its own. The pearlescent glowing ball at the bottom just stayed stationary, as if waiting for it.

The vigorously renewed drilling through the bone didn't hurt but felt undeniably real and entirely physical. The whole unexpected, unprecedented, lightning-speeded event was just too much. I panicked. "It's going to break my back!" I thought.

Immediately the phenomena stopped. "Damn!" was my next subjective response. "It was probably going to heal my back, and I just blew it!"

I calmed my breathing. My eyes had been opening and closing during this as I checked my surroundings. Helen sat quietly observing me.

I closed my eyes once more and focussed on my belly. The ball of energy again cropped up out of nowhere and rose to my chest, contorting my body around it. It didn't have the same intense electrical charge, but it was still solidly there. It bounced up and down inside my torso, repeatedly throwing me back against the wall as I relaxed around it. The other glowing ball at the base of my pelvis didn't reappear.

I don't know how long I stayed with this ball moving up and down inside of me. In the meantime, Helen relaxed her posture, lit up a cigarette, and just watched.

Eventually, I became exhausted. The phenomenon petered out. I limply sat there, sweating and panting. I looked at Helen. She spoke for the first time since it started.

"My, you certainly do have a lot of energy," she said lightly. "Now you just have to learn how to do it without the drugs."

Her use of the plural was curious but I didn't ask. There was so much more to sort out.

While I was in the ten-day retreat, Helen had arranged for me to stay, if I wished to, with an elderly ascetic outside of Kandy in a 500 years-old temple built by the last of the Singhalese queens. It sat on a knoll surrounded by rice paddies. I was happy to continue my education with the Anagarika Tibotuwawa.

He was a tiny Singhalese yogi in his early seventies with large blue eyes set in his shiny brown bald head. *Anagarika* means 'homeless one' in Pali, an ancient title for a Buddhist yogi with certain vows. His voice was deep, and his English was perfect with long colonial diphthongs on his 'o's, pronouncing them in two parts.

Our meditation would start well before dawn. He took me back to the basics of observing the breath at the nose. He always sat in full-lotus but his ankles were calloused on the outsides like the pads of a dog's paw from a decade of first sitting in half-lotus on a cave floor. He walked so quickly that only I could keep up with him, the young monks and novices trailing behind. His burnt umber sarong and matching ascetic's shirt set him apart as a serious meditator.

At one point, the Anagarika took me to the Forest Hermitage in Udawattakele, a patch of virgin rainforest behind the Temple of the Tooth in Kandy, to ask the Venerable Nyanaponika to sponsor my visa so I could continue learning meditation. The old German monk lived alone in a small two-story house with musty bookshelves and no electricity. We had an appointment, and he was aware of our intentions.

We bowed three times each to show our respect to the aged monk. Just as the Anagarika started introducing me, a dramatically theatrical Swiss monk named Bhikkhu Sumedha[2] arrived. His robes were a dark chocolate brown like the German monk's. He carried a large type of dried palm leaf for an umbrella that folded sideways in on itself. His whole manner was that of a fiercely artistic intellectual. His Swiss-German accented English was also perfect.

After several minutes of pleasantries, the Nyanaponika turned to me. Leaning forward in his chair, he asked, "So why do you want to learn how to meditate?"

The answer occurred to me in the moment, "I want to learn how to die. I figure if I know how to die, then I'll know how to live."

This answer, coming from a lad in his early twenties, surprised this man in his eighties. He sat back and looked at the Bhikkhu Sumedha, who indicated with a nod his approval. They both looked at the Anagarika for a moment, then back to me.

The Nyanaponika remained seated as he reached up to a bookshelf beside us and extracted a white envelope from it. "Here you go," he said lightly, handing the already-prepared letter to me.

A couple of weeks later, during Helen's usual Tuesday morning work visit to him, a Sri Lankan meditation teacher brought a German man to request visa sponsorship. The Nyanaponika refused. "I don't know this man. How can I vouch for him?" was his answer, which she related to me.

[2] *Bhikkhu* – Pali for 'monk'.

Leaving the Anagarika's temple, I moved into an empty colonial era house with pillars out front and an old stable underneath on a back road into Udawattakele right up against the jungle. Daily, a band of monkeys swung through the trees up to the house. The mothers would pull their clinging babies from their bellies, then push them through the bars on the windows, which were there to keep the big ones out, to steal fruit from the table. The Nyanaponika became my nearest neighbour a mile further up the road. Helen's house was a mile away in the opposite direction.

Every day I would visit Helen, bring some small cakes, drink instant coffee with her, smoke a joint, and talk. I never asked her to sit with me again as the stipulation had been quite clear before I went into that meditation course; she would sit with me once.

After a week or so, an American friend of hers who was a little older than me, came over to my place one afternoon for a visit. We smoked a joint, sat in meditation together for a short bit, and I told him my back hurt. He showed me a few yoga poses out on the lawn, then said, "Lie down on your stomach and let me massage your back."

I lay down on the camping foam I'd just used for the yoga. He put one hand on my lower back and took a deep breath. Suddenly, I felt the same energy as when Helen had put her hand on my arm over a month earlier come through his, albeit only as a minor dribbling spurt that stayed under it. I immediately sat up and faced him.

"I recognise that energy! Have you been sitting with Helen?" I knew she didn't sit with anyone, and the similarity surprised me.

"Yeah," he said, surprised back, "last night, for the first time."

"Did she blow you off your cushion?"

Fresh with the memory of it, he shook his head vigorously and laughed, "Yeah, she sure did!"

I went over to Helen's place that evening. Intrigued, I told her what had happened. She looked at me thoughtfully, and then said, "If you can identify my energy coming through his hand when I only touched you once like that, well over a month ago... I take this as a sign that I should be your teacher and help you every way I can."

And thus, my apprenticeship started.

Chapter 6

Lucky Puppy

Helen and I were already the best of friends, but now our relationship entered a deeper phase beyond anything I'd ever experienced. The tone became archetypically teacher/student, and we wholeheartedly embraced it.

The subject: "The Great Work" as Helen said the Egyptian hermetic orders called it.

The method: uniquely culturally woven, as it probably always has to be.

My parents' small estate, which was poorly invested and I couldn't touch until my mid-twenties, would have paid for university, but I wasn't interested. At the time, I considered it to be merely mainstream societal indoctrination. This tutorship was entirely different. I knew I was getting tools that were indispensable for my success in life, whatever path that would take.

Here was the teacher who had been missing in my formal education. With esoteric knowledge of different traditions and impressively articulate, Helen was passionate in her understanding of Buddhism. She embodied the art of teaching: that rare alchemical marriage of pertinent information with joyful inspiration which is pure gold for any student.

My inspiration stemmed from the speed of our communication due to a similar cultural framework and a fluently shared vocabulary for accurately expressing our ideas. The joy existed because there's a naturally occurring, mutual respect between friends that automatically enables a cooperative aspect in exploring ideas together. It creates a harmony in communication. This harmony underlies all mutually profitable human interaction.

Incidentally, in Theravada, the giver of the meditation subject isn't called a guru but the 'good friend' (*Kalyanamitta*). This distinction makes all the difference. Friends feel inherently equal.

The next months were a whirlwind of lessons. Helen was a master of Samadhi. She could travel through the frequencies with ease. She'd bounce me into different states that were always incredibly charged electrically and more vivid than my normal waking state of awareness. Helen could slice, dice, and julienne the explanations every way imaginable for me to understand what was happening. The subjects ranged from Buddhist cosmology to the principles of magic.

At one point, she said to me, "I'd like to make you an amulet to make you easier to work with."

I thought about it for a few minutes. "Well," I replied, "I'll accept one only because I refuse to get attached to it."

She laughed. "I knew that, or I wouldn't have offered."

Helen loaned me obscure books on metaphysical teachings to take home that I pored over. We settled into an easy rhythm of me spending the days alone reading and meditating before going over to her place for the evenings. She'd ask me what I'd read that interested me. After discussing it briefly, whether it was Pythagoras, the Tibetan Book of the Dead, ancient Egypt or whatever, we'd then smoke a joint and go to her meditation room to sit. She said the smoking "lowered some of the veils" for me and made me easier to work with.

Helen repeated many times that it was all about creating energy, storing it, and directing it. She would throw a force at me while sitting across from me that often registered as a blinding flash of light. It was always extremely fast.

If I didn't mentally blink or duck, which is an entirely natural reaction when faced with such a blast, even when expecting it, I'd have a full-blown experience of access into other dimensions/states of consciousness. Accompanying this would be an incredible intake of information about that system of ancient knowledge we'd just discussed.

I always left her place completely energised. I could see light glowing around me as I walked home afterwards. The neighbourhood dogs would surround me as I passed by, snarling and barking, night after night. When I came from anywhere else, they'd just ignore me.

Her clear musical voice would change quite often. Sometimes, Helen channelled different entities who instructed me in ways to focus better for access into absorption. Other times the instructions would be hers but at a level of resonance that our normal atmosphere doesn't support as she spoke of the nature of reality. There would be a corresponding shift of visual contrast and definition into sharper imaging in the room along with it. The expression 'the ring of truth' took on a very literal meaning.

If I'd been away for a while in India or another part of the island, I'd feel my mind and body retuning into a finer frequency by the sound of her voice when I returned. I wouldn't realise the dissonance that my system had become until it was recalibrating into alert resonance. I came to expect this phenomenon as well as many others.

For example, regularly while talking about meditation Helen would say something like, "...and then I shift like this ...and (blah-blah) happens."

As soon as she'd say, "...like this...," her whole face and body would rearrange its structure so swiftly that visually I could only register her form as a dancing triangle of strobing images before settling into continuity again. I knew every molecule in her had rearranged itself in a moment of expansion, but I was too slow to see it in any other way than this three-step process, a triangle being the most basic of geometric forms. She giggled when I said it was like seeing Pythagoras' theorem in action.

All manner of different phenomena happened during our sitting together. Some examples demonstrate the range of experiences.

We sat to meditate in her shrine room. Helen's voice changed completely in cadence and tone. I knew in that moment that she was channelling an entity as it gave me a different instruction than I'd ever received from her.

We'd discussed that day how the pineal gland has crystals in it[1] that need aligning to open the 'third eye'. The pituitary gland sits directly in front of the pineal gland. Focussing on the connection between the two aligns these crystals, turning the inside of the back of the skull into a satellite dish. I'd already experienced at times various sensations, sometimes throbbing and painful, in the back of my skull as if the increased energy moved the plates around.

Helen's voice rang in a different spatial resonance as I was told to look directly back into the centre of vision. I thought, "That's simple enough." As soon as I did that, the next sensation was of my entire awareness dropping down a central shaft, complete with the pit of my stomach feeling like an elevator suddenly fell.

The next thing I knew, it was as if I was pressed up against a plate glass window, on the other side of which there was an enormous sea of pale yellow light. I was just a point like a fly speck on that glass vibrating with the syllable 'i-i-i... i-i-i...' in stunned self-reference. I knew that was what was keeping me from becoming part of that sea.

Then in the next moment, I was sucked from this experience, spiralling downward through a handful of scenes in bubbles. They seemed totally disconnected from each other but made sense in those brief moments of being in them. I abruptly landed in my own form sitting in half-lotus. My eyes popped open, and I looked down at my crossed legs.

"Quick! Avert! *This is the one it gets stuck in!*" was my immediate first reaction in sheer panic. My next thought was wordless, total shock at this being my first thought. I closed my eyes, repeating, "Avert! Avert!" in this charged state of extreme

---

[1] Calcite microcrystals in the pineal gland of the human brain: first physical and chemical studies, Baconnier S.; http://www.ncbi.nlm.nih.gov/pubmed/12224052

alarm. My awareness went nowhere but manifested as longing followed by pressing existential danger.

My eyes again opened. I was aware of the Earth hurtling through space and the passing of a few seconds. I felt like I had moved too far from the point at which I dropped into this continuum to escape back out from this, "...*the one it gets stuck in!*"

The feeling of separation from all that matters welled up inside. It burst out with a grief that ripped my chest open. I sobbed uncontrollably over losing something I couldn't even remember. Helen just sat across from me, smiling compassionately.

Such immediate, overwhelming sorrow was completely out of character for me as were the tears. I was no stranger to loss and pain. A postscript to this story takes place over twenty years later, related in Chapter 14.

Another time, we were sitting when I heard Helen move in the room. I kept my eyes closed. The next thing I knew, a small, heavy metal object dropped into my right hand which was folded over my left, palms upward on my lap in half-lotus. I felt it start to emit an energy that had the sensation of a thick form of electricity to it. A beam of this same energy shot up as a column inside of my torso. It stayed there like a solid pole.

Another thinner beam then emerged from the pool of energy in my hands. It came up diagonally into my liver which started to fill with it. This experience lasted about half an hour before dissipating. I'd contracted hepatitis A in Nepal many months earlier, and I knew it was helping my liver to recover.

When I opened my eyes, I was surprised to see a small bronze *Dorje* sitting in my palm which I hadn't noticed in the room before.

Dorje is the Tibetan word for a symbolic ritual tool used by lamas in their tantric ceremonies. Among other esoteric meanings, it represents both the indestructibility of a diamond and the irresistible force of a lightning bolt. The Sanskrit word for it is *Vajra*. It's also known in Hinduism.

I looked enquiringly at Helen, who just sat there, grinning. She asked me what happened. She said she got the message to take it off of the shrine and put it in my hands.

"I was also told that in a past life you were a master of what was called 'the bolt of lightning technique', so your system would recognise it and know what to do with it. I wondered what it was for when I bought it a couple of weeks ago, as I don't usually gravitate towards them. Now I know. It was for you."

Once, while sitting with Helen, I heard an unusual swoosh. I opened my eyes. In the next moment, we both saw a 'doorway' appear in the room in front of me. It was a large rectangular hole with absolutely straight sides and ninety-degree angles at the corners. Looking into its fathomless black depths, I saw something even blacker sparkle like a dark star in the emptiness. No way was I going through it. Neither one of us moved. It disappeared after about ten minutes.

At the start of one sitting, Helen threw a force at me. Behind closed eyes, my vision immediately brightened. Then, with a white flash, a huge star-shaped hole suddenly appeared. It was stable and unmoving, as real as any opening between one room and another, but this was from the inside of my head into a different world. Lines of fork lightning rippled along its edges. Through it, I looked up into a thundercloud-filled sky flashing with sheet lightning.

I was awestruck. The power I felt in that sky was ominous in its scope. I knew I was no match for anything hostile I might encounter in such a foreign environment. My mind recoiled with a twinge of fear. The experience abruptly ended. My eyes popped open.

The hole in the fabric of my reality had been no wavering, psychedelic hallucination. It, like the rectangular doorway, imposed itself as uncompromisingly real. 'Right there!', with clearly defined perfect edges and angles.

Shaking my head in disbelief, I asked Helen, "Why a pentagram?"

"I don't know. I do know you accessed a frequency just above ours called 'the Realm of the Four Kings'. I don't usually bother with such levels. I prefer to explore finer spheres in my own practice."

I started seeing auras around people, sometimes multi-coloured and other times cloudy. The most magnificent I ever saw was around the Nyanaponika, and I wasn't looking for it.

We were alone in his cottage, the 'Forest Hermitage', at the end of a visit. As it grew dark, he lit a kerosene lamp, the place having no electricity. We were sharing a hot drink before I left. The Nyanaponika sat behind his desk ten feet from me.

As we chatted, I became aware of a sheen around his shoulders. Then, the entire field came into focus. What I could see extended over four feet on either side of him with a rounded bump on top, two feet wide around his head. I just continued talking while I examined this without telling him what I was seeing.

The glow I saw was actually innumerable, extremely close, hair-thin lines of burnt orange-golden light extending off into space. They alternated one straight, one squiggly. They didn't stop at four feet but after that grew finer than my ability to see them. I knew they continued, but it was just because they weren't so densely packed after that point that I couldn't detect them. Helen was delighted that I'd seen this.

I developed an appreciation for nuances of translation as well during my education with Helen. For instance, the Pali word *bhavana* was translated by the first Catholic priests to study Pali in the late nineteenth century as meaning 'meditation'. Recent translators such as the Nyanaponika, who were meditators, which is so important, as well as more advanced as scholars, came to realise it more accurately renders into English as meaning 'becoming'. So instead of practising meditation, one practises becoming. I consider this to be a crucial clarification of intention that leads to more immediate results.

Perhaps the best known word in Pali that is hard to translate is *dukkha*. It's commonly left untranslated into English sentences as a consequence. The standard translation of it is 'suffering'. The best known use of it is in saying the Buddha said, "Life is *dukkha*." As a result, his teaching is dismissed by many as being depressing.

Helen taught me it more accurately translates as 'inseparable from suffering'. That entirely changes the perspective. Being an intellectual, she said, "It most accurately means 'inherently insufficient as to give lasting pleasure,'" but that's rather unwieldy.

In the discourse documenting the Buddha's death, he said seventeen times (and I paraphrase), "This is a delightful place. Anyone who develops and perfects the bases for certain supernormal powers can live out the aeon, if he wants to. I've developed and perfected those bases, and I could live out the aeon if I wanted to."[2]

After all, if life is only suffering then why would anyone ever cling to it or crave for it in the first place?

This renders the classical four noble truths of the Buddha as:

> 1) Life is inseparable from suffering.
>
> 2) The cause of suffering is attaching.
>
> 3) To end suffering, stop attaching.
>
> 4) There is a path of becoming which leads a person to number three, the end of suffering; ultimately: Nibbana.

The Buddha taught this fourth truth as 'the eightfold noble path'. Helen preferred to group it into 'remorseless conduct, concentration and understanding', as the developmental cycle that the eight factors fold into. She liked to laugh about how a threefold division is so much easier to remember than an eightfold one.

It was the combination of direct transmission of incredible energy while sitting with Helen, then discussing the resultant experiences in depth that I valued as the most extraordinary learning opportunity possible. Regularly I'd shake my head and say,

---

[2] Digha Nikaya 16, 3.3. A few translators disagree about the word 'aeon', as they can't accept the idea of such a 'great miracle', even though the meaning and usage are clear.

"All of this is going so fast. I don't know how I'll remember everything."

Her answer was always the same. "I feel our time together is going to be quite short, so I'm giving you an imprint of everything I can. When you need it, it'll be there for you."

Spontaneously, paranormal abilities started to manifest which freaked me out. I'd stop meditating for several days and not come around. Seeing auras, beings from other dimensions in places, and reading minds were just fine. It was affecting the physical world without thinking that concerned me. You'd think I'd be delighted, but the effects of throwing a force on impulse at targets scared me.

My anger could flare out of control. I'd proven this when I took a six-inch knife in the guts at sixteen, stupidly avenging the honour of a girl who didn't have any. I was beating on a guy with a hardwood stick, so pumped on adrenaline that I didn't realise he'd stabbed me until after I let him go. I realised then I could make drastic mistakes recklessly. The ramifications of developing myself into a loaded gun, so to speak, deeply upset me.

I said to Helen more than once, "I'm not ready for these things! I have a really nasty temper. I could really hurt somebody! Doing so with something like this would be really heavy karma."

She always reassured me with the same words. "If you weren't ready for it, it wouldn't be happening."

I wasn't convinced. There are so many examples of minor abilities going to someone's head and their impetuous use leading to disaster as to be cliché. A cliché is just a well-worn truth. For those familiar with the Pali canon, Devadatta is the perfect example.[3] He felt his development of 'mere supernormal powers' entitled him to kill the Buddha and lead the monks in his place.

Helen had come into her paranormal abilities spontaneously. She and Bob had left upstate New York for Malaysia where she had a short tenure teaching at a university. One evening they smoked a

---

[3] *The Book of Discipline* (Vinaya-Pitaka), Vol. V: Cullavagga, I.B Horner, pp. 259-285. London Luzac, 1963

joint - their daughter had introduced them to pot years before over a Christmas break - and Helen closed her eyes. As she opened them a short while later, Bob was staring at her very oddly. Asking him what was wrong; he said a voice had just come out of her for the last fifteen minutes that wasn't hers.

It happened the next night again. Bob started asking the voice questions and writing down the answers, night after night. Her descriptions of the blissful states she went into while this took place prompted him to want to learn how to experience them himself. As she said, not only did he learn but then he went further himself and taught her how.

They smoked ganja and ate it to help them get into these states. They were both brilliant, mature individuals who'd already raised a family when they took to using cannabis to explore different realms. Ancient Egypt became their fascination. They once ate some pot, left their bodies while meditating and went to ancient Egypt for three days. Waking up three days later, they talked about it like others talk about their last long weekend trip together.

Bob had been a Wall Street broker whose adrenal glands got turned on by the stress and wouldn't turn off. He was expected to die of kidney failure within six months which is what usually happens. He lived for over eleven years. As his time grew near, he was approached by an Egyptian master from another frequency. He resisted the request put to him, often pounding the table forcefully that he wouldn't do it.

The Egyptian was nearing the end of his term of service stationed in an information realm for meditators who reached that far. He wanted Bob to take over his position. Finally, Bob acquiesced.

About this and other matters, Helen repeatedly said, "The universe is a giant computer. If you know how to ask the right questions, you'll always get the right answers."

For the last week of Bob's life, the Egyptian was 'hologrammed', as Helen called it, into a corner of the room. Others could see him. A few asked who the little man in swami's clothes was.

While sitting propped up with cushions, spine erect, Bob's final words were "It's alright. I can unify my mind."

Twenty minutes later, he breathed his last. Arriving an hour later, the doctor asked incredulously, "Did he die like this?"

This story came out piece by piece one night in front of a trusted mutual friend who had a background in the occult. Helen mentioned the name of the Egyptian. Our friend stammered in surprise. He knew the name from a book written in the 1920s by a European mystic. Helen had never encountered it anywhere before.

At the end of his life, Bob taught Helen everything he could about different teachings he found to be vitally important, especially the Greeks with the esoteric side of their geometry. She had discovered liberation from rebirth in the Buddha's teaching and taught him what she could of it.

I once saw an old servant come to visit Helen, see Bob's picture on the wall and start praying to it, tears rolling down the old man's face. She loved to tell me numerous stories of their explorations together. Everything I heard let me know they were quite the couple, completely in love with each other.

After a couple of years on her own, Helen started telling me that it was better alone. She withdrew in that direction.

She stopped smoking ganja. I'd come back from rural southern India, and she wouldn't have had a toke during the months I was gone. It held no more interest for her. She'd go into absorption night after night on her own to the finest immaterial realm there is, the state called 'neither perception nor non-perception'. She did smoke with me as was our custom.

At one point, I returned from India to find Helen distraught. She knew she'd made a big mistake and wondered what the repercussions would be. I couldn't believe Helen slipped up like she did. Neither could she. Two weeks before, her neighbour, a Sinhalese woman, begged her to sit in meditation with her. Helen directed a force of energy at her which bounced her into a deep absorption.

The woman couldn't handle it. She started raving. Confusion lingered, and she couldn't function in her life. I watched her walk by with her husband holding her. Obviously fragmented, she kept looking at the house with fear. I felt this mistake was born of too much time alone coupled with the desire for companionship.

Helen's loneliness was becoming more and more apparent. Her emotional world became her dogs, strays she had rescued.

She once said to me, "The reason to have pets is to show them human emotions. That way, when they die, they'll be reborn as humans because they identify on our emotional matrix. A human life is so valuable as it's the only one that allows for the examination of motives. This ability is what separates us from the animals. It gives us the opportunity to become enlightened."

Helen's connection with the Nyanaponika and editing for Buddhist Publication Society kept her mind occupied. She typed and retyped complete manuscripts and translations, all with one finger. All so fast, her hand would only be a blur as it raced over the keys on an old manual typewriter. Eventually, she taught herself to use both index fingers.

We continued to write regularly after I went back as a layman to Thailand from my home country those first two years to practice with Phra George. Our correspondence thinned out over time although she always answered my letters promptly. I had less and less to write about, living in a different world, having returned to the West out of economic necessity.

Helen was delighted to 'enter the robes' in 1987. The Nyanaponika created an ordination ceremony for her as there wasn't one anymore for nuns. It gave her security in Sri Lanka. He passed away in 1994. Our last letters were in 1996. She passed away in 2004.

A search on the web brings up very little on her. Only references to her work with BPS and a couple of brief eulogies.

There's nothing that even hints at the abilities of this incredible adept.

This tale of Helen wouldn't be complete without the following story.

Chapter 7

My Brother, Freddy

It was four months into my first period of training with Helen. I had no wish to return to the West but did desire to see my brother, whom I'll call Freddy. Although four years older than me, we were quite close as we were all we had left to each other as immediate blood family. We'd been through a lot together.

Physically, he was the thicker, darker version of me. I grew up across the table from a full-face beard since he was sixteen. Our communication was lightning fast; sentences rarely needed finishing. I offered to pay from the first instalment of my inheritance for part of his trip to visit me for a month.

Freddy jumped at the chance. Married and with a small toddler, he was on summer break from university. He was a year past his Master's degree in English and Philosophy, the same subjects Helen had taught. A gifted academic, the government kept throwing grants at him to keep him in school although all Freddy would be qualified to do would be to teach what he'd learnt. We planned two weeks in Sri Lanka followed by two in southern India.

The two weeks in Sri Lanka were magical. Renting a motorcycle, I took him to visit the Nyanaponika, Bhikkhu Sumedha, and the Anagarika. Freddy and Helen hit it off fabulously, both sharing a vocabulary of European philosophers' ideas. We toured tea country and snorkelled on brightly coloured coral reefs together. Formerly only a lake swimmer, he'd never seen anything like it.

A village of fishermen, buddies of mine from the year before, barbequed a haunch of wild boar for us one night. Even the beach dogs were too stuffed to move when we tripped over them in the dark. Helen's friend with the guest house put on a birthday party for

Freddy with my favourite curries and a chocolate cake. He turned twenty-eight, a happy, big bear of a man.

A strange, unpleasant incident occurred two days before we were to leave for India. We were high up in the mountain town of Nuwara Eliya. While we were leaving the tiny post office, the postmaster jumped on my back with a scream for no apparent reason. I flipped him off of me without a problem, and he quietly stormed back to behind the counter. Bewildered by this bizarre attack, the two of us just left, determined not to let it interfere with our good moods.

I felt unusual as if I were floating and couldn't get grounded. A half an hour later back at our lodge, I realised I was missing the amulet from around my neck.

We retraced our footprints without finding it. As we re-entered the post office, the surprised postmaster looked spooked as if he couldn't understand what had come over him. The Sri Lankans are very superstitious people. They call their country 'the island of demons'.

"You aren't in any danger," I assured him, "but I'm missing a powerful amulet. It got pulled off of me in your attack."

He blanched. Now meekly cooperative with us, we all quietly searched the room for it, but to no avail.

For the next thirty-six hours, I felt I was in an energetic free fall from a high-velocity state to slower wavelengths I'd forgotten about. I said at the time it was as if dirt clots or giant scabs were re-attaching themselves to my face and head, filtering my perception.

We flew into Trivandrum, now called Thiruvananthapuram, in Kerala, southern India, on a warm moist tropical evening. We took a motorised rickshaw to Kovalam Beach where I had been five months before. The twenty-kilometre trip on a rough road was slow in the three-wheeled vehicle, but it gave Freddy the chance to savour our lush, rural surroundings.

"It's such great karma to be here," he said excitedly, after just half an hour.

I was surprised by Freddy's choice of words. It just wasn't in his vocabulary. My brother had never spoken once in terms of karma before. He took to repeating this sentence every hour over the course of that night and the next day. I didn't encourage him with it. Striking me as curious, I just put it down to his delight with our exotic location.

That first day, we body-surfed up and down the bays of the area. Freddy was blown away by the whole experience. Mid-afternoon, we were resting in the shade of a palm tree looking out at the ocean when I said, on a whim, "Let me see your hand." I'd picked up a little palm reading in my travels there.

"Whoa!" I exclaimed, stunned by the appearance of his left palm. "Let me see your other one. Wow! Have they always been like this?"

Freddy, who only used glasses for distance, lifted his hands to examine them carefully. He couldn't focus to see. It looked like he was in a dream. His eyes went narrow, then wider as he moved them over his palms, closer, then farther away with no success.

Still trying, he said, "I think so. I dunno. I guess so."

I recalled a palm reader on the banks of the Ganges earlier that year who by reading my aura tried to tell me I had VD. I laughed at him as that was impossible. I later learned I did have a prostate infection. For some reason, I thought what he said then appropriate to repeat in this moment.

"Well, drop it for now."

Freddy's hands were identical. They were void of all lines except one on each which slashed deeply across his blank palms, perfectly straight from one side to the other.

We sat in silence. The oddity of it lingered in the air for me. To break it a minute later, I jumped up. "I'm going to get wet. Want to join me?"

"No. I'm just going to rest here a bit," he replied.

I turned and walked into the ocean up to my waist. A two-foot wave curled lazily towards me. With pleasure, I dove under it. As soon as my head was in the water, I heard Freddy's voice urgently telling me something. I couldn't make it out through the fizz of the bubbles engulfing my ears.

"He's in the water, and he's in danger!" was my first thought. By the time I formulated that, a few more syllables had continued. I realised, no, this was a message of some sort. I went limp as I strained to understand what I was hearing. Freddy's voice continued for about ten more seconds, insistently repeating the same sentences over and over.

As the wave passed and the bubbles stopped so did his voice. I stood up fast, spinning around to look for him. He was peacefully lying down with his eyes closed, in the shade, right where I'd left him.

I faced out to the ocean again. I took a few steps, but the water had lost its appeal. I headed for shore to collect Freddy. We went back to swim in the bay in front of our guest house.

We were in the water long enough to catch a good-sized wave together. We watched it continue onto the beach, just licking the corner of my bag which held our passports and money. I went to move the bag further up on the sand.

Freddy came out of the water until it was only up to his knees. A servant from the guest house approached me asking how we wanted our fish cooked that evening. Unconcerned, Freddy turned to go back in deeper.

"Please, sir, be careful," the young man said, worry in his voice.

"It's okay," I replied confidently. "He knows about the conditions. We discussed them last night."

In this bay, the waves went out with a white cap as well as came in with one. It was monsoon season here on the Malabar Coast of the Arabian Sea.

As we talked about dinner, I heard a shout from the bay. Freddy was two hundred feet out on a six-foot wave that he couldn't handle. A massive set had sprung out of nowhere. I couldn't believe he'd gotten so far out so fast. I watched as he stood up in chest-deep water. I thought, "Good, he's got a footing," when a wave washed him back out.

I ran into the ocean to swim to him. The fishermen on the shore were all shouting for me to go, go, go! I was one hundred feet from him when a six-footer took me under. As I struggled to the surface, another one took me back down. When I surfaced, Freddy was gone. I screamed for him. I swam to where I saw him last.

Visibility was zero in the tossed-up water. The fishermen were waving me in. I floated, trying to find him in the choppy ocean. I didn't want to believe he'd disappeared under the waves.

After some minutes, I can't tell you how many; I swam to shore hoping the fishermen were watching him floating further out than I could see. They just looked at me, answering my unspoken question with sad shakes of their heads.

The servant threw buckets of water on me to rinse me off as I stood in shock, absorbing the situation. Together, we went to the police, who, bizarrely, wouldn't believe Freddy was my brother. Returning to our bay, I went to the five-star hotel on the point to make an international call. Against all the odds of getting through I wanted to speak with Helen. Being 1982, in a pair of third world countries, it was going to take a miracle in telecommunications to do so.

A Sri Lankan operator found the guest house next to Helen's place. She came to the phone, "Alex! Where are you? What's up?"

"I'm in India. It's Freddy. He just drowned."

She gasped, then, "Are *you* alright?"'

"Yeah, I'm fine." What else was I to say? Comparatively, I was fine.

A moment's silence, "What do want me to do?"

"From our studies of the Tibetan Book of the Dead, I know the *Bardo* (the state between lives) starts off blissful, and then it turns terrorising. I want to spare him that. Can you arrange a guide for him to help him through it?"

79

"Don't you do anything. Let me do everything. I was just going into retreat today since you were gone. I'll take care of this instead. When are you coming back here?"

"They say there's a ten-mile undertow where he went down, and there's a fifty/fifty chance of the body coming up. If so, it'll be within five days. I'll be back in a week."

"Okay, I'll see you then. You take care of yourself."

"Thank you... for everything. I'll see you then."

That night, alone on the porch of our room, I smoked a joint, pondering the day's tragedy. I thought about hearing Freddy's voice while I was in the water and he was on the shore. A veil dropped. The insistently repeated words came back ringing clearly now.

"Alex! There was nothing you could do. I'm alright! Alex! There was nothing you could do. I'm alright! Alex! There was nothing you could do. I'm alright!"

Freddy's body never came up. It was food for the sharks.

Seven days later, Helen greeted me at her door with a smile and a hug. As we sat down, she said, "I wrote it all down while it was fresh so I wouldn't lose any of it. Let me show you."

She picked up an envelope from the coffee table and handed it to me. Inside was a small typewritten sheet of paper. Smiling, she motioned for me to read it.

'Right after you called, I returned home and lit the candles and incense that I had prepared to start my retreat. Wondering what to do, I opened the Book of the Dead and read that the first thing that appears is the white light. So I closed the book, sat and went into the white light to look for Freddy.

The white light turned to amethyst. Out of the amethyst light stepped Freddy. He was wearing blue Adidas shorts, a blue T-shirt, his glasses and a gold chain around his neck. I walked up to him and put my hand on his shoulder. "Do you know who I am?" I asked him.

"Yes, Madam, er, Helen," he replied.'

I smiled. The shorts and blue T-shirt were his favourite clothes. The gold chain his wife had given him instead of a wedding ring, and he wore it always. An ongoing expression of loving respect for Helen from me was formally calling her "Madam." Here he used it to show his recognition. I continued reading.

'"Good," I said and with my hand still on his shoulder, started to walk with him.

At this point, I watched myself pull out of myself and continue talking to him as they walked away. The watcher/I could not follow. They both disappeared into the amethyst light together.

I then went to an information realm to find out what had happened. I was informed that a mind-made body of myself imprinted with all of the Dhamma [the Buddha's teaching] *that I know had been created, and it would stay with him for the forty-nine days of the Bardo. Then he would be reborn, and it would just dissolve for lack of nutrition.'*

"Why an amethyst light?" I asked. There's no mention in the Book of the Dead about a light of that colour.

"Good question," she answered. "I wondered the same thing, so I asked the Nyanaponika about it. He said that, quite simply, he'd missed the white light so he'd be reborn."

If someone doesn't recognise the initial white light for what it is, which is the purpose of mental training, then other lights appear, and events play out as the discorporate electric flux of consciousness winds down in frequency. Eventually, it magnetically matches up with a form. This process goes through forty-nine stages, called 'days' in the book. Even if a rebirth takes years, the tightest lingering connection to and from this frequency is said to last for seven weeks.

Although Helen and I never discussed it, the Buddha taught his monks how to create mind-made bodies.[1] Different phenomena manifested quite spontaneously for Helen. Such were usually of an

---

[1] Majjhima Nikaya 77.30

Egyptian flavour. Two years later in London, I read that hierophants used mind-made bodies for various tasks.

The next night, Helen and I sat together in meditation with no particular intention. When she threw a force at me, I managed to not mentally blink. Instead, I took it like a cream pie in the face. I found myself going very far in a direction I didn't recognise.

Suddenly, a room appeared around me. I was sitting in a chair. It felt like an office. The walls were beige, and there was a man in a brown suit sitting on the other side of a dark brown desk. He opened his mouth, but only a musical tone came out.

I opened my mouth to say, "I'm sorry, I don't understand you," but instead, a corresponding tone an octave higher emerged. As I sat back surprised, he too sat back, looking satisfied. The room dissolved into nothing.

Another room with the same office feel to it appeared around me. This time, though, the walls were light yellow. A woman sat across from me, behind a different, straw-coloured desk. She too was dressed in a shade of yellow.

She opened her mouth, and a higher octave musical tone than what the man had voiced emerged. I went to answer her that I couldn't understand but another corresponding tone, an octave higher than hers, came from my mouth. As she sat back satisfied, this room also dissolved.

Out of the darkness, a lit space appeared around me. In it, stood Freddy. I shouted his name and hugged him. Pulling back but still holding him, I said, "But... how did I get here?"

I turned to look behind me. Suddenly, I was back in Helen's meditation room, sitting on a cushion.

Immediately I shut my eyes. As before; I went through the same rooms with the same man and the same woman behind their desks, exchanging corresponding tones. Freddy appeared. I grabbed his arm.

Disoriented, I couldn't help thinking again, "But... how did I...?"

Glancing around as a matter of reflex, there was a flurry of movement. My eyes popped open once more. I was back in Helen's place. Closing them didn't take me anywhere. My sense of loss was overwhelming.

I returned to the West to tell Freddy's wife, whom I'll call Clare, about what happened. Her brother was contacted right away by the consulate. He'd broken the news to her but didn't know the details.

Freddy had been born on the same day as our father. Clare said that when she saw his plane ticket was the same date our father died; she knew she'd never see him again. She didn't try to stop him.

For two weeks after he drowned, Clare continued getting letters from Freddy because of the delay in the mail. She said he was the happiest she'd ever known him to be.

She was up at her family's cottage when he drowned. A neighbour was taking care of their place and was unaware of Freddy's accident. He told me that when he stepped into the house that day, he felt there was someone in it. He checked every room in the place, coming last to Freddy's bedroom.

As the man paused in his story, tangled emotions swirled through me over this discovery about Freddy's world. I didn't know they weren't sleeping together. Freddy told me the morning he died that he'd never regretted for a second being married. It shocked me as I'd locked horns with Clare countless times over her rough treatment of him right in front of me. Hearing he had his own bedroom, his devotion to her amazed me even more.

When the neighbour had watered a plant in there some days before, everything was normal. This time, the covers on the bed were pulled back on one side as if someone had started to get into it. He ran from the house. His wife told me that he was as white as a ghost. It scared her badly as he's a very black man.

Friends saw an amethyst light around me that first month I was back. While going to the bathroom in the middle of the night, I also saw it glowing around me, a half-inch-high sheen hovering a half inch above my skin.

I continued to get night-time visits from Freddy while I slept over the next two years in India and Sri Lanka. The experiences were too vivid to be considered just dreams. One time, in a brightly lit space, I hugged him. Pulling back but still touching his shoulder, I said carefully, "You know you're dead, don't you?"

He answered calmly, "Yeah, I know. I just wanted to see how you're doing…"

Chapter 8

The Dragon in Bangkok

The library of the headquarters of the World Fellowship of Buddhists on Sukhumvit Rd. was about half full on this Tuesday evening as was usually the case. There were the few ex-pat regulars and several Thais that spoke English, but mostly the audience consisted of Western tourists who had somehow found their way in from the humidity to this air-conditioned space. Some of them scattered around the room sat with closed eyes meditating while they waited for the lecture to begin. A couple of those sat with their legs tucked up in loose yoga positions, their spines painfully erect, feigning nonchalance.

In other words, I saw no surprises as Phra George, resident house speaker, arranged his robes around him while sitting in half-lotus on a desk at the front.

He cleared his throat, and his evenly paced, rich British baritone gently filled the air. "Good evening ladies and gentlemen. Will all those who want to be holy please leave the room."

After a long pause, during which no one moved, he continued, "There is no use in that. It is merely impurity contemplating purity. This can only lead to an impure picture. It's better just to remove the impurity and purity results."

This was classic George. To the point and a hair abrasive if you had an edge that his words could catch on. He delighted in his refined diamond-in-the-rough sense of humour, not caring if the listener did or not. He didn't care for mysticism either, quipping that its problem was it started with 'mystery' and ended in 'schism'. Likewise: neither for ambiguities or egos.

Many months before this, I'd returned to London. The pain in my spine from an unnamed, serious degenerative condition of the vertebrae and discs was spreading. Not having found any solutions for it in India or Sri Lanka, I wanted to see if Western medicine had anything new to offer me. It didn't. I took a train north for a tour.

I visited a Theravadin community in Newcastle. This transplanted model sure wasn't for me. I hitchhiked up into Scotland. Camping in a grotto by a stream, I got it into my head to return to Lanka and be a monk. The idea stunned me. I knew better than to take it lightly.

So, I retired up to a set of windswept crags on the Scottish-English border to mull it over for a handful of days. It happened to be the summer solstice, the sun just briefly dipping below the horizon at night. It was a peaceful spot in a barren sort of way.

In the long hours of unbroken silence, I reviewed my experiences of sitting with Helen, the magical power spots I'd found in Lanka and India, and the exotic cultural journey through them. Also, the theory behind actively practising non-clinging and non-craving, and all of the clinging and craving I'd exercised everywhere and where all that had gotten me.

I remembered fondly generous doses of sex and drugs. I was the only person I knew who had gone to Asia to dry out. Friends warned me that sex on the road would be a rare thing. It was.

Knowing it would be, I stocked up on indulging for a couple of months before going. That sometimes meant two to three times a day among the different women my age that I'd been intimate with over the years.

After Freddy's death, a girlfriend I'd met back in the West joined me in Sri Lanka. Our vigorous sex in a lovely tropical home in the hills of Kandy eventually felt empty and confining. The relationship only interrupted my apprenticeship with Helen. When I sent her home months later, her last words before getting on the plane were "Whatever you do, don't become a monk." I'd laughed at the time at what seemed like an utterly ludicrous idea.

Now, after a year of exploring Sri Lanka and the south of India as a meditating yogi, what appealed to me was that I'd never tried giving up my options and jumping onto the solo path as a committed way of life. It didn't feel like a crash and burn idea. It felt like there was everything else in life, and then there was THAT. It felt like it required bravery like no other adventure ever had.

The unpredictable consequences of letting go of my culture intrigued me. Anticipating a self-imposed discipline that I'd never known terrified me. I knew I could leave the monkhood after a while if I wanted to. But then, isn't THAT the opportunity that everything else isn't? I felt it was now or never. It was radical, but I wasn't afraid, except of my untested shortcomings.

I dropped in on a Tibetan Buddhist community in northern England. I saw another transplanted model that didn't suit me. But it was interesting to see the Dalai Lama show up there and hold court for a day.

One resident lama had a giant, clear bubble around his head for an aura. It made me think of a thin crystal fishbowl. I found it to be unusual and his manner charming. I just wanted to go back to a quiet jungle cave in robes.

I also decided that I should visit my home city to say goodbye to some friends. I thought this was a good idea because if I wished to visit at some point in the future, it'd be harder to do so as a monk. Eastern-robed Western aspirants on Western city streets had always amused me as clownish. I didn't want to stand out like that. Best I got the last look out of my system then.

At a family wedding, I encountered an uncle by marriage. For many years a widower, he was the personal executor of my parent's small estate. The last time I'd seen him was at my grandmother's eighty-second birthday party four years before. I'd told him then that I'd looked into the financial market, and I wished to buy gold with my inheritance. The way it was invested it would be worth nothing by the time I got it.

Without missing a beat, my uncle had answered, "You don't know what you're talking about. Learn a trade, and I'll buy you a screwdriver for Christmas."

Needless to say, I wasn't impressed. Gold went up three hundred percent within the year.

Remaining distant with him at the reception somehow upped me in his eyes. In front of a tableful of relatives, he said he could tell I was now able to handle the money. He made the astonishing declaration that I should contact the institution it was invested through to release it to me. Figuring it was about time that finally happened, I phoned the trust officer a few days later. I continued spending freely as I kept travelling, expecting more funds to be available when I needed them.

Thousands of miles later, I was sleeping on the floor of a childhood friend's when I made the follow-up call for cash. The woman in charge of the account solemnly informed me that my uncle said he didn't know what I was talking about. Calling him, he denied to me he'd ever said such a thing! Confrontational, he demanded I come back to discuss it with him and the lawyer who drew up the will. "Perhaps he was just drunk at the wedding…" was my most charitable thought.

I didn't have enough for a ticket directly to Sri Lanka. I found an incredibly cheap ticket to Bangkok. I expected Bangkok would be like London (it isn't), full of 'bucket shops' where one could buy highly discounted last-minute tickets to other places. I wouldn't have enough for a hotel but knew an insider secret of Asia.

Back then it was supposed to work. If a person went into a temple of any stripe, put their hands together in prayer salute and requested to stay three days, the answer had to be yes. I'd heard this from an older, completely crippled, American ex-pat acid-head, with whom I occasionally tripped on full moons in his lush garden in Kandy. He'd assured me this was an unwritten rule all across Asia.

I told my friend I'd put this secret rule to the test.

He kept trying to give me an obscure guidebook, one of those multi-country ones for Southeast Asia, and I kept refusing. Finally, he said, "Fine. I want to see where you're going."

A minute later, he gloated, "Here. First page for Bangkok. Three temples you can stay in." I razored out the page.

The flight was the 'milk run' to get there which is why it was so cheap. There were incredibly long stopovers in way too many airports for good taste. Thirty-six hours later I landed in Thailand.

I grabbed a tourist map of Bangkok from a brochure rack and walked up to an airport guard. "Do you speak English?" I asked.

"Yes, yes!" he replied.

"Do you know where these three temples are?"

He looked at the page I gave him, "Yes, yes!"

I handed him a pen. "Will you please mark on this map where they are?"

"Yes, yes!"

"Which one is the nicest?"

He pointed to Wat Mahadhatu. I thanked him and caught a shared taxi.

Over time, I discovered the other two didn't exist. Not by name or location. Curious about it, I was thorough in my search with many inside resources at my disposal.

I eventually learned it's rude in Thai culture to say no. One has to learn how to ask a question so 'yes' will be the right answer. Very tricky; indeed.

I got out of the taxi on a busy street looking very 'big and pink and not like me', with a trench coat over one arm, and a brown boar-skin travel bag in my other hand. I stood in front of a large gate lined on either side with many small shops. Going through it, I could find no one who spoke English. Giggling Thai school girls in their uniforms ran away from me. Nuns in white bent over sweeping with short brooms shook their bald heads at me. Young monks wrapped up in bright orange robes hurriedly went about their own business without a glance.

Eventually, I found a group of four obese monks who spoke English getting into a minivan with a driver. By their haughty manner, I knew they were politicos. I was already aware of the marriage of Church and State in Asia.

"Could you please tell me where I can find the abbot?" I asked.

By their quick, quizzical chatter with each other, I could tell this really intrigued them.

"What do you want to see the abbot for?" asked one as he settled into his seat in the back.

"I want to ask his permission to stay for three days."

They roared with laughter. Without even looking at me again, the monk closed the door, and then waved his hand for their driver to leave. Later when I learned where I was, I realised this was the same as going into the Vatican and asking for the Pope.

For fun, I eventually took to calling Wat Mahadhatu "Vatican City-Bangkok," due to its political significance as the traditional seat of the Thai national religion. It sits across from the Royal Palace but the tourists never see it, although they can. For centuries, its abbots have been the *Sangharajs*, 'Supreme Patriarchs', who are to Thai national church politics what the Popes in Rome are to Catholic government.

That was until King Rama the Fourth gave the honour to another temple during his reign 150 years ago. Imagine the furore. Now the *Sangharaj* comes from one then the other in tandem. It was Wat Mahadhatu's turn at the time.

After the minivan had left, I noticed another monk, a skinny one in just his *sarong* and one-shouldered undershirt, sweeping nearby, watching me. He motioned for me to come over. "Engrit? Engrit?" he inquired, nodding.

I nodded back. The monk indicated that I should follow him, and he led me through a rabbit warren of alleyways. I was beginning to wonder at the size of the place when we arrived in front of yet another whitewashed building. Pointing up the stairs, he repeated the only words he'd said to me, "Engrit. Engrit."

Thanking him, I went inside. There, amongst the bustle sat a very tidy Thai monk in orange robes behind a desk. "Do you speak English?" I asked.

"Yes."

I sat down across from him. I put my hands together in prayer salute in front of me. "I'm on my way to Sri Lanka to be a monk. May I please stay for three days?"

He was shocked. He didn't know what to say. Apparently, this had never happened before, but he was bound by the unwritten rule to say yes. In that moment, I knew it too. I stayed silent with my hands held in front of me, smiling.

The monk hemmed and hawed. He asked for my passport and flipped through the pages in it while looking off, trying to buy time while he thought. I just kept smiling. Finally, he said yes. Producing a large book, he had me sign in.

"We have some European monks here. Would you like to meet them?" he asked.

I assured him I would.

We headed upstairs where he showed me the large room with curtained off sections that I could stay in. After dropping my bag and coat there, he took me next door to a screen door that had an old brown robe thrown over it for privacy.

"Phra George? Phra George?" he timidly called while tapping lightly on the door frame.

The reply from inside was fast and very gruff, "Who is it?" I recognised the accent as British.

"It's... it's me, Phra George."

Equally gruff, "What do you want?"

"There's a foreigner here with me. He's going to be staying with us for three days."

Incredulous surprise; unpleasant, threatening tone, "What! Who let him in?"

I leaned my head against the door frame. I was way too tired for this. I'd done acid the night before my flight, for what I thought might be the last time ever. I'd been up for at least sixty hours by this point.

"I… I… I did… venerable sir."

A moment's pause, and then a relenting tone, "Oh, alright then. Let's have a look at him."

Relieved, the Thai monk opened the door and stepped aside. Thick smoke billowed out through it. As it cleared, I looked inside.

There, in the middle of an oversized broom closet with the corners piled high with books and a disproportionately large shrine illuminated with Christmas tree lights, on an irregular scrap of Oriental carpet, not a square angle to it, sat two shaven-headed, bare-chested Western monks. One was young, the other old. They sat side by side in the yoga posture called 'the pundit's pose', in just their brown *sarongs*, big smiles on their faces, smoking big, black, oily cigars. The scene was too mondo for words.

Silently stepping inside, I didn't bow three times to the monks, as is traditional, as it was just too weird for such a formality. Instead, crossing my ankles, I dropped straight down into the same pundit's pose facing them, which is always an impressive move. It was the only way to do it in such confined quarters. I raised my hands in a simple prayer salute. They looked at each other, nodding once in approval. Looking back to me, the older one lifted a thermos jug and enquired lightly, "Coffee?"

I could smell it was real and not instant. Somehow, I felt I'd arrived. I still didn't know that anyone wanting to stay had to have this older monk's permission and that very few got it. No one, but no one, slid past 'The Dragon'.

After a long conversation, I asked Phra George if he knew of a healer monk I'd heard about up the Chao Phraya River, a stone's throw from where we were. The monk was an empath that sucked people's diseases into himself. Phra George said no and asked me why.

I told him about how my knees were degenerating along with my spine. He replied that he'd had trouble with his own knees but that at the hospital across the river a woman acupuncturist fixed them for him, and he'd been fine ever since. He went on to explain that it was a public hospital, so the treatment which took three weeks was free. If I liked, I could stay there for free; they'd feed me downstairs, and I could go through the acupuncture series. It would only cost me thirty cents per day for the ferry.

"We can go together tomorrow and enquire," Phra George offered magnanimously.

I didn't hesitate to agree.

"There's only one catch." He continued, "While you're here you have to practice meditation under my direction."

That caught me off guard. I figured that he knew his stuff from our conversation, but I already had a practice of Samadhi. "I guess I could do some Vipassana as well. That could be interesting…"

"No smorgasbording. Only Vipassana as I teach it. It has to be a full retreat or not at all."

I stammered, but his tone was final. I figured that at worst I had nothing to lose but a few weeks, and so far our conversation had been great. I wasn't convinced about the acupuncture, though, which was the bait on the hook. "Let's see what she says at the hospital tomorrow," I replied cautiously, "It still sounds good to me."

My reluctance was because of the rigours of practising Vipassana in full retreat. The ten-day retreat I did in Sri Lanka before Helen sat with me for that first time was another form of Vipassana, so I had a little experience with it. That had been lightweight with no real supervision and was interesting.

But this, I'd learned in our conversation up to that point, was an extreme form of practice. It meant sixteen or more hours per day of sitting and slow-motion walking in a curtained off section of the large room next door with progress reports twice a day. One is supposed to just watch the current action and label it without thinking about anything else.

You soon discover you're best at thinking about everything else rather than just watching and labelling. You drive yourself up the wall with your thinking while trying not to, even though the practice gives you the tools to stop it. This challenge isn't for everyone.

Phra George, a culturally transplanted urban ascetic, was one of those unique individuals so grounded in what he was, that in all of the affectations he presented there was an element of theatre for the fast-minded. If one really wants to know the meaning of 'eccentric', one has to think of the English. The English just laugh when I say that. Then there's a brilliance that bounces off the finest of edges between genius and eccentricity. That was Phra George, riding that edge for his own entertainment.

Lightning-witted, a ball of shining energy (or was it simply profuse sweating in the heat?), sitting in half-lotus or pundit's pose, spontaneously expressive with his face, precise gestures, and belly-shaking laugh, George was a character. His rich voice came from deep in his chest, resonating clearly as he played with the English language as only one that loves communicating knowledge born of personal experience can. High voltage, George could get loud quickly, enjoying a joke or a serious discussion.

I soon saw that if something wasn't happening and he thought it should be, Phra George would stir it up! He had one purpose in mind: results in those he agreed to teach. His understanding of the human condition, the Western mind in relation to that, and how to drop a Westerner's mind into a moment removed from all reference points was unparalleled pure genius. The familiar river of personal reality became the treacherous rapids of rocky koans. Phra George aimed to fling his students over the falls.

I also came to see that all of the theatre was equally for the student's benefit as well as for George's own entertainment although, in some moments, I wasn't always sure. With mock ferocity, he would kick us if we weren't paying attention while sitting, telling us that for the Zen it was an honour to die from your teacher beating you for the sake of your own enlightenment. All of this while plaguing you with bad puns. These were the cultivated, cloistered circumstances of practising Vipassana for thirty days at a time with no contact with the outside world.

In one regard, life in this busy Thai temple was anything but peaceful. On the main floor, there was a constant cacophony of noise from people milling about. Upstairs, monks came and went, either to classes or about their city lives. Everyone walked through the main entrance and past a long, raised platform where lay meditators in white practised sitting or slow-motion walking. Then they went past the always-full main meeting hall to the dining and kitchen areas in the back or to get upstairs.

The volunteer-staffed kitchen fed meals from donated food to at least fifty monks and meditators every day, twice per day. In Theravadin temples, no one eats after noon. No group of people in the world can do that much on-location preparation and turnover quietly. The Thais did it efficiently, but early morning banging pots and clattering dishes were facts of life.

Upstairs, foreign residents were allowed to meditate in closed-door privacy, but the din never stopped. Any complaint about it landed you in the middle aisle downstairs until further notice. There, the old ladies bumped past you continually. It could take a couple of weeks until none of it mattered anymore. Trying to fake that it didn't matter never worked.

To mention any old chronic pains that might pop up would be met with Phra George's standard yet serious quip delivered deadpan, "Congratulations! You have a built-in object of awareness for meditation."

I had no idea what I was getting into. I knew it wasn't going to be an easy trip, but I didn't know the tough parts which were inevitable could be used to such full advantage. But that's why it worked, along with knowing that everyone really did have my best interests at heart.

After breakfast, that first morning in Section Five of Wat Mahadhatu, Phra George and I boarded the crowded public ferry across the Chao Phraya. The acupuncturist examined me and sadly told the both of us that she could take away my pain for the length of the treatment but then it would come back.

High-energy George bowled right over her pessimistic response, "Fine, madam! You take away his pain, and I'll do the rest!"

You don't argue with a monk, and you most certainly didn't argue with Phra George. Charmed by this, and in no position to refuse, she told me to go back into the examination room and lie down on the table.

And so my routine of early morning practice, breakfast, ferry, ten block walk, needles, and back for lunch and the rest of the day in Section Five began.

My back and knees responded well. With almost no discomfort I was able to sit alternately in half-lotus or easy posture (an open half-lotus) for an hour. I'd start with an hour of slow-motion walking meditation for four metres, turn, four more metres, turn, four more metres. This was for up to six-hour blocks at a time.

In total, I was usually practising twelve hours per day for those first three weeks. George would take a meditation report three times a day. My instructions usually changed twice a day.

Phra George was fully interactive as a teacher. Always available for conversation when I wasn't sitting or walking, he said he could keep the meditation practice on track and moving faster that way, wherever it was going. He also said it was at cross purposes to give me too much theory to think about. He just wanted me watching and labelling the watching while it happened exactly as he instructed.

George told me that with this method if you were really quick, an experience of Nibbana could happen in one week. If you were average, it took a month. That seems incredibly short until you start doing the mindfulness practice. Time takes on a whole new meaning with the intensity of the method. I was doing restricted hours because of my mornings away. The usual sixteen hours per day was considered a minimum. The Burmese kept you at it for more.

He said if you were slow, it could take three months if it was going to work at all, which was a very long time with this method and he wouldn't keep a student at it past a month. Then he'd tell them to go to the beach, have a rest, and if they felt like it, come back and try again. He felt a meditator's mind lost its incisive punch after that length of time in retreat.

Phra George kept me interested and kept me practising. I was glad when the acupuncture treatments finished so I could practice without interruption. A week later, I had the breakthrough experience.

Afterwards, we were sitting on the scrap of Oriental carpet that also served as his mattress, drinking coffee and talking about the experience of Nibbana.

"I don't think much of this 'nothing' of yours," I said flatly. "It doesn't even warrant a capital 'N'."

He laughed. "Now you're quoting famous responses. What'd you expect? Bright lights? Big city?"

For an in-depth treatment of the path to Nibbana, please read Theory and Practice C, 'The Insight Knowledges'.

For a brief treatment on the ramifications of experiencing Nibbana, *please read Theory and Practice D, 'Grokking Nibbana'.*

For insights into the Thai method of Vipassana, please read Theory and Practice E, 'Inner Sanctum Secrets of Vipassana'.

Chapter 9

The Meditation Teacher for all of Thailand

First, it's important to put Phra George and Section Five of Wat Mahadhatu into greater perspective. And that perspective giver is whose section it was: Phra Tepsiddhimuni. That was the man's name during my time there so that's how I'm going to mostly refer to him, 'Phra Tep' for short. His name changed several times throughout his life according to his advancing formal rank in the Thai clergy. His final name was Phra Dhamma Theerarach Mahamuni. His royally bestowed title of 'The Meditation Teacher for all of Thailand' remained constant.

George met Phra Tep in 1964 on Phra Tep's (then called Phra Rajsiddhimuni) first visit to London. George was the one in the Buddhist scene who showed the foreign dignitary monks around. He'd studied with some eminent meditation teachers, and Vipassana became his preferred form of practice. He respected Phra Raj's's to-the-point approach, benefitting greatly from his instruction.

George felt a deep affinity for the tiny, always cheerful monk. Phra Tep returned every year to teach at the Thai temple in London and other European cities until his many duties in Wat Mahadhatu made it impossible. During those years, he was the head of the Thai clergy in Britain.

Phra Tep was an important Pali scholar who in the 1950s was chosen to attend the two years long Sixth Buddhist Council in Burma on behalf of Wat Mahadhatu. The official purpose of this Sixth Council in 2500 years was to confirm the texts and practices of the Theravada. The Nyanaponika and his teacher, the Nyanatiloka, were the only Western monks of the eight countries and 2500 monastics attending.[1]

The unofficial purpose was to introduce the Vipassana meditation technique to the world that the Mahasi Sayadaw, the Burmese monk who organised the council, learned from his teacher and had developed further. Any such method needed canonical support which was the Council's job to scrutinise. A Council's official endorsement is the bottom line in Theravada for acceptability. Phra Tep returned to Thailand to report to his superiors that through personal experience the method did indeed work and was validated by canonical analysis.

Here was another firebrand whom it was hard to keep up with when he walked, but I did. It was especially challenging in crowds which he could flit through with ease because of his size. Patient with all and approachable, always enthusiastic in his teaching, he was an exemplary monk on every level. The Thai people adored him.

George stopped at Wat Mahadhatu on his way to Burma to become a monk. Also having been a student of the Mahasi Sayadaw's, he expected to go on to his centre to ordain. Walking in on Phra Tep in the large main temple delivering a discourse over a microphone to the Thai laity, the revered monk spotted him. Still holding the microphone, Phra Tep asked George what he was doing there. When George replied that he wanted to become a monk himself, Phra Tep welcomed him to Wat Mahadhatu and his section. If you have any respect, you don't say no.

That was nine years before I came along. Phra George shared the senior instructor's enthusiasm for teaching. Phra Tep sometimes told George upon admittance which Western students would ultimately be successful and which ones wouldn't.

Section Five was quite unassuming in appearance but unequivocal in accomplishing its task of maintaining the Buddha's

---

[1] *The Chatta Sanghayana Souvenir Album*, p. 92. Union Buddha Sasana Council Press, Yegu, Rangoon, Burma

teaching as a living, working reality. No gaudy splash in those halls steeped in the humble tradition of worldly renunciation, it was a very no-airs Thai spiritual community centre.

There was no fanfare either. On the ground floor, in the plain central meeting area, a few flat-sided, white pillars were part of the construction. On one side of a pillar at the edge of the hall, hung maybe ten black and white pictures, about six inches by four inches each, of individual monks sitting in meditation. They were just ordinary snapshots, taken by different cameras at different times in slightly different plain frames with no explanation, almost insignificant except for their puzzling presence. I wondered about them for a year before I finally asked who the monks were.

Phra George told me the photos were taken at the twenty-three hour and fifty-nine minute mark. The monks in them had mastered the incredible ability to sit in *Nirodha Samapatti*, the 'attainment of cessation'. Each monk sat making the intention to enter the state and sit for exactly twenty-four hours. In a few minutes, their breathing would stop. Then they'd turn ashen grey with no signs of life while they remained upright, motionless.

At precisely the twenty-four-hour mark, they'd suddenly start breathing again. Their normal colour would return a few minutes later; then they'd open their eyes, just fine. An ancient commentary advises not to enter the state for more than seven days at a time because then the suspended animation is too hard on the body.[2]

I have no idea how many month-long retreats I did during my first seventeen months in Thailand and when coming back two more years in a row for six months each as a layman. Phra Tep's final teaching manifested a handful of months after I left that second year. It was a posthumous affair. George told me the story when he came to my house in the West to lead a retreat a month later.

---

[2] Vism-mht 903 (Paramatthamanjusa, Visuddhimagga Attakatha), *Visuddhimagga* XXIII, footnote 14

Phra George suddenly got the insistent idea that he should leave the robes and return to the West. Two Austrian doctors were trying to convince him to come to Vienna to establish a centre.

Leaving the robes is a huge decision, the biggest possible for a serious monk. Only by living it can one know the full opportunity that comes with that way of life. There is no parallel. George felt he had to trust his gut instincts, though. He didn't know how Phra Tep would respond.

Phra Tep's response turned out to be, "what took you so long?" He always expected George would return to the West to teach.

George was still in Bangkok when Phra Tep died less than two weeks later, apparently of a heart attack. He'd just completed translating the entire Pali canon into Thai as his last contribution to the world, which was no small feat. The Pali canon is thirteen and a half times the length of the old and new testaments combined. It doesn't contradict itself once on the point of doctrine.

George said that if he were still in robes, he'd never have been able to leave as duty would have required him to stay out of respect. The assumed obligations of Oriental culture absorb into a person's system after a while.

Word about Phra Tep's death spread like a shock wave through Bangkok. People started pouring in as the monks began preparing his body for the numerous ceremonies that would follow. Not only would such ceremonies be to pay respect, but they would also pay handsomely. The more important the monk, the more money the body is worth. In this case, it would be worth untold thousands of dollars, potentially hundreds of thousands.

That's because of a modern-day version of the 'water ceremony'. The water ceremony is the oldest ritual done between the clergy and the laity, dating directly from the Buddha himself.[3] After offering food, robes or anything to a monk or a group of them, sometimes the donor then pours water from a container over his or

---

[3] Khuddaka Nikaya, Khuddaka Patha 7 = Petavatthu 1, Uraga Vagga 5

her own finger into another container while the monk(s) chant a blessing. While pouring the water, the donor considers to whom she or he wishes to transfer the 'merit' (profitable karma) for the generous action. The collected water is then poured over a living plant to complete matters.

Never mind that the Buddha said merit could only be transferred to beings stuck in the realm of the 'hungry ghosts',[4] today donors take this as an opportunity to send it to anyone. That can include one's spouse so that they can win the lottery. You even 'make merit' for transferring it. The self-interested making of merit on the part of the laity supports the entire Buddhist world. You can never have too much good karma in the bank.

In this lucrative, contemporary version of the water ceremony, the corpse of a revered monk is dressed in new robes then put on display. For a contribution, fitting to the prestige of the monk and the ability of the donor, a donor can pour water over the dead monk's hand which hangs over the side of the display into a container while a group of at least four monks chant a blessing. The more important the monk, the more merit one makes.

So, just as they were getting the corpse and the hall ready that night, some men from a local university showed up with Phra Tep's signature on a document. He'd donated his body to science to be cut up like any other cadaver for teaching anatomy. The monks freaked out. The men took the body. But guess what? *The monks bought it back!*

To no avail. The Thais are master embalmers. A monk's gold-leafed body can sit on display for years without a problem, as described in the next chapter. Not in this case, though. No matter what they tried, the body wouldn't stop decomposing. His corpse rotted so quickly that they didn't have a chance to put it on display once. It bubbled, it smoked. It reduced to a puddle of goo within days. No one had ever seen or heard of anything like it.

---

[4] Anguttara Nikaya 10.177

This gives us some interesting food for thought. *Theory and Practice E, 'Inner Sanctum Secrets of Vipassana'*, reveals that the Thais added the ability to make intentions (*aditthanas*) an integral working part of their Vipassana technique. What sort of intention did this Thai meditation master make, and why, to have such a phenomenon occur with his body?

Did he sign it over to the university so it would be under accredited observation when it decomposed in this fashion? Or did he sign it over because he disapproved of this variation of the water ceremony that he knew would take place, and that was his definitive statement about the matter without any confrontation? Did he set it up so that if this event occurred, he would have known well the character of the monks around him, then the body was to self-destruct?

We'll never know, but one thing's for sure: even if you're not around to watch, there's nothing like having the last laugh.

Chapter 10

Mysterious Secrets of the Northern Monastery

Phra George knew I wasn't interested in basing myself in Bangkok and that I was still considering continuing on to Sri Lanka to be a monk. He started offering daily to take me up north to a rural temple to ordain where the abbot whom he utmost respected had recently died. He figured I'd find my way into the jungle from there easily enough. I hesitated because I loved Lanka dearly.

He told me wonderful stories of the old forest monk. For example, when George was in London considering entering the Order himself, the monk heard of him and sent him a set of robes as encouragement. He was delighted when I agreed to have a look. We set off by overnight train for Chiang Mai. We would arrive just in time for the one-hundred-day ceremony after the old monk's death. Such celebrations were always a major event.

A van met us at the train station. Before we even arrived at Wat Phra Buddha Bat Tak Pah, I knew I'd entered a different world of the Thai monkhood than that of 'Vatican City-Bangkok' or that I'd seen in Sri Lanka. It may have been at this point that I started to fall in love with northern Thailand.

We came across a young monk from the temple out on the road for a walk. The driver stopped to speak with him. The first thing I noticed was the way he wore his robe and the 108 brown-bead necklace around his neck. I'd seen beads like this on Tibetan monks and Hindu yogis but never before on a Theravadin monk. They're a tool for meditation.

Not only was his rectangular robe worn with his right shoulder bare, which is strictly reserved for inside a temple, but the folding of it was unique to my eye. Pleated lengthwise with the bulk of it draping over his left shoulder, he had a short 'sleeve' pulled out of the folded stack down to his elbow. A single layer from underneath of the stack wrapped around his body and then tucked back in. A four-inch wide woven band tied him into the whole affair. It cinched his waist with a stylised, asymmetrical knot, its loose ends rendered into equal lengths. The whole presentation looked very formal, like an Oriental warrior from a bygone era.

I asked Phra George about it. "This is the traditional style of the *Mahanikaya* [the main denomination of Theravada in Thailand] of old," he replied. "Only in this region do they still wear their robes like this. It's permissible to wear one shoulder bare outside of the temple. It always makes me feel good to see this."

I would be given one of these beaded necklaces at my ordination. The first time I wore it into Wat Mahadhatu, a city monk chastised me harshly. In no uncertain terms, he told me it was utterly improper for a monk to have such a practice with its heretical associations. I left it out of the equation when I went down there from then on.

His objections stemmed from it being an aid for Samadhi meditation using a mantra that is popularly associated with the northeastern forest sect, even though they don't use beaded necklaces in their lineage. In that sect, they have developed a cosmology that has no canonical basis. In it, Samadhi absorptions equal levels of attainment in understanding Nibbana. The mantra they use is '*Buddho*', for the state of mind of a Buddha.

The quality of a Buddha's mind is a Samadhi meditation subject detailed in the *Visuddhimagga* as 'recollection of the Buddha'.[1] It specifies the subject will bring you to access concentration but not to full absorption as it relies on specific characteristics. One needs to change the object of awareness from the contemplated characteristics to what arises as the 'counterpart sign'. Whether that sign is light, a feeling of increased energy or something else, an increase in phenomena occurs which allows for a leap through it

---

[1] *Visuddhimagga* VII, 1, 2*ff.*

into full absorption. How to work with the counterpart sign is detailed in the book as well.[2]

The recollection of the Buddha is as close as Theravada gets to the become-the-deity practice of Tantra although it doesn't have a particular frequency as the destination. In this northern Thai version, one holds the beaded necklace in the right hand. The index finger moves one bead at a time while reciting 'Bud-dho, Bud-dho'. The bead slides across the small gap between contact and placement, anchoring the attention. Rejection of this ancient tool for Samadhi showed me how a new form of fundamentalism was arising in the main denomination of Thai Buddhism that embraced only Vipassana.

Wat Phra Buddha Bat Tak Pah itself is quite large. It's set back from the road up on the rise at the foot of 'Lying Elephant Hill'. The gates have an enormous mythological beast on either side that I hadn't seen before. Phra George told me these were traditional temple guardians in the North.

The Thais treated us like visiting dignitaries. Phra George was well known and respected. They gave us a cottage built out of carved basalt blocks with a tile roof right behind the main meeting hall. The white lace curtains charmed me. The place was nothing fancy, but George said that they reserved this one for important monks because of its location. I understood and appreciated the intended honour when they gave it to me for over a year after my ordination.

I explored the temple with Phra George as my guide. In the main hall with its very high vaulted ceiling, in front of the giant golden Buddha statue and shrine, lay Krubar Brahmachako's gold-leafed body. Wrapped in their traditional draping of robes, it lay in a large, gilded white coffin on a high raised dais. A full-length mirror was horizontally tilted over it at a forty-five degrees angle so that the entire hall of people could see the body. Huge flower arrangements and many large candles surrounded the coffin.

---

[2] *Visuddhimagga* IV, 31*ff.*

On the floor in front were tiers of small candles as well as lots of smoking incense sticks in ceramic pots lit by the laity. Throngs of kneeling Thais dressed in white with hands in prayer salute bowed three times each on a humungous, wool Oriental carpet. Covering a fifth of the floor, it could hold sixty people.

The old monk's body remained like this on display for the next two years while they built a shrine on top of the hill out back. Then the body was cremated, and the ashes interred up there.

The shrine for the Krubar's remains would be the last monument built by the province's ecclesiastical governor, Maha Khun. He once won an award from the King for his temples designed in the traditional fashion, including one in Los Angeles, California. It fit that his crowning contribution was to be a tribute to the last of the great forest monks.

Four hundred and fifty broad steps carved out of basalt rock blocks lead to the top. Flanking these on either side are two huge seven-headed protector dragons who face pilgrims at the bottom. The dragons' undulating bodies run up the hill to its crest. Their scales are green-glazed tiles topped with a brown-glazed ridge up their backs.

Large protector 'demons' stand at the top to scare away evil spirits. The temples have multi-tiered, orange-tiled roofs with stylised dragons (very art deco-ish) on every corner of every tier. This arrangement is common in Thailand. These particular temples are quite enchanting, looking like fairy tale gingerbread structures.

Exquisitely gilded filigree covers the many pillars both inside and outside of the buildings. Dominating all of it is the golden dome of the enormous stupa over the Krubar's relics. This small yet magnificent complex has a commanding view over the countryside.

The grounds of the monastery below are extensive with more than one hundred cottages, all constructed with carved basalt blocks. The place is spotlessly clean with a large reservoir in the back, aerated by a tall fountain. Mango trees and flowering bougainvillaea are sprinkled throughout the grounds.

In 1984, Wat Phra Buddha Bat Tak Pah was the fifth largest temple outside of Bangkok. It was home to one hundred and fifty young novices as well as thirty or more monks and twenty or so nuns. Often, the education as a novice is the only schooling a poor farm boy gets before returning to work his father's paddy fields. Temples serve many functions in Thailand. This one quickly became a popular pilgrimage point after the Krubar's death with large tour busses pulling in daily.

There are two other large buildings of note besides the main meeting hall. One tall, pillared affair with large, gilded, carved wooden windows is for official acts of the monkhood. I was ordained there two months after that first visit.

The other building was a curiosity with four entrances. Both buildings have the multi-tiered, orange-tiled roofs like most Thai temples as well as the ornate mosaics of coloured glass inside and out. I wasn't prepared though for what I found inside of this four-entranced hall.

'Wat Phra Buddha Bat Tak Pah' means 'Temple of the Buddha's footprint and robe drying place'. Under an elaborately mosaicked structure inside with a golden Buddha statue pointing in each of the four directions are two large carved footprints in the rock. They say these are the Buddha's astral footprints as, of course, he never set physical foot in Thailand. Hmmm... well, his astral right foot was almost twice as big at nearly two metres in length than his astral left foot! A quaint pamphlet in English assured one they were real.

The carving of the right foot with its lotus-petalled border I recognised as done in an ancient Indian style dating back 2,000 years. I'd seen many carvings in this style throughout India, especially in the south where I stayed the longest. What was this doing here as Buddhism in this area is only supposed to date from the eleventh century CE?

The 'robe drying' carving is equally an enigma. According to the local myth, after his meal during that astral visit, Ananda, his attendant who was there with him, washed the Buddha's robe and laid it on the ground to dry where it left this impression. This 'astral impression' is unmistakably a likeness of a robe of the Theravadin Order. 'Robes' were simply cloaks of patches stylised into rectangular panels for easy identification as belonging to the Order. These were easy to come by, low-maintenance, all-weather tropical camping gear circa 2500 years ago.

This robe, though, has a different number of panels than they do today, and the carving was primitively hacked into the rock. It gives a person the sense that it was hastily done which is very unusual for an ancient sacred site. I've been in rock temples in India that took generations of master carvers to hollow out of hills as royally sponsored works of devotion. As monuments of religious art, they were meticulously executed.

Holes in the rock show where wooden posts once stood. There are more holes on the next empty hill. A small natural cave lies between the footprints and the robe carvings. The current building over the footprints was constructed in the early part of the twentieth century CE, but this was obviously the site of a monastery whose story is lost in antiquity.

Over my time there, which spanned the next fifteen months, different Thai forest monks passed through to pay their respects. Sometimes they'd get further practice instruction from the meditation teacher whom the Krubar appointed to succeed him. They'd usually only stay a night or two at the most. Sometimes not even, preferring to sleep under their traditional large umbrellas with mosquito nets over them, hung from trees in the jungle. I understood. I had a quiet cave by a waterfall far off in the jungle that I liked to practice in.

I'd converse with these forest monks having a resident monk translate as my Thai was limited. I always enquired about the places that they frequented and if other spots had similar footprints. They told me there were jungle caves in a string through the north of Thailand where there were also carved footprints of the same sort with lotus-petalled borders. They informed me that this was the only preserved one. The others were quite eroded due to weather exposure, some almost entirely destroyed. As far as I know, all of the other well-known Buddha footprints in Thailand are from much later periods and lack the border.

Time, in the form of devotion, took its toll on this carving as well. While I was a monk at the wat, a tree root poked up through the bottom of the footprint. All of the water that was poured on it in ceremonies over the years attracted the thirsty tree. Maha Khun ordered the tree cut down, and the bottom of the carving cemented.

The footprint was a Buddhist symbol before the first statues of him appeared approximately six hundred years after he lived. Emperor Asoka of India sent Buddhist missionaries into Southeast Asia in the third century BCE, but no one knows what became of them. The Burmese at one point controlled Chiang Mai, which is less than fifty kilometres away. They claim Buddhism has been part of their culture since the time of the Buddha. Whoever was responsible for this carving in the Indian style left an enduring symbol of their Buddhist faith on this site long before history records it in this region.

I speculate that as this original form of Buddhism in the area was dying out, the last remaining monks grew concerned that the meaning of this footprint might fall into obscurity over time. Perhaps they were even concerned that someday people might think this was a Jain site. The footprint was also a symbol of the Jains, a sect of naked ascetics whose founder was an older contemporary of the Buddha.

The Pali canon mentions the Jains. The Buddha considered them to be a threat to the longevity of his teaching as people are always impressed with asceticism which the Jains epitomised. I believe the Buddhist robe was quickly carved to make sure there'd be no mistake by whoever should find this site deep in the jungle. Thick forest covered the area complete with small jungle cats (civets) right up through the first years of the Krubar residing there.

In the rock near the carved footprints and the robe carvings, there is a handful of weathered impressions that look like degraded footprints of different sizes, including one the size of a small child's.

111

Legend has it they were put there over different centuries to show the accomplishment of mental powers. Extrapolating on a demonstration I was privy to years later in Bali, if the small one is real, it could have been set there by a child holding an accomplished monk's hand.

The one-hundred-day ceremony I recognised as an honouring of a much-loved monk's passing. A few venerated, old, wizened contemporaries of the late abbot were there with their entourages. Visiting their temples with Phra George in the days following the ceremony, one shared remarkable similarity always caught my eye. Each had large black and white photos of themselves with swirling solid lines of pure white surrounding them. It was as if a laser light pen had scribbled wildly over the negative at lightning speed the moment someone snapped the shutter.

Many monks of all ages milled around. There was even a young monk from somewhere in the backwoods with the wild looks of a witch doctor who had a table of amulets for sale. I was surprised to see him there with his wares as such isn't considered right livelihood for a monk, by any stretch. He must have filled a niche in a jungle society far removed from the mainstream.

Forest-dwelling monks, called 'tudong monks' from the Pali *dhutanga*, which means 'ascetic practices', have formed the backbone of the Buddha's teaching in Asia for millennia. Today the tradition is much lionised as temple life easily allows for complacency. At Wat Mahadhatu, I heard that only ten percent of the monks ever make it to the forest, and only ten percent of the monkhood meditate. Not that they are the same monks either. None the less, the Thais feel supporting all monks is worth it to preserve this core of serious practitioners.

Personally, I think they're generous with their count. From what I saw at that time, I came to expect that two percent of the monks ever went to the jungle and that only two percent ever meditated. These percentages overlap. There's not near the jungle left now either that there was then. No species survives out of its habitat.

The cynical curiosity for me was the young, too confident, too smooth, too good-looking, famous forest monk. Tall, with piercing eyes and sporting a manly five o'clock shadow (very unusual for a Thai), his almost-khaki shade of robe, the perfect weight of cotton for a rugged roamer, was tossed over his shoulder with flair. He looked like he just stepped off of the cover of a GQ magazine for monks.

Following Phra Yantra Amaro was a battalion of younger, eager, new, devoted forest monks with the same distinctive shade of robes and some fawning female lay supporters. The King had even given him a national park to roam around in as its resident teacher. He invited me to please come anytime. I knew better. Phra George laughed long and low when I remarked that he had the polish of a rich lawyer.

Phra Yantra Amaro became quite a charismatic celebrity before eventually going down in flames over too many gnarly sex scandals and was unwillingly defrocked. The scandals included rape accusations, an illegitimate daughter in Belgrade, and credit card receipts from New Zealand brothels where the girls called him "Batman" as he always kept his robes on. When the Thai government wanted him on criminal charges, the Americans gave him asylum as he claimed he'd never get a fair trial.

His outrageous story saddened when he blew through a stop sign driving a car, killing a young woman in Minnesota. After doing time for that one, Yantra Amaro became a California guru in uniquely green robes, claiming millions of international followers. He quietly returned to Thailand twenty years later to visit after the statute of limitations on his legal problems expired.

In the monastery, there is another footprint that is an astonishing jaw-dropper. It sits in rock in a back corner, surrounded by a simple, small, knee-high concrete wall, four concrete pillars, and a roof on top to protect it. Maha Khun had the structure built during my time at the wat. I'd have preferred to see the footprint enshrined in something more grandly spacious, more fitting as a tribute to what it is. I consider it to be one of the wonders of the world.

Krubar Brahmachako, aka Phra Subrohmyan, ordained as a novice at a young age and then continued straight on into the monkhood. 'Krubar' is an honorific reserved for deeply respected elderly monks who start off as novices. There's only ever one at a time in a region.

His forest-dwelling life occurred in a bygone era of Indo-China. He wandered on jungle paths for twenty-eight years avoiding people. To sit near him, one apparently got 'high', so he stayed on the move as people would swarm him after a short time in any one location. After so many years of living in this taxing fashion, he agreed to an abbotship at Wat Phra Buddha Bat Tak Pah. A couple of decades before that, it had a new building constructed over the carved footprints.

When something is donated in the name of the teaching, if it's an allowable gift, one doesn't or can't say no. Because of this, a huge monastery sprung up around him, complete with an impressive water system. That included an ornate cottage with marble panels inside and a screened marble floored walkway surrounding it. As it was the same donor and the water system was important, the Krubar would spend one symbolic night a week in the 'marble cottage' to express his gratitude. I'm sure the donor felt he made immeasurable merit for both of his contributions.

Meanwhile, the Krubar, who already had a very simple cottage as is fitting for a humble monk, had another small, simple cottage built. This one was in a far corner from the rest of what had sprung up around him so he could get some solitude. A walking meditation path around seven metres long constructed of large, flat stone blocks was set into the uneven rocks for him to practice on beside the cottage.

One morning, the monks came back to find him sitting beside this path. In the solid rock next to it was a footprint that wasn't there the day before. When asked about it, all he'd do is smile.

Talking about such things is improper. A demonstration to anyone - monks or laity - is completely out of the question.

I've placed my right foot into this impression many times. It looks like an ordinary footprint anyone could make in soft mud, but this is in hard basalt rock. Think about it. It's an incredible marvel to be in the presence of, especially the longer it's contemplated. It's genuine in every regard, including the splayed toes and thick callous-ridged heel of a person who goes barefoot their whole life. Phra George told me the Krubar did the same thing at his brother's temple in the next county as well.

The *Visuddhimagga* gives detailed instruction on how to dive in and out the earth by creating a pool of water.[3] Likewise, how you can walk on water by creating the firmament under your feet as you go.[4] For leaving a footprint in rock, one enters an absorption into 'water totality'. As soon as you start to sink, you avert out of it.

The proof that this is possible is set in stone at this temple in Pasang district, Lamphun province, less than fifty kilometres south-east of Chiang Mai on a well-paved road.[5] The footprint sits in the back-right corner. It's a tribute to the Krubar that he broke the code of silence about such powers at the end of his life in this quiet way to show what's possible.

There were many stories about the Krubar's consideration for everyone. There were many other stories as well. The monks would whisper in private about how he could come in out of a pouring monsoon rain without a drop of water on him. It's quite a useful ability for a forest dweller.

They considered his greatest gift his ability to teach. Commonly, he'd send for a monk from the far side of the monastery. He'd say something to the effect of, "You're not doing your meditation right this afternoon. You're doing that... you should be doing this. Now go back and practice."

---

[3] *Visuddhimagga* V, 29
[4] *Ibid.*, V, 28
[5] Highway H106, 'Wat Phraphutthabat Tak Pah' on Google maps.

When I returned as a layman the first year after I left the monkhood, they'd cremated his corpse because the shrine for his ashes was complete.

"Would you like to see the gems that came out of his body?" two monks whom I'd eaten lunch with for over a year asked me in English.

I immediately knew what they were talking about and voiced my appreciation of their offer.

They led me to a sacred place. In front of me was a collection of what looked like rough, uncut topazes of different colours, perhaps thirty or so in a small dish. I had no doubt they took them from the Krubar's ashes, probably representing only a portion of what they found.

These were completely honest monks who had surrounded him and stayed on. They had proven their character to me on a daily basis. Any fraud in such a matter was out of the question.

I'd heard about this phenomenon before in Thailand. The Tibetans write about it and years later I saw a travelling display of such which I thought was of dubious origins. They looked nothing like these.

When an accomplished meditator dies, his or her body is cremated. Then the cremators sift through the ashes searching for relics. The highest form of relic is small crystal gemstones. The Thais say that you can tell the supernormal powers the monk or nun had by the colour of the stones.

This is my preferred explanation: calcium is a crystalline structure. Cut in half, bones look like frothy porridge with lumps; all made out of calcium and other minerals. When an accomplished meditator masters Samadhi, their physicality changes to accommodate the shift in frequency. The small lumps turn into different crystalline structures to facilitate the finer frequencies.

Think of early crystal radios. Some needed no batteries or power supply. The crystal was the first type of semiconductor diode which in the 1920s made radio publicly available. To get the radio signal, a wire was plugged into the crystal. Millions were made. Kits are still available for educational purposes.

Deeper in the countryside I visited the meditation teacher from Wat Phra Buddha Bat Tak Pah in the small temple to which he'd been transferred.

"So, did you get any of the gems from the Krubar's ashes?" I asked.

"I only took one," came the soft reply from this exemplary monk who'd been my 'babysitter' as Phra George called him, for when I wasn't in retreat in Bangkok.

"May I see it?"

"Of course."

He went to a cabinet, and then returned with a small, grey silk cloth wrapped around something. Smiling and with a twinkle in his eye, he presented me with what was inside.

I held in my hand another wonder of the world: a small fragment of bone, perhaps from a foot or hand. At one end, it had shrunk back during the cremation, revealing a smooth, shiny, pure black crystal. The receding of the bone left tiny talons holding the gem, like claws on a diamond ring.

We just smiled at each other. There was no need for comment. Speaking for itself, there was really nothing else left to say.

In 1999, I returned to Thailand for my first visit since 1988. Over tea with this monk we talked about the Krubar. The depth of secrecy surrounding intense meditation practices came to the surface as I was made privy to information that's usually learned only on a need-to-know basis. My status as an old friend allowed for such at this time. While I was a monk, everyone treated me with consideration and even honour, which was hard to accept at times, but some things don't make it into conversation with outsiders.

"For four years, the Krubar kept his eyes closed to develop his other senses," he told me in his quiet, sing-song voice in English. "Other monks would lead him at the end of a stick on the jungle paths."

I was shocked. I'd never heard of such an ascetic practice in any yogic tradition. The Buddha taught 'the Middle Path' between sensual indulgence and self-mortification. Not that this was the latter, he wasn't hurting himself by it, but it's an extreme discipline by anyone's standards.

The Krubar could've opened his eyes at any time. Just remembering to keep them shut would require constant mindfulness, let alone unmitigated patience. He must have achieved total peace with the self-imposed limitation. Four years is way past trying out something like that just to see if anything happens. Somehow, before he started, he knew it would potentially bear distinctive fruit worth the effort. 'Other senses' indeed. A universe full of them, I'm sure.

Who the Krubar's teachers were in the forest lineage of the region is unknown. The Thai monks would wander up through the jungles of what's now Myanmar (Burma) on the map between China and where the Rangoon government has no influence all the way to India. Their robes were their passports.

Wat Phra Buddha Bat Tak Pah sits at the linguistic edge of the region known as 'Lanna-Thai'. The people there speak 'phasa muang', also called 'phasa yuan'. Phasa muang was the language of the Lanna Kingdom 700 years ago. I was always surprised that when I'd go to Chiang Mai speaking what I thought was Thai, the shopkeepers would cheerfully inform me that they couldn't understand me as I was speaking phasa muang.

According to Maha Khun, the province's ecclesiastical governor in 1985, there were over 300,000 speakers of this language living on the other side of the Burmese border in those territories cut off from Thailand. That translates into an indeterminable number of villages and towns spread across an unimaginable amount of hilly terrain. The melding of other tongues and traditions is endemic. Unknown, ancient languages that are long lost still embroider certain hill tribes' garments.

Maha Khun took me into border areas in his large, chauffeured, air-conditioned Land Rover. The hill tribes could understand my basic Thai but I couldn't understand them as they all mixed a handful of languages into their conversation. Maha Khun's multilingualism seemed natural to him as well. For the assorted 'locals', communication with strangers wasn't an issue. The Krubar could have gotten his meditation instruction anywhere from Laos to the foothills of the Chinese Himalayas.

This region of Indo-China is part of the fourth world on the planet: unnamed tribal nation-states resisting foreign domination. The UN never recognised these areas as separate from Burma nor now from Myanmar. The local chiefs had a truce with the British but no one else ever since.

Only the bottom territory has a known name: the Shan States. In the mid-80s, it had a well-equipped standing army of 5,000 men financed by heroin. It's part of the infamous 'Golden Triangle'. Jade and rubies supposedly anchored the finances of the other states. Who knows if they still exist?

No information comes out. Monks told me some of these territories even printed their own money and had their own post offices. That was over thirty years ago. A lot of the jungle trails are now landmined. The last two monks to go there from the temple while I was a monk came back with cerebral malaria. One recovered just fine; the other never spoke clearly again.

If there are any 'indigenous meditation practices' still in that vast, disputed jungle region that have been developed over the millennia and absorbed under the umbrella of Buddhism, one thing is for sure: we'll never know.

When I returned to Thailand in 2008 with the woman who would become my wife, another layer of secrecy peeled away. Meeting with this monk for an afternoon, we delighted in seeing each other once again. I asked him to confirm for her what he told me years before about the Krubar's practice of keeping his eyes shut.

After he had done so, he paused for a moment before continuing, "Not only that, but for twenty years he had a sitter's practice. He stopped it a few years before he died."

I was completely surprised but by then not shocked that I hadn't heard this before. The sitter's practice is the thirteenth and last of the ascetic practices listed in the *Visuddhimagga*[6] and a form of training sanctioned by the Buddha.[7]

To clarify what this meant for my girlfriend's benefit, I replied, "So he didn't lie down to sleep for twenty years but would sit in meditation at night instead?"

With an old, familiar twinkle in his eye and soft music in his voice, he replied, "That's right. For twenty years."

---

[6] *Visuddhimagga* II, 2, 73*ff.*
[7] Majjhima Nikaya 113.18

Chapter 11

The Ever-Morphing Face of Buddha

If I say, "think of the Buddha," you probably picture a guy with super-long earlobes and his hair piled on top of his head in a neat bun. In reality, the facts completely contradict this image. First of all, there are no references in the Pali canon to his earlobes being an extraordinary length or stretched by plugs, or heavy earrings. Secondly, he was a shaven-headed ascetic.[1]

The first images of the Buddha in human form popped up in a region of India owned by the Greeks in their style of statuary six hundred years after he died. Some even depicted him with a moustache, as to have any important status among the locals; a man had to have one. Likewise with long hair, so they piled a bunch neatly on top.[2]

Famously, the Buddha was born with 32 marks that were prophetic of his destiny, but many are metaphorical, such as 'legs like an antelope', and 'the torso of a lion'.[3] The last one is a fleshy bump on top of his head, but that's as close as they come to bestowing upon him a top knot. Contradictory, together they all render him both a perfect physical specimen and a bizarre-looking freak of nature. For instance, he has webbed fingers on hands that extended past his knees, and a tongue that can cover his forehead.[4]

These 32 marks are augmented centuries later with 80 more minor marks, many of them poetic accolades. Like number 49: 'His

---

[1] Digha Nikaya 3, 1.10
[2] *Critical Terms for the Study of Buddhism* edited by Donald S. Lopez Jr., p. 22. University of Chicago Press, Chicago, 2005
[3] Majjhima Nikaya 91.9
[4] *Ibid.*, 91.7

ears are long like lotus petals'.[5] That's all it took to paste them on his head for these thousands of years since.

What we do know is that he wasn't immediately distinguishable from the other monks.[6]

At one point, he said, "Why do you want to see this nasty body? He who sees the *Dhamma* [his teaching of the nature and laws of the universe] sees me; he who sees me sees the *Dhamma*."[7]

By this, we can expect he wouldn't care that his appearance changed as his fame travelled around the world over these millennia. Maybe he'd even be amused by it, especially the ear thing. Perhaps as well with being morphed obese in China.

It does help us to appropriately apply his discoveries to compare the original face and culture of Buddhism before the moustache appeared with what's happened since.

2500 years ago Siddartha Gautama did what was considered noble in some circles, shocking in others and extreme by anyone's standards. He renounced the safety of his community where he was the son of the locally elected governor,[8] shaved off his hair and beard, and went 'forth from home to homelessness'[9] in the pursuit of enlightenment.

Renunciation wasn't a new idea at the time. It was the prerequisite method considered to work in those days. The accompanying usual ascetic practices in vogue were revolting and certainly not for the weak-willed. Finally rejecting those as not working six years into his new way of life, Sid had his breakthrough. He then established an order of monks with a codified, rational approach and rules of conduct to keep them on track.

---

[5] *The Concept of the Buddha: Its Evolution from Early Buddhism to the Trikaya Theory*, Guang Xing, p. 32. Routledge, London, 2004
[6] Digha Nikaya 2.11/1:50; Majjhima Nikaya 128.8f.
[7] Samyutta Nikaya 22.87
[8] *The Historical Buddha*, H.W. Schumann, English translation by M.O'C. Walshe, 1989, pages 6, 17. Motilal Banarsidass Publishers, India, 2004
[9] Majjhima Nikaya 1.240

Kapilavatthu, the community he walked away from, bears little resemblance to any in our so-called civilised world today. It was small; the city moat protected an area less than 400 metres by 500 metres, not even twenty blocks.[10] Everyone knew everyone, and most were related. Nuclear families in multi-generational, extended-family habitats were the norm. The expression "It takes a whole village to raise a child" springs from such societies.

Agrarian with minimally traded goods, Kapilavatthu functioned with completely interlaced duties. The sun went up on one side of the fields and down on the other. Other than wars and weather, life was predictable. Walking away from this safety net with no guarantees of food, medicine, shelter or clothing wasn't just a life-changing decision, but most likely a self-imposed death sentence. It wasn't for the faint of heart.

Although the lessons in suffering and death are the same as ours, living in such a different world, the people then were physically almost entirely different human beings than most people today. They consumed no refined foods, caffeine or junk, and virtually no sugar. No freaky preservatives or hormone-disrupting chemicals crossed their lips. Everything was nutritious even though limited in variety, which guts appreciate. Their primitive diet helped them avoid so many of the diseases that plague modern humanity.[11]

With no electric lights to keep them up at night, their natural circadian rhythms were unaltered. They slept with their spines adequately supported on firm, electrically grounded surfaces, rising with the break of day.[12] They spent a lot of time in the sunshine and fresh air.

Researchers estimate that people in agrarian communities sit for an average of three hours per day instead of the twelve to fifteen hours sat daily by a typical office worker.[13] Walking almost

---

[10] *The Historical Buddha*, H.W. Schumann, English translation by M.O'C. Walshe, 1989, p. 16. Motilal Banarsidass Publishers, India, 2004

[11] http://www.westonaprice.org/health-topics/the-scientific-approach-of-weston-price/

[12] http://www.ncbi.nlm.nih.gov/pmc/articles/PMC3265077/?tool=pubmed

everywhere, their postures would have been entirely different. They moved around the world upright and open-chested instead of slouched over a steering wheel or a personal device. That makes it harder to be depressed.[14]

Their hips were used to a full range of motion by squatting for bowel functions, which work better lined up in that position, every day of their entire lives. There's no record of the first monks practising physical yoga to be able to sit upright in meditation postures. There simply was no need as every healthy person's hips rotated freely.

Even their facial structure would have been different. Humans who have never eaten white flour, white sugar or other refined foods have broader palates and uncrowded teeth. Those change with the DNA inherited from first-generational exposure.[15]

Their teeth would have had almost no cavities, these being a product of our modern diet. If they got any cavities from a period of malnutrition, their teeth healed themselves once they were eating properly again.[16] Think of the ramifications for the rest of the organism.

Nor would they have had any sodium fluoride in their system that first and foremost calcifies the pineal gland.[17] This gland was considered the 'seat of the soul' by Descartes[18] in the seventeenth century CE and for thousands of years the location of the 'third eye'

---

[13] http://www.scientificamerican.com/article/killer-chairs-how-desk-jobs-ruin-your-health/

[14] https://biofeedbackhealth.files.wordpress.com/2011/01/a-published-increase-or-decrease-depression.pdf

[15] *Root Canal Cover-Up*, George Meinig, Price Pottenger Nutrition Foundation, Lemon Grove, CA, 2004. Referred to as 'dental deformities' under 'PRICE'S CENTRAL FINDING' and '...it compromises the development of the face and dental arch.' as well as '...and an underdeveloped middle third of the face,' under 'THE SCOPE OF PRICE'S WORK' at http://www.westonaprice.org/health-topics/the-scientific-approach-of-weston-price/

[16] http://www.westonaprice.org/health-topics/the-scientific-approach-of-weston-price/

[17] http://www.icnr.com/articles/fluoride-deposition.html

[18] *Treatise of Man*, Rene Descartes

by Easterners. Between fluoridated toothpaste and drinking water, it's a wonder the pineal still functions now at all. Or does it?

Everyone walked barefoot or in sandals of natural materials that didn't insulate them from the planet's electromagnetic field. There's a transfer of negative electrons between the ground and our bodies when we aren't insulated from it which has many health-giving benefits, such as thinning the blood and reducing inflammation.[19] They were all electrically grounded with the Earth's magnetic field twenty-four hours a day, and it was far stronger than it is today. We know it was, but we don't know why.[20]

There were no pulsing electromagnetic frequencies from electronic devices bombarding them like we have today. We have no idea of the effects of these on us as the large, bioelectric organisms that we are.

When I first returned to the West, I knew whenever I drove under large power lines as the hair on the back of my neck would stand up. This sensitivity passed quickly with repeated exposure.

As a monk, I went barefoot for over a year. I appreciate the feel of being grounded with the Earth's magnetic field. It supports a balanced sanity. I still live a lot of my life barefoot for this reason.

At first, there were no rules for the Buddha's monks as the band of like-minded individuals was small and they understood the spirit of the endeavour. As their communities grew, new monks sometimes behaved ignorantly. The Buddha formulated rules for when such actions happened again, which was expected, knowing humans. The rules were all in line with how a fully enlightened person would behave in various circumstances according to the cultural acceptability of the day.

Eventually, there came to be 227 rules recited every two weeks on full and new moons. On his deathbed, the Buddha told the monks they could abolish the minor rules.[21] They couldn't decide which ones those were so they just kept all of them instead.

---

[19] http://www.ncbi.nlm.nih.gov/pmc/articles/PMC3265077/?tool=pubmed
[20] http://www.livescience.com/46694-magnetic-field-weakens.html

The rules still get recited every two weeks. The preferred monk to perform the task is the one who can whip through it in Pali from memory without sacrificing annunciation for speed. He then gets paid a stipend in an envelope for doing so even though he's just recited the rule about not accepting money. Still, some monks, one offshoot sect in particular, have lay servants in white carry their money for them, so they don't technically touch it. If these monks need to count it themselves, some will use chopsticks.

The original *sangha* (community of monks) vowed in their ordination ceremony to wander and camp for the rest of their lives at the roots of trees with just what they could carry comfortably. The climate and terrain lent itself to such an idea. Think of Florida's latitude with a mix of virgin forest, farmland and dirt tracks with animal carts instead of apartment blocks, asphalt and air-conditioned cars.

Their uniform and gear were essential, easy to come by necessities for subtropical camping. Each wrapped himself in a large rectangular sheet of smaller, rectangular pieces of cloth, often just rags that were found, sewn together in a simple, uniform patchwork that identified him as belonging to the Buddha's Order.

Two of the same patchwork sheets tacked into a double thickness also served as a sleeping bag. It could be draped over one shoulder or worn over both as an "overcoat", as Phra George the Londoner called his. Under these cloaks of patches, a shorter cloth that came below the knees was wrapped around the waist and tied with a cloth belt. This completed a presentation of common decency.

All of these were dyed using the heartwood from trees. I watched this process using jackfruit wood by some young, ardent forest monks. It was a lot of work. The result is a dull, reedy yellow stain that doesn't last through many washes.

These ancient ascetics carried a plain bowl made out of anything from a coconut to clay for collecting alms food from

---

[21] Digha Nikaya 16, 6.3

villagers. Small items were limited to a needle and thread for repairing the 'robes', a water flask and strainer, a razor and sharpening stone for shaving the head and face. These they carried in the bowl.

Hair was kept to two fingers' width at most or for two moons, whichever came first. Teeth were brushed using a green twig with a chewed end, preferably from the neem tree for its antiseptic properties. These dedicated jungle yogis vowed that they would use only their own urine, fresh, stale and fermented, as medicine for all of their maladies for the rest of their lives. Sometimes, they fortified it with 'broken gallnuts', which are hardened pockets of sap secretions from certain trees, mixed into the urine.

The Buddha established an order of nuns as well. Eventually, grisly rapes and mutilations sometimes happened to them in their camping way of life. In light of this, their dedication to pursuing enlightenment is exceptionally extraordinary.

These first wandering separate bands of monks and nuns, living in the forest and going to villages just for food, developed Samadhi to the point that incredible mental powers manifested. They refined the science for such. Demonstrations to the laity were strictly forbidden.[22] The specifics of these paranormal abilities are listed many places in the Pali canon.[23] Although difficult for us to imagine, again, they were very different human creatures in tune with a very different world.

Just as we filter and absorb physical nutrition, we also filter and absorb mental nutrition.

Think of the arms that result from eating the right supplements, going to a gym and working out on the machines under the direction of a personal trainer. At the same time, you decide to learn to play the piano, taking lessons from a skilled teacher to do so.

---

[22] Cullavagga 5.8.2

[23] Digha Nikaya 2.85*ff.*; Majjhima Nikaya 77.30*ff.*, as two examples.

Extrapolate just these to the mental muscle and focus developable with the right mental nutrition combined with the right concentration exercises worked at all day free of distractions under the direction of accomplished yogis who could personally show you how.

This easy to understand analogy, '...just as a strong man bends or straightens his arm...' pops up in many places in the Pali canon regarding the Buddha's and others' ability to change frequencies or locations like we change TV channels.[24]

There were no microsecond attention spans from TV, internet surfing and computer games in these mendicants. They'd probably be initially overwhelmed standing on a busy city street corner today, but this wasn't their world. We selectively process some types of information much more rapidly out of necessity and familiarity in our complex environment, but that doesn't mean we've developed penetrative sustainable attention. We've developed different skills to survive.

These ascetics were dedicated to mastering their mental abilities with the opportunity to do so. They taught their less experienced companions techniques for not losing their concentrative gains in Samadhi by distractions when walking into a village for food. Now that's juggling!

The forest monks conducted meetings of the community for serious matters or rites such as ordinations within 'sacred space'. They chanted the boundaries of it into existence around them and then dissolved those afterwards. The delineated space extended from the nadir to the zenith, the lowest point directly below them in this celestial sphere to the highest point directly above. These were always and only on 'land owned by no man'. Any breach of the Order's rules had to be confessed before such ceremonies to ensure they all resonated in purity of conduct for the success of the proceeding's intention.

---

[24] Udana iii. 2. 21-24, for example.

Village life, with all of its securities in place and shared agrarian tasks continued to roll on. The people supported the Buddha's monks as living examples of the epitome of human development in ethical conduct, concentrative ability and resultant wisdom. A mutually beneficial relationship was understood to be taking place. Monks weren't even allowed to store food overnight so that they had to face their supporters every day. Their lives wove through each other in this way.

The laity made 'merit' (cosmically bankable good karma) for supporting the monks. They expected there would be rewards, if not this lifetime then another, for doing so. Ideally, by being reborn with the opportunity to be a monk oneself, without too much hardship.

If they were like most villagers I've met, most everybody, actually, they probably just wanted to be reborn in the heavenly realms of sensual indulgence. They heard that even those are impermanent, but hey, they're for a long time, and a lengthy luxury vacation always sounds great now, doesn't it?

Accounts in the Pali canon of anybody other than monks meditating in the Buddha's day are rare. *Very rare.* They called the laity 'householders'. When you're holding a house together without modern labour-saving devices, there's always someone needing attention or something to be done. Even with, quite often.

As time passed, the subtropical camping gear of the forest monk became augmented with buildings for residences, a variety of medicines, and luxuries until finally all of the accoutrements of modern living have crept in. For example, televisions for watching Thai boxing, contrary to the rule forbidding going to shows. But then, they aren't going to it; it's coming to them!

All boys enjoy their toys. The contemporary Theravadin order, like the Tibetans and the Zen with all of their uniquely stylised embroideries, is no exception. I've seen finely-wrought ceremonial fans with mother-of-pearl inlay on carved hardwood handles with matching stands.

The best addition to the forest monk's essential gear we can attribute to the Thais. That's the large umbrella with a mosquito net for meditating and sleeping under in the jungle. As well, the bowl has gotten much bigger to carry extras in (a flashlight is good, so is a bar of soap) or to bring food back to the monastery. The sling for carrying it has become a piece of luggage in its own right, complete with an intricate wicker stand, so it doesn't get dirty sitting on the ground.

This arrangement of householders supporting communities of Buddhist monks who in return were supposed to be examples of what humans could aspire to be continued for centuries stretching into millennia throughout Asia. There was only one problem: for the most part, thankfully not all, the monks stopped being living examples of the Buddha's teaching along the way. As early as sometime between 104-88 BCE, at a meeting of high-ranking monks in Sri Lanka, they decided that care and preaching of the texts were more important than practising their contents.[25]

A Burmese monk known as Ledi Sayadaw entered the picture in the late 1800s. He saw that the current order of monks in many places had become a lazy boys' club, solely catering to the superstitions of the people through the performance of rituals. He knew that supporting them wasn't as profitable merit-wise for lay people as the original arrangement intended, nor were the householders spiritually fed with role models.

As a solution, Ledi Sayadaw created the Vipassana retreat wherein a layperson could enter a monastery for a short period of intensive meditation practice with knowledgeable instruction. Ideally, they'd become stream-enterers (*see Theory and Practice D, 'Grokking Nibbana'*), taking home a daily practice to maintain their gains in mindfulness until the next time they could enter a temple for another retreat so as to progress further.

This form of meditation practice was the start of all modern 'spiritual' retreats. Not only in the different Buddhist schools, but

---

[25] *Visuddhimagga*, Introduction, p. xxix

every New Age weekend workshop, and Tantra 'playshop' in an exotic vacation spot package. I suspect Christian Bible camps as well, perhaps brought West by a Brit as Burma was a crown colony and they always paid close attention to local spiritual movements. There's no record of Bible camps existing before that time. They too probably have their origins in this concept pioneered by Ledi Sayadaw.

This brings us to the Information Age.

Chapter 12

Info Delivery

In this unprecedented Age, we're very different creatures than the human beings with their society that produced Siddhattha Gotama. The truths he discovered and taught about the nature of the universe are still applicable because truth doesn't change whether you know it or not. The delivery system for us to be able to absorb those truths did need to change and has.

Processing information through some of the sensory doors more quickly than any other culture in history makes us more wired for hyper-speed emotional stimulation as well. This modern phenomenon has been taken advantage of by every marketing department in the world. Think of the amount of sexual stimulation thrown at us as an example. Hyperstimulation is a reality as is information overload.

Thoughtless reaction to stimuli is the norm as our filters for selective awareness try to sort through this onslaught. This reactivity is taken advantage of as well. As a result, a lot of our mental circuitry connects up in such a way that an intense impact is required to make an impression through the habitual responses to stimuli that we have no conscious awareness of.

That level of impact is the basis of Vipassana retreats. Isolated from all of its usual information, the contemporary mind which sifts so much so quickly, suddenly hits a wall with such a limited variety of objects of awareness to choose from. Attention spins from one frame of personal reference to another, endlessly interrupting focus on the recommended objects. This generates extremely intense emotional reactions, propelling a person through the insight knowledges. *See Theory and Practice C.*

Phra George once said, "Intensity of feeling is necessary for intensity of focus." He was absolutely right.

As I wrote earlier, this isn't a challenge for everybody. And working yourself up into a lather doesn't get you anywhere either.

Keeping the intensifying emotional reactions funnelled into renewed focus depends on the teacher. I consider personal contact with the student to be an absolute necessity for progress in Vipassana. Only then can a teacher tailor the process to fit the student who's out of his or her usual frame of reference and requires guidance through the difficult, uncharted stages. It's tough to remember the initial objective was to drain the mental swamp when you're up to your ass in alligators.

A word of caution: 'the guru from afar' can exploit the student's unfamiliarity with the emotional environment to his or her own end. Some always will although this is more prevalent in other types of retreats, 'New Age' ones in particular. The retreat leader knows the venue better than the student as it's his or her own territory.

All retreats exist to shift a student's frame of reference. So the student has to trust this person at a certain level to have their best interests at heart as well as a more thorough understanding of the subject, or there's no point in being there. A student just has to be sure they aren't being danced right into the teacher's pocket for the guru's own gain.

An older woman who managed the office of a retreat centre for several years summed it up well to me after it closed due to the owner's exhaustion. Shaking her head, she said, "I took this job because I thought it'd be interesting because of the people who pass through. And you know what? All these New Age 'teachers of enlightenment'? They all want somethin' for nothin'! They all work you for whatever they can get. You want to know what was straight forward? The hairdresser retreats! They were on the level."

But I digress…

The supreme objective of a Vipassana retreat is for a person to experience Nibbana at the first level of understanding it, establishing her or him as a stream-enterer. If this happens, a beneficial fate is sealed. Eventually, the continuum of that person will unwind as desires naturally unravel, resulting in no more momentum towards rebirth which is inseparable from suffering. *See Theory and Practice D, 'Grokking Nibbana'.*

The Buddha said that after experiencing Nibbana, if that continuous flux of states acting as rebirth-linking factors we call a person doesn't unwind in this life, then it's certain to within seven lifetimes.[1] This is considered monumental compared to endlessly recurring lives as the alternative. Only a few sequels probably makes the last ones all that more remarkable to experience.

Phra George once called Wat Mahadhatu, "a *sotapanna*[2] factory." He considered it to be a practical contribution to humanity in this Age. Thankfully, he was skilled at catapulting a person into an experience of the here and now free of definition. A person only needs to achieve 'momentary concentrative absorption' (*khanika-Samadhi*) to reach the first experiential level of Nibbana. This momentary Samadhi is within reach for many today. *See Theory and Practice E, 'Inner Sanctum Secrets of Vipassana'.*

So many interdependent states (mental, physical, environmental, and social) which acted as conditions for the original

---

[1] Samyutta Nikaya 13.1
[2] 'Sotapanna': Pali for 'stream-enterer'. See *Theory and Practice D.*

form of Buddhism to arise have changed that parts of what the Buddha taught by example as a profitable way of life and its rewards aren't feasible now.

Some argue that the ability to progress to the more refined experiential levels of Nibbana requires full Samadhi absorption ability. Having fun with supernormal powers requires developing a mental dexterity with a sequence of Samadhi absorptions. These abilities aren't going to happen anytime soon for most of us. Hyperstimulated and confused microsecond attention spans don't incline towards sustained concentration.

Also, I don't expect that 'going forth from home to homelessness' in your neighbourhood, or anybody else's for that matter, is a viable option for most spiritual aspirants today. Not only does the West not honour its renunciants, to say the least, but as technologically coddled creatures we don't weather discomfort well as a way of life. Establishing a serene, concentrative absorption long enough to make up for the missing material comfort that a lot of us are used to, like just a hot shower, isn't likely to happen.

Becoming a Buddhist monk in a foreign culture with all of its unfamiliarity, resultant isolation due to language difficulties, and need to reorient on basic standards of living is far too upsetting for most personality types to be profitable. Deep existential angst is a useful tool in retreat circumstances for Westerners but experiencing it as a way of life, day in and day out, in a distant land is just too dismal as a navigating mindset to be useful for most.

A lot of people today haven't been brought up in nurturing nuclear families and extended multi-generational habitats. This lack of beneficial role modelling in dealing wholesomely with procreation, coexistence, and other challenges makes it tough to develop the nobler emotional responses.

Isolation from considerate touch is a fundamental issue in our world, realised or not. For many, that translates into a lack of kindly sexual exposure as well. This deprivation has shaped a lot of our contemporary personality types. I don't expect most of them would be fulfilled trying to refine thoughts and feelings living alone with only superficial friends and the internet for companionship. Nor do many jive with the idea of belonging to a meditation club.

Now stuff lust, that heavily manipulated and incredibly powerful biological drive, underneath of that deprivation. Repression kinks and denial warps a person's emotional development in our hyperstimulated times. All this realistically means that our desire for intimate contact and sexual pleasure requires a pragmatic approach. Just plain abstinence isn't going to help.

Do I have a prescription for adjusting to these changes so as to better absorb the Buddha's truths other than undertaking a Vipassana retreat with a trustworthy teacher?

As my story shows, I was very privileged in my exposure. Landing back in the First World merely impregnated with a permanent shift in perception doesn't grant me the authority to pontificate. Neither does just having an imprinting of Samadhi experiences with a cosmological framework for reference. Still being imbued with a full capacity for desire colours any advice I might have, even as my hair greys and my hormones slow in working their magic.

As it's the privilege of the informed to apply ancient wisdom to a modern-day situation, let's look at this. As Socrates supposedly said or should have if he didn't (I can't find this famous quote in Plato's works), "I can't teach anybody anything: I can only make them think."

A 'healthy, working relationship' is a great start. In healthy, working relationships, we refine our deepest, most intense feelings through constructively playing out the dramatic genres that have always categorised human interaction: tragedy, comedy, and the 'satyr play', as the ancient Greeks classified them. Only instead of the burlesque nature of the Greeks' satyr plays, refining passion with sexual polarity transforms the working relationship into our own symbolic amphitheatre at the centre of the mandala. It becomes the archetypal stage upon which we learn of our ensnaring attachments to drama while celebrating the freedom that comes from letting them go once we understand them for what they are.

Respectful, intimate human contact stimulates and nurtures in us the 'doable responses' of loving-kindness (friendliness), compassion (proactive empathy), sympathetic (or congratulatory) joy, and equanimity (or 'recourse to neutrality regarding a specific phenomenon'). The Buddha called this range of four emotional frequencies 'the divine abidings' (*Brahmavihara*).[3]

Helen said they're also known as 'the boundless states' (*appamanna*) because they're boundless sources of energy. She taught me that all reactions in any situation could be transformed through mindfulness - being intently present - into one of these four emotional responses. This always results in an increase of bioelectricity or, at least, no diminishing of it.

Consider this transformative process to be a valuable spiritual practice in and of itself. These frequencies give us a taste of the archetypal emotional matrices that form the basis of the divine part of the human blueprint. It feeds us to hang out in them. *See the*

---

[3] Anguttara Nikaya 4.125*f.*

second half of Theory and Practice F, 'Formal Samadhi Practice' for instruction on developing them.

They're simply all forms of 'having consideration for others' although, with equanimity, consideration is a result of the frequency rather than the cause for it. Equanimity manifests as patience with shortcomings, or sometimes, just not caring enough to respond anymore. For it to be a boundless source of energy, though, first the other three ways of responding to someone or a situation (with loving-kindness, compassion, or sympathetic joy) need to be tried and found to not work. Otherwise, not being bothered enough to care becomes a cop out, short-circuiting its spiritual usefulness. Hence there's the term '*recourse* to specific neutrality'. It's the 'last resort' option.

To become boundless sources of energy, all forms of consideration except equanimity require fully wishing for the other person the level of happiness you wish for yourself.

If you think responding with 'wrathful compassion' is ultimately going to help you out of a rough moment in an intimate relationship, you better think again before acting.

Sex, or more precisely making love, that fusion of respectful consideration with passionate sexual polarity, is the great healer for couples in healthy, working relationships. Responsibly undertaken, mutually pleasurable sex classically results in both parties having each other's interests at heart. It creates the emotional space necessary to fulfil those interests. This mutual support makes the working relationship a healthy garden in which beneficial mental nutrition grows.

The Buddha discovered that a person reaches the end of suffering through nonattachment. Then he applied the laws of the universe that he'd uncovered in such a way that his teaching would be around for millennia. That was his gift to us.

In this age with our highly developed intellectual filters, we can readily acknowledge that attachment, to anything or anyone, even to just desiring, ultimately leads to suffering. Attachment and suffering are inseparable. This fact forms the basis for the Buddha's still applicable prescribed approach to living: develop the ability to stop attaching to stop suffering. Do understand that developing this ability does take practice.

To be able to love without attachment is the tantric goal as preparation for achieving freedom from suffering. In these times, sex without attachment is easily confused for love without attachment as love is the most bandied-about word in the English language.

Let me define it: love *is* consideration. Period. Behaving considerately without attachment will lead you to a lighter, more energised state of mind and probably body as well.

Fully feeling love without attachment is possible. But fully feeling love isn't possible without sacrifice. If there is no sacrifice, then it isn't love; it's merely momentary pleasure. To become a spiritual path, the sacrifice love requires is the commitment to consideration.

One immense challenge in making the working relationship a path of successful development is for each to assume full responsibility for their behaviour - their responses - towards the other. There is no "I couldn't help it. You left me no choice but to react negatively."

That makes and takes maturity and is the basis of consideration. Only then can the relationship be healthy. If this proves impossible, then the healthy thing to do is call it all off and go your separate ways as the emotional slavery in it isn't profitable for either individual.

Having a formal practice of meditation, either Samadhi, which you can teach yourself or Vipassana, radically increases a couple's sense of fulfilment in daily living. Meditating together is profound. It anchors their togetherness. *See Theory and Practice F, 'Formal Samadhi Practice', for suggestions. 'F' is for fun.*

Entheogens, 'substances that generate the divine within',[4] are a touchy subject in traditional Buddhist circles. The Buddha declared alcohol to be unsuitable for mental training, but that's never been news anywhere on this planet. He mentions no other psychotropic substance, pro or con. I tend to leave alcohol completely out of the equation in almost every situation. I treat all poisons with respect.

Substances that help a person integrate the *Brahmavihara*, the emotional frequencies of the gods, have been considered to be sacred tools by elders respected for their humanitarian wisdom all over the world. 'Spiritual equipment' takes many forms. This subject deserves a fresh examination. *Chapter 13, 'Sacred Substances: Medicine for Becoming'*, is but an introduction to the topic. Dangers, some deadly, are not detailed but are everyone's personal responsibility to research.

Responsibly engaged in, healthy, working relationships, meditation practices, and entheogen use are valuable forms of intense impact for beneficially cutting through manufactured habitual responses. Used in conjunction to energise, expand, and enlighten, how helpful are they?

They rock.

---

[4] http://dictionary.reference.com/browse/entheogen

Chapter 13

Sacred Substances: Medicine for Becoming

Want to know the best entheogen for transformative psychedelic sex?

First of all, other than cannabis, the entheogens I'm most familiar with are LSD and MDMA. That includes a few of MDMA's close analogues, alas. I've taken LSD at least three hundred times. My first LSD experience was at a rock concert at sixteen, in and of an era.

MDMA, I've taken at least four hundred times. I've never been to a rave. Dancing it up with hundreds of my suddenly closest friends to electronic trance music, high on something that may or may not be MDMA, never had any appeal, even if it may be a lesson in empathy. I've been blessed in that 99% of my experiences with MDMA centred on ritualised tantric sex, as have many of my LSD trips.

Secondly, I'm not a chemist, an ethnobotanist or claim any expertise in the field of entheogens. Nor do I consider myself to be an avid psychonaut. I'm merely an experienced researcher of some re-creational substances who values the shifts in becoming that they've granted me. It's from this limited subjective perspective that I cautiously wade into this tricky subject. I'm well aware there are all sorts of sharks swimming in the vast depths of our digital pond who will gleefully tear me apart for my naiveté, ignorance, and audacity. My karma is my refuge.

What determines a substance to be useful for refining thoughts and feelings is its compatibility with the human body as well as its mental effects. What are generally recognised as such are plant-based compounds that have no logically ascertainable LD50 level. 'LD50' is an abbreviation for 'lethal dose 50%'. It's the scientific term for measuring the toxicity of substances. It refers to the amount required to kill half of the test subjects.

What amounts to a lethal dose varies from individual to individual. It depends on many factors such as body mass, age, exposure time, etc., so an LD50 level is merely a benchmark. In common street parlance, the answer to the question, "Does it have an LD50 level?" determines a substance as being potentially dangerous or not. Even water has an LD50 level, as does arsenic. Knowing the differences can mean life or death.

For practical purposes, it boils down to this question: how much of a substance - a substance for which your brain has receptor sites and that induces a shift in perception considered valuable - does it take to kill you? For spiritual purposes, that means ideally positive mental development is safely facilitated chemically by compatible biology transpersonally resonating with an archetypal 'plant teacher' for an ennobling shift of perception.

That said, there are organically-derived, recreational psychotropic substances traditionally used for spiritual purposes which are generally regarded as safe (GRAS). The margin of exposure (MOE, how much a person takes for how long) for them is so high that it's impossible to die from consuming them (reach their LD50 levels) unless you're really trying to.

These are cannabis, LSD25 (always modified from organic bases), psilocybin, psilocin, peyote, and its derivative mescaline. Ayahuasca, which hails from the shamanic tradition of the Amazon and contains DMT, is also considered safe. That's when it's brewed without additives such as datura, commonly called 'deadly nightshade' for a good reason. This doesn't mean that you may not come down sideways from where you went up if you ingest a massive amount of any of the above or the set and setting aren't suitable.

'Set and setting' refer to the mental state of the consumer and the physical circumstances while taking the substance. The appropriate intention, emotional condition, as well as physical jurisprudence, such as being healthy and drinking enough water, are all essential.

The other extreme which also isn't desirable is best summed up by the statement, "Beware the deadly underdose," apocryphally attributed to the late Terence McKenna.

MDMA takes the prize as the best tantric entheogen. Once commonly known as 'Ecstasy', it's strictly sourced from safrole, the essential oil of the sassafras plant. Safrole can be manipulated from other base materials such as nutmeg. It does have an LD50 level well within the range of potentially lethal overdosing. It serves one to remember that modern pharmacology tells us the difference between medicine and poison is the dosage, echoing Paracelsus.[1]

Medical researchers consider MDMA to have extremely beneficial therapeutic value, as they do all of the other substances mentioned above.

As I write this, different governments are legalizing the medical and recreational use of cannabis. Some are considering the therapeutic use of MDMA and psilocybin for PTSD. And still, way beyond the medical model lays the laser-lit spiritual model. To reap its potential benefits entails great personal responsibility and maturity, as true freedom always does.

Sassafras was the root in root beer until the law stepped in. Safrole contains other compounds known to cause liver and esophageal cancers in mice and rats upon 'chronic feeding'.[2] Its psychoactive crystalline extract has an easily identifiable taste and smell, distinctly bitter due to its high alkaloid content.

I don't know if safrole's crystalline extract contains these carcinogenic compounds. It feels just as well tolerated by the body as MDMA is when taken in similar milligramme dosages, the polar opposite of 'chronic feeding'. Although these two vehicles are alike, if pure MDMA is a private jet, "Sass" is a bi-plane.

---

[1] *Dosis facit venenum* (Latin), 'The dose makes the poison'. Paracelsus, Swiss physician, 1493-1541

[2] https://www.ncbi.nlm.nih.gov/pubmed/14259070 by EC Hagan, 1965

Synthetic analogues (frauds) with unpredictable effects of all of these entheogens abound on the black market except, as far as I know, for the recently arrived Sass, but I expect that's just a matter of time. I usually maintained the prudent habit of avoiding analogues, tablets of unknown mixtures and knowing the trustworthy source of supply had personally taken the substance. Just the smart behaviour developed by alert 'heads' in the Psychedelic 60s and passed on. Nobody needs a 'bummer'.

One wholly synthetic exception generally regarded as safe (GRAS) with extreme therapeutic value is 2C-B. Especially when it's taken the day after a MDMA experience to help establish the neural pathways that were imprinted while on that.

There are major problems in our day with sourcing these products on the black market. Those include but are not limited to bad quality due to illicit labs not having standards of purity, poor base materials due to unavailability of proper ones, paranoia, criminal element, rip-offs, synthetic frauds (especially amphetamine-type substances), violence, jail, irreparable physical and mental damage, and even death.

Entheogens do exist made by dedicated chemists who devote themselves to its production as a sacred trust and a labour of love. For example, MDMA cleaned through seven ketone washes to ensure its purity is, quite simply, an incredible vehicle for refining thoughts and feelings.

As vehicles for spiritual development, it's best to ingest entheogens with a purposeful intention based on an accessible format. Otherwise, time spent influenced by them can be likened to getting into a car in an icy parking lot, putting the pedal to the metal, yanking on the steering wheel, and spinning in circles for several hours. Initially exciting, it's probably disorienting, and not much use of the opportunity at hand. Chapter 15, *Sacred Sex: Theory and Practice of Archetypal Access*, details one format of intending.

Personally, the desire for chemically-based experiences has dwindled over the years except for those available through cannabis, MDMA, and LSD. All of the negative factors listed above played into it, but others did as well. Even with safe, millennially proven 'sacraments'.

I haven't taken peyote since the dozen times, or so, I did as a teen, even though it's been available in a 'Red Road' traditional format if I'd wished to seek it out. Throwing up was always tough for me and usually comes with it. Cleaning out all of the little 'hairs' helped, but still, for me, puking is never simple. Often, 'roadmen' of the Native American Church who work with it come through the more liberal major urban centres throughout the world. For psychedelic sexual purposes, the initial stomach discomfort or vomiting doesn't make it particularly appealing.

The same stomach issues rule out ayahuasca as well for sacred sex. As for DMT smoked? Being knocked right out of the body doesn't create a lover. Please read the next chapter for my brief personal accounts of investigating DMT and ayahuasca.

I'm deeply grateful for the resets to my system 'magic mushrooms' of various genera have blessed me with over the years. They've continued to be available, often just for the picking or offered as presents, but I'm no longer attracted to them. Sex while on them is not reliably formative. Psilocybin can be a trickster ally, especially in heroic doses.

Of significant historical note is that by most accredited scholarly accounts, the Buddha chose to end his life by knowingly consuming poisonous mushrooms. We can assume that any deadly mushroom is also going to have an extremely psychotropic effect. All poisons do if they aren't immediately lethal. The marvellous story was recorded in great detail in the Pali canon.[3]

The salient feature for our purposes in this chapter is that the Buddha was offered lunch along with his retinue of monks for the next day by a householder. Starting before dawn, the man prepared a lot of something called 'pig's delight' (*sukara-maddava*) for the monks as well as some other dishes.

---

[3] Digha Nikaya 16, 4.13*ff*.

Most contemporary Pali scholars agree that this term refers to a type of wild mushroom. Probably like truffles are, they were a delicacy which pigs were trained to sniff out in the forest floor. A few academics think what killed the Buddha may have been a type of pork that had gone bad. To them, I say this: there's nothing subtle about foul raw meat, even at the slightest turning. Nor would someone take such a chance serving a revered guest. Wild mushrooms are famous for varieties being mistaken for each other, often fatally.

First, a piece of background: approximately two months earlier the Buddha announced he would discorporate the force that held his body together within three months.[4]

That day of his last meal, the Buddha told the man to serve the 'pig's delight' to him alone, then to bury the rest as nobody anywhere could digest it. After discarding it in a pit, the man fed the other monks the other dishes. Sid then proceeded to eat what had been placed in his bowl, as he did with everything that had been put there for forty-five years.

After finishing, his guts immediately reacted. Undaunted, he gave an inspiring talk on universal law to the householder. Then Sid got up, and with his attendant Ananda walked away, leaving everyone behind. Many hours later, on a shady hillside after quietly enduring the bodily pains, he died peacefully. First, though, he flew up and down and back up through all of the frequencies one last time. The full details of this final journey of his awareness were diligently recorded by the monks who caught up with him.[5]

This accurate identification of a fungus demonstrates such a knowledge of mushrooms that even cooked into a dish he recognised it as toxic although others didn't. Scholars expect psychotropic mushrooms have a shamanic history stretching back many millennia across the Indian subcontinent.[6]

---

[4] Digha Nikaya 16, 3.9, 3.37
[5] Digha Nikaya, 6.8*ff.*
[6] Hallucinogens: A Forensic Drug Handbook by Richard R. Laing, 1.4.1. Academic Press, London, 2003

Even I've eaten a 'magic mushroom' omelette at a backpacker restaurant on the shores of Phewa Tal, a lake in Nepal. I ended up going for a roll on top of the lake as I couldn't sink into it more than a couple of inches. This part of the Himalayas isn't far from where the Buddha lived, ethnomycologically. Considering he initially explored realms of consciousness among a large field of wandering seekers of enlightenment, one can expect he was well aware of the perception-altering properties of certain species of fungi. Probably all of the local dreadlocks were.

The Buddha taught his son, Rahula, that the ultimate point of living was to be able to watch one's last in-breath and out-breath with total awareness.[7] I can't imagine him knowingly consuming something that would sabotage his ability to be completely alert for such an event.

Besides, he lived his life as an example for others. He wouldn't have set a bad example at the last moment. What would be the point in that?

Radical right to the end, Sid the Good Friend chose to go out surfing the edges of perception (*sannya*) on a massive chemical wave into final discorporation (*Parinibbana*). I'm sure it was a rush...

We can also expect these ancient ascetics were also aware of ganja in all of its different forms. Hemp is as old as humanity in the Himalayas and just as widespread. In a Nepalese village, far from any road, I've walked up to a two-stories-tall wild hash plant and rubbed off some amazing *charras* in the timeless tradition of their roaming renunciates. "Boom!" as they say now, to invoke Shiva, the natty-dreaded, tantric lord of yoga and Hindu solar god, to come and share it with them...

The only cannabis smoking tool of the wandering Indian mendicant, since time immemorial, is the sacred straight clay chimney pipe known as a chillum. Kept meticulously clean, they use it with a wet cloth wrapped around it to cool and filter the smoke. As India today is culturally Hindustan for its pantheon, this plain

---

[7] Majjhima Nikaya 62.30

pipe is called a '*Shiva lingam*'.[8] Never do you hear this most respectful, sacred title used for the tourist souvenir chillums decorated with carved wrapped cobras, inset semi-precious stones, etc.

The Ayurvedic pharmacopoeia includes ganja. No one knows when the laity started eating it as snacks. When I was in Varanasi, the holiest city in India on the banks of the Ganges, I had a *bhang lassi* in a government licensed tea shop. I expect you still can. A *lassi* is a yoghurt shake with fruit or rosewater. *Bhang* is tender young leaves of ganja rolled into spiced balls and called such for several thousand years.[9]

When the Buddha taught there, Varanasi was named Kasi. Timeless in so many ways, I expect I could have ordered a *bhang lassi* there then as well. But then, eating it to get high never really appealed to me. As the Malaysian sorcerer said to Helen, "The secret is to burn it hot."

And so, the bong replaces the chillum, the original hot combustion chamber. Dabbing shatter replaces hot knifing hash for younger generations. For the record, I prefer my herb neither manipulated nor handled by persons I don't know, when possible.

The Buddha's dictate that alcohol wasn't suitable for a person undergoing mental training was specified by him to be because it's 'a cause for heedlessness.' This clause is always included as the reason when reciting the precept.[10] Contemporary commentaries extend this to mean all psychotropic substances, which is entirely poetic licence.

---

[8] Lingam (Sanskrit): 'Wand of Light': a dignified term for a penis.
[9] The Great Book of Hemp by Rowan Robinson, p. 107. Park Street Press, Rochester, Vermont, 1995
[10] *Suramerayamajjapamadatthana veramani sikkhapadam samadiyami,* "I undertake the rule of training to abstain from fermented and distilled alcoholic beverages which are a cause for heedlessness." This is the last of the 'Five Precepts' of conduct for lay Buddhists. The others translate loosely as abstaining from 1) impinging on breathing creatures, 2) taking what isn't offered, 3) sexual misconduct, and 4) lying, harsh speech, and gossip.

Clear euphoric shifts from non-toxic entheogens and alcohol-induced, mundane slurry slides are two completely different vectors. We're very different creatures in our sophisticated Information Age. We can use a boost to put space into our habitual responses to stimuli for better balance in becoming.

A person energised with the right substances and making the right intentions can fill that space with refined thoughts and feelings that accelerate their spiritual development. When that happens, a finer frequency response system manifests in their coarser mundane consciousness. A variety of medicines for becoming actualise this fertile space. For this reason, many psychoactive substances have been considered sacred tools in societies around the world for countless ages.

Interestingly, the word 'shaman' in English derives from the Evenki word *saman*. The Evenki are a northern Russian (mainly Siberian) nomadic tribe of reindeer herders. Their medicine men are known for eating the world's most famous toxic psychoactive mushroom, *Amanita muscaria*. All scholars agree that migrated Buddhism directly influenced them. Most expect their word *saman* originates from the Pali *samana* which means 'wandering ascetic'.[11]

The figure of Santa Claus with his sleigh pulled by flying reindeer originated with these people. Santa's red and white suit comes from their shamans' ceremonial costumes worn while collecting the mushrooms which have red tops with white spots.[12]

All of which begs two questions: "Why did the Evenki medicine men with their indigenous practices identify so strongly with Buddhist monks that they adopted their title for themselves?" and "What makes reindeer fly?" It could well be that the monks

---

[11] Psychomental Complex of the Tungus by S.M. Shirokogoroff. Kegan Paul, Trench, Trubner & Co., London, 1935; The Beauty of the Primitive: Shamanism and the Western Imagination by Andrei A. Znamenski. Oxford University Press, 2007; Indo-European Language and Culture: An Introduction by Benjamin W. Fortson. John Wiley & Sons, West Sussex, UK, 2011

[12] http://www.atlanteanconspiracy.com/2008/09/santa-claus-magic-mushroom.html

knew how to soar higher on the herdsmen's favourite fuel than they did and taught them how to use it better.

In my own pedestrian existence, my history with cannabis in all of its forms stems from first smoking black hash with my new friends during lunch at a new school while still just eleven years old. I credit Helen with showing me its true potential.

LSD's suitability as a tantric entheogen depends on established neural pathways and dosage. Erections can be elusive on LSD if a person gets lost in space and interest wanes. It doesn't provide the ejaculatory control that MDMA does. Mixing it with MDMA, a practice called 'candy flipping', is a perennial favourite among aficionados. As one accomplished friend on the tantric Path said to me over twenty-five years ago, "If they're both top quality, then it's kind of a waste of both."

As matters can get a little confused as people tend to find themselves quite heroically dosed, I agree.

When 'candy-flipping', it's best to take the MDMA first and a couple of hours later take the LSD. That way the warmth and closeness of the MDMA is established before introducing the element of Space.

In the most basic of terms, what makes MDMA so well-suited as a tantric entheogen is that it works by squeezing, all at once, all of the polyps in the brain that hold serotonin which is the pleasure neurotransmitter. The serotonin floods the brain, electrifying all of the sense doors, including the mind door, in a thrilling manner. This flood makes it easy to surf pleasurably and productively the stream of consciousness. The pure substance well deserves its original street name: 'Ecstasy'.

It also pumps out dopamine and noradrenaline. So now we have surging pleasure mixed with motivation and focus.[13] Talk about energised enthusiasm!

---

[13] Effects of methylenedioxymethamphetamine on the release of monoamines from rat brain slices.
www.sciencedirect.com/science/article/pii/001429999094150V

While on MDMA, if a man gets an erection, which is dependent on the individual having well-established neural pathways for such, he can easily maintain it for hours. He also has incredibly increased control over his ability to not ejaculate. Combining this with the other effects, including increased physical energy, renders him a powerful and sensitive lover if he learns how to direct his attention. No wonder some say, "Bring on the Tantra party!"

If a man doesn't attain an erection as he expands 'out the top' instead of the bottom, it may be several hours until he can come down enough to achieve one. That's truly a waste of an opportunity if the circumstances were otherwise favourable for it. If a man expands 'out the bottom', he will expand 'out the top' as well. To that end, it's useful while the first glimmers of its effects are being felt to stimulate him sexually. Then the pathway is established.

A little Viagra taken beforehand ensures the erection will happen if there's any question in the moment although it makes a penis less sensitive. Don't indiscriminately disparage synthetic chemical products. Some do make life easier. If you must, know your heart health before boarding the bus. Always remember: **due diligence is everyone's personal responsibility.**

Not specifically a hallucinogen, there are always visual effects of a most pleasurable nature. Cannabis used with MDMA facilitates those. Lovers morph for each other in a more appealing sexual manner according to our archetypal blueprint. Primarily, MDMA acts as an 'empathogen', generating feelings of empathy or open-heartedness with sensual awareness.

WARNING: On the average, it takes two weeks for the serotonin to be replaced in the brain of a healthy person after taking MDMA. During this time, depression can be a problem as can diminished physical energy. A third-day 'crash' afterwards is typical. That which goes up must come down. After so much expansion some contraction can be expected. If you want to play, be prepared to pay, sometimes in spades.

Although a methamphetamine, MDMA has a unique signature of effects compared with others in that class. Nor is it as rough on the system, I hear, probably due to its organic base being the essential oil safrole.

I've never had any interest in smoking 'crystal meth' or taking any other methamphetamine. One twist of a molecular chain and you get an entirely different beast. 'Ice' addicts are called 'tweakers' because they always look tweaked about something, stoned or not.

From time to time as a teenager, I took amphetamine pills (Dexedrine) while drinking in nightclubs. When I was twenty, my bodyguard-chauffer said to me, "I know you don't have any interest in shooting speed because it fucks people up, but you really should just once, so you know what it's about."

So, my girlfriend and I did - once. We had sex until we both bled. We laughed about it, but it was, ahem, hardly beneficial, other than learning our limits, which wasn't necessary. That bodyguard eventually died from Hepatitis C contracted from sharing needles before I met him.

As so many others discover, I too can say, "Sometimes, I learned how far to go by going too far."

Moments of expanded awareness loan us a valuable perspective on ourselves by slicing through our habitual responses. We freshly reconsider our headlong rush through decisions and reactions by allowing for other possibilities. With our highly developed intellectual filters, conjecturing about their mystical, euphoric qualities makes for supportive conversation and deeper comprehension. Ultimately, though, these moments too, just like all experiences in meditation, need to be examined in the light of the three characteristics of all phenomena (*tilakkhana*).[14]

Manifesting the 'boundless states' (*appamanna*), aka 'the emotional frequencies of the gods' (*Brahmavihara*), while influenced by an entheogen is an incredibly profound experience.

---

[14] *Theory and Practice B*

One can bypass the usual governors for maintaining them within a familiar range. This can result in an experience of unparalleled intensity overwhelming the user, restructuring his or her response systems to stimuli.

Being overwhelmed by a positive emotion is both liberating and empowering. Unfortunately, it has the potential to be entirely inappropriate in action, especially with an uninformed bystander. Being able to process such in private and then return to a biologically uninfluenced state before interacting with others is an absolute necessity. One definition of shamanism is 'technique of religious ecstasy'.[15] It can be rather unsettling for the casual observer...

A person can't solely rely on entheogens for progress in meditation or 'practising becoming'. Even cannabis, like all of the substances mentioned above, is beneficial up to a point for accessing other frequencies (Samadhi) but counterproductive for discorporating the entire mundane sphere (Vipassana). Entheogens can enhance concentration (exclusive focus), but they interfere with mindfulness (juggling perceptions). It's always great fun to ponder the universal truths of impermanence (*anicca*) and no self anywhere (*anatta*) while high, but don't expect the 'aha!' moments to last. Maintaining the accessed frequencies gets tricky, especially for an undisciplined mind.

Entheogens are great for a ride, but it's also necessary to walk to the top of the mountain, so to speak, in full mindfulness to learn the way. One issue being that chemically shifting can become essential to get there. This is a reliance you don't need. Success with becoming requires a discipline of regular mental exercise to build mental muscle and sustainable focus. Sometimes in life, though, it helps to hitch a ride.

A weak analogy goes like this: let's say you're stressed to the max for any number of reasons, including fighting with your significant other, if you have one. You love to ski or snorkel

---

[15] Shamanism: Archaic Techniques of Ecstasy by Mircea Eliade, Bollingen, pp. 3–7, Series LXXVI. Princeton University Press, New Jersey, 1972

surrounded by beautiful, fascinating nature because it helps you unwind. It recharges your batteries while you relax like nothing else does, even with some serious exertion manoeuvring around. This helps you face your working week creatively and re-establishes a festive glow in your relationship that excites you. It also feeds a deep part of you that brings peace from a less verbal place within that you'd like to be more familiar with.

There's only one catch: you just have a weekend or a few days, and the place you need to go for this activity is far away. Perhaps you need to drive for many hours to get there or catch a plane. Self-declared purists smugly citing their authority tell you that your communion with nature can't be a valid rejuvenating spiritual pilgrimage unless you walk there as that's a prerequisite for it to mean anything.

But you've got logistics to consider for maybe two people for the journey. Also, you have to be back ready to work well rested on Monday morning. The technology is available to get you there and home in that time. What are you going to do?

To sum up the situation: the traditional, all-consuming, dedicated way of life that allows one to reach certain, rarefied mental states which bestow beneficial shifts of perspective is no longer available or even desirable to most everyone. These states can be experienced briefly by safely altering one's body and brain chemistry. Integrating them enriches one's understanding of existence for the benefit of all beings via the ripple effect. So why not chemically experience them?

Merely ingesting an entheogen doesn't guarantee a spiritual quality to the experience. A satisfying weekend on the slopes or diving on a reef is weather and other conditions dependent. Another factor is one's level of navigational skill in the medium. So too, is a constructive chemical journey dependent on many conditions. Only a tiny percentage of LSD users at its height of popularity ever reached 'the white light'. Even fewer understood it.

Intending from the outset to integrate lessons from these altered states into our daily living and reviewing them afterwards for that purpose provides us with the opportunity to ennoble our interactions with others. As the direction of any conversation belongs to the most conscious person engaged in it, we can then better influence others for the benefit of everyone.

There's always a physical price to pay. Just as an athletic weekend takes time to recover from, so does a journey on a chemical compound which blows a lot of energy through a person's circuits. This is a significant factor in the loss of appeal for such experiences in many enthusiasts as they age. **Fact:** older bodies are more fragile and repair themselves more slowly.

Early in the last century, a collection of accomplished yogis in the Himalayas all agreed the most challenging daily spiritual practice (*sadhana*) is taking care of the body.[16] It's marvellous to fly the realms, but common sense dictates physical care is of primary importance.

The reason I'm not 'burnt out' or even a little crispy around the edges from the use of entheogens is because of specific physical practices that went with them as *modus operandi*. Proper hydration was a must. Early on, well-researched intensive nutritional supplementation became an obligation to my system. Decent rest before and after was always necessary. That included prudent spacing between experiences to allow the body time to recover and the mind to integrate. Enjoyable exercise remains a way of life.

I'm not going to quote studies and make statistics dance extolling the virtues of entheogens. Experimenting with such may be a bad idea for you, period. Bizarre interactions with unpredictable effects between substances, including alcohol and pharmaceuticals, can and do occur.

Do not misconstrue this chapter nor the next as encouragement for cavalier experimentation. Re-read the legal disclaimer. The following conclusion is merely my opinion based on personal investigation:

---

[16] At the Eleventh Hour: The Biography of Swami Rama by Pandit Rajmani Tigunait, PhD. Himalayan Institute Press, 2004

Approached with the right attitude in the right setting while in good health, properly ingesting entheogens makes a profitable difference in a person's life. Not just to return to balance, as conventional medicines are supposed to do with a person's physical system, but even better than ever before for integrating moments of expanded awareness as mental nutrition. As medicines for becoming a more integrated, functioning human being, entheogens can be unparalleled, breakthrough mental nutraceuticals.

***

'The future might teach us to exercise a direct influence, by means of particular substances, on the amounts of energy and their distribution in the mental apparatus. It may be that there are other still undreamed-of possibilities of therapy.'

Dr. Sigmund Freud, 'An Outline of Psychoanalysis', p. 192, 1938.

***

'There are experiences that most of us are hesitant to speak about because they do not conform to everyday reality and defy rational explanation. …. I believe that if people would learn to use LSD's vision-inducing capability more wisely, under suitable conditions, in medical practice and in conjunction with meditation, then in the future this problem child could become a wonder child.'

Dr. Albert Hofmann, the Swiss inventor of LSD, beginning and ending the forward to his book 'LSD My Problem Child'.

***

2500 years ago, the Buddha taught 'the Middle Path' between self-mortifying asceticism and sensual indulgence. Consider a broad and responsible interpretation of this wise directive in our so very different era.

In Vienna, in 1994, after my seven weeks in retreat under George's direction was finished, we met up with some of his students in a local pub. They were all considerate people who had treated me exceptionally well.

George and I, by nature abstainers, watched them sipping their beers and enjoying each other's company. I turned and asked him what he thought now, back in the West, of the training precept declaring alcohol to be unsuitable as it causes carelessness.

He looked at me and shrugged. "Simple," he said. "If you drink don't drive."

Chapter 14

DMT and Ayahuasca

Of special mention, although my times with them have been very limited by choice, are DMT and ayahuasca, the sacred tea containing DMT. DMT, arguably the world's most powerful hallucinogenic, occurs naturally throughout the plant kingdom, animals, and in humans. In us, its precursor is the neurotransmitter serotonin synthesised in the pineal gland.[1] I've smoked a few different forms of DMT, but the whole genre just isn't my medicine.

That said, I heartily respect DMT's powerful impact on a person's system and the often serious level of enquiry undertaken by the 'meditators of ayahuasca'. Ayahuasca is the most widespread form of the substance. It certainly is an available experience in many Western countries as well as in any of the countries that meet in the Amazon.

Internationally, legal systems have been kind to churches using it as a holy sacrament. Addiction centres do great work with it. Sometimes it can be found in 'luxury' jungle lodges bookable over the internet, complete with shady characters. It's usually taken in a group ritual with a leader, native Amazonian Indian or not, in a traditional modified format reflective of the circumstances.

First, I'd like to share my DMT exposures, as those preceded the ayahuasca adventures. Neither were extensive explorations. I'll let you determine their relative importances. Due to these moments of exposure being so few and brief, I can't weigh in with a valid opinion. I don't need to.

An old friend of a girlfriend, known for his taste in and resources for exotic substances, treated me to a synthetic form of

---

[1] *The Scientific Basis of Integrative Medicine, Second Edition*, Leonard A. Wisneski and Lucy Anderson, p. 147. CRC Press, Boca Raton, Florida, 2009

DMT while we were visiting with him one afternoon. The stuff had a distinctive flavour that I heard from others afterwards is characteristic of it.

He lit me up with a pipeful of this powder that tasted like mothballs. It left what felt like a plastic film on my lungs. Perched on a corner of the couch, I fell back into my girlfriend's arms, utterly incapacitated. The visual kaleidoscope of colours and fractal constructions of her beautiful, smiling face made me laugh uncontrollably, but I didn't know why.

At the same time, my inner urban guerrilla, altered-state survivalist knew that if the cops walked through the door that moment, I was toast. I experienced no expansion or clarity that I associate with psychedelics; just the opposite.

Another time, a man who travelled the 'ayahuasca trail' in the Amazon gave this same girlfriend, with whom I was living, some "natural DMT" from down there and a pipe for it as a gesture of respect. It also was a crystalline powder. Exactly what its source was, I can't say.

Already experienced in the use of DMT and considering it to be enjoyable, she wanted to 'hold space' for me while I smoked some. Sitting on our bed, I lit the pipe and was struck by the similar mothball taste to it. I looked up, and the small, wooden, winged Balinese goddess that hung overhead took flight from her string as if she could. Then, without warning, the room vanished.

Surrounding me was electric, glaring white light, an impenetrable wall of sparks. In that moment I 'knew' that every point of its flaring mass was functionally a fibre-optic thread from my perception to a different reality. I was overwhelmed at the prospect of following any one of them to perhaps never making it back to this reality.

What stunned me about this sudden encounter with a multi-dimensional exit from my existence was, quite simply, my attachment to being 'here'! With all of its familiar reference points and the woman I loved, my world was instantly more important to me than I'd ever realised. The whole event was way too fast for good taste as far as I was concerned.

My eyes had closed. Opening them, my lover appeared completely unfamiliar. Instead, she looked like a goddess I'd never met with a purple universe for Her headdress, extending into infinity. Her voice sounded normal as she asked me what I was seeing.

Before I could answer her, the enrapturing goddess in front of me started to shift into a nightmare visage of snarling, pointed teeth with vicious, female monster's eyes. "Dial it back!" I thought to myself. The visuals complied, much to my relief. From there, matters slowly returned over the next handful of minutes to my being with my usual darling, in our usual home.

I told my supplier of liquid LSD, a high energy raw-fooder, about the experience. I likened the onslaught of it to being hit over the head with a baseball bat.

"Nope," he laughed in recognition. It seemed everyone I spoke to about it had a horror story of their own or somebody else's. "You won't find people lining up for that stuff!"

A couple of weeks later, I tried some more at the same dosage in the same setting. My girlfriend sat across from me, watching me intently.

After a few moments, she asked, "I look funny, don't I?"

"Ummm, yeah. How can you tell?"

"By the expression on your face," she replied.

Her face had sprouted large, green, warty growths, one after another in a few seconds. They looked like pickles dangling from their ends attached to her cheeks, nose, and chin. While she spoke, they jiggled as if possessed of real weight, moving in real time.

My thinking seemed completely lucid. I knew I'd just smoked a powerful substance that was responsible for this disturbingly real hallucination. I tried to examine this phenomenon impartially, but my revulsion at the silliness of her appearance was getting the best of me. I was intrigued by the uncanny realism but didn't see the point. Again, it wore off after some minutes.

Not finding these incidents to be particularly inviting, it was a couple of years before I was talked into trying DMT again.

I sat at a small table outside of a café in my village having breakfast with a bulbous-nosed gnome of a beautiful hippy. He was older than me, of indeterminable age in baggy, blue velvet trousers and jacket, with long, dark hair traditionally parted in the middle. I'd known him peripherally for five or six years. A dealer of all things psychedelic, three people approached us during our chat, each calling him by a different name than the one I knew him by. He was nonchalant about it.

As soon as he heard that I didn't care for DMT, he got sweetly animated. "It all comes down to set and setting," murmured my companion in a sympathetic, brotherly tone. "You need to be out in nature. The sound of running water is critical. Tell you what: I have this great, vegetable-sourced, 5-MeO-DMT. I know this place by a stream nearby where we could go, and you can try it. We can go right now. What do you say?

What could I say? This good-hearted bro wanted me to soar, immaculate. I trusted him and thought I might never have another opportunity, so I agreed. He led me up a babbling brook to some large rocks overlooking a small, tree-lined pool. He was delighted to be my guide. With an air of satisfaction, he put a pinch of black paste into a small brass pipe from another era.

Sitting with my legs tucked up into a half-lotus on the stone ledge, I took a deep toke and leaned back against another rock, waiting. Everything was quiet except for the stream and an audible buzzing that started from deep inside of my head.

As the buzzing grew in intensity, I heard my cell phone start to ring. I silently laughed at myself as I knew it was off. It kept ringing. Yep, that was my phone alright, but I knew it was off. It kept ringing. As the buzzing subsided, so did the distracting sound I knew well. I couldn't believe that was all that happened, but it was.

The setting and my gnome's enthusiasm were the best parts. I thanked Brother Blue Velvet and bought a little to be polite about it. That wasn't his intention, but with a shrug, he accommodated me, pleased I'd liked it. Once home, I threw it in the freezer and never tried it again.

Not many people end up with ayahuasca outside of the rituals. When the chance came to buy a wine bottle of the 'vine of death', as a friend in Peru called it, purportedly brewed by Terence McKenna himself, I jumped at it. In private, that same DMT-savvy girlfriend (who had also drunk ayahuasca once before) and I ripped up our relationship on it for the first journey.

The second journey, a month later on my own, was possibly the most profound bummer I've ever had. I couldn't throw up either time which is supposed to bring relief. I gladly disposed of the last dose of it.

Like I said, I've never thrown up easily, which, many say, is a prerequisite for the full experience. I even lost my gag reflex in India from sticking my finger down my throat so many times to dump out bad food. Up to that point for me, ayahuasca was like having the psychedelic stomach flu.

So, I didn't go looking for more ayahuasca, but it found me. An ex-girlfriend I trusted repeatedly asked me to meet a Peruvian trained, travelling Spanish 'shaman' whom she and her current boyfriend had drunk the sacred tea with a few times before. I liked the guy's sincere vibe. So I agreed to a warm, full moon, outdoor ceremony in a small circle set on a large deck at a private home overlooking entirely natural surroundings.

It was to coincide with the end of a personal health retreat. I broke an eight-day raw juice fast on a brew that was chanted over by a coven of indigenous grandmothers as they prepared it. I threw up alright, although, after that, it was still like having the psychedelic stomach flu.

This time, I did go into the white light. When I emerged, I immediately recognised my surroundings in a moment of intense, unmistakable déjà vu. Here was one of the scenes in the bubbles I'd found myself spiralling down through back into my body over twenty years earlier while sitting with Helen. When I'd screamed in my head, "Quick! Avert! *This is the one it gets stuck in!*" right before sobbing uncontrollably for feeling fragmented and trapped in this blinkered reality.

At that moment in Sri Lanka inside this scene, it made sense to be here just like it did now with a linear history. I was shocked. It was as if different corners of the fabric of time and space were grabbed up in a bunch for just an instant and threaded through with a needle of awareness.

Did the experience leave me feeling like I was in the right place at the right time? Not really. There was our hostess, a New Age whale of a 'tantric educator', cackling like the wicked witch of the North while rocking back and forth on her mat. Who knows for how long, as it didn't matter how many times the Spaniard screamed at her to shut up, she wouldn't. If I'd known it was at her place, I'd never have come.

On my other side, there was a young guy who was successfully pulling off a psychic act in Japan thanks to his abnormally long eyebrows. He was listening to the wind in his wires in wide-eyed wonder. Everybody else was in varying levels of semi-able cooperation and having bodies for launching pads. No one felt the need for the second-offered shot of brew.

None the less, that inexplicable experience of the non-linear nature of The Mystery lingers as a memory that doesn't shake off. And it is wondrous.

Chapter 15

Sacred Sex:
Theory and Practice of
Archetypal Access

This chapter doesn't teach techniques for men to not ejaculate or for women to awaken their own response to.

To women, I would like to say female ejaculation isn't 'icky'. It's your sexual birthright. Be prepared that the first one may contain urine as the liquid flows through the bladder. Urine is always sterile in a healthy person. If a blocked emotion needs clearing, the ejaculation may have a strong smell. Otherwise, it's odourless when fresh. Being living fluid, it spoils quickly.

As one smart woman said to me, "If your man doesn't support you in this, you're evolving out of his league."

Re: professional personal instruction for awakening this response; Caveat Emptor. Remember: the brighter the light, the darker the shadow right next to it.

I was sitting in meditation at the back of the monastery on the enclosed marble floored walkway of the 'marble cottage' that was built for the Krubar. This was a regular place for me to do so. It was always quiet, and as I'd witnessed, the screening kept the poisonous snakes off. Months would go by without any guests in it.

In a flash, I understood something crucial. My eyes popped open. Looking out at the woods, I said to myself, "Aha! I get it! Having children is a daily spiritual practice. One that you ideally undertake with another person for a minimum of, say, eighteen years but it never really ends."

I looked down at my hands folded on top of each other resting in my lap as I sat there in half-lotus, in only a brown *sarong*. I blinked, taking in my surroundings. "Well, I already have a spiritual practice."

I felt into my past, my proclivities, then into the future. I'd only been a monk for a few months or so. I was still very much in it open ended as a way of life with no plans to leave. I surprised myself with the next thought, "If I ever leave the robes, I'll get a vasectomy. It's the responsible thing to do."

And I did, my second day out of robes in Sri Lanka about a year later. I went to the old guy in the public health system as a friend told me that he was the one with all of the experience. His extremely thick glasses unnerved me a little for starters. In honour of me paying, which was a novelty, he used a fresh scalpel. I haven't regretted my decision for half a heartbeat.

And thus, our chapter on sacred sex starts with responsibility. I'm not pushing my decision to be a culturally modified male on anyone. Responsibility lies within the parameters of what it means *to the utmost degree* to every individual. That's where the concept of sacred sexuality really begins.

In nature, there are actions and there are the results of actions. In between the result of an action and a fresh one, there is a pivotal moment of choice. This is the karma-generating moment. It's also the fulcrum point of power. Responsibility is being accountable for the potential consequences of your choices so as to support open-heartedly those affected by them. Understanding this form of respect will be tested to the maximum depth possible by the very nature of the ocean of living and dying itself.

Your understanding earns you the right to love and be loved moment to moment while striving for that great rush of the heart opening to the universe in full acceptance of life's passage. Just so you know how it feels and what to do with it. This challenge is where you learn to have confidence in your ability to swim for setting out in life's floods. Practice makes better.

The next non-negotiable ingredient is trust. Trust is the act of faith that the other person is entering this act of union with the best of intentions, just like you are, and is open to improving them as well, just like you are. Mixing with responsibility, the first ingredient, results in the indispensable tantric alchemical compound called 'mirrored trustworthiness'.

Then comes total privacy in the setting, so there are no distractions while establishing an erotic frequency. The primal generator required to establish an erotic frequency is mutually permitted and encouraged sensual lust, aka, reciprocal, passionate, polarised desire for sexual intercourse. Whipped up together and let bake, this is the basic recipe for a wholesome adult party cake. It's sacred in and of itself thanks to the first two ingredients.

Now add a symbolic ritual as icing on top, and you have an offering fit for a Goddess. If you wish, sprinkle on some MDMA or other entheogens for a little star dust and rocket fuel. Blessed be! May She arrive in full glory for the honours at Her party.

Sacred sex is all about 'descension' into the body, as in, the opposite of ascension into the mind. This state of descending into the body with full attention to the point of manifesting a frequency of divinity here and now depends on three things for starters:

> The first is the participants' joint attitude based on the intention of the symbolic ritual.
>
> The second is the male *Tantrika*'s ability to control his ejaculation.
>
> The third is the ability of the female *Tantrika* to run her sexual energy orgasmically.

Ultimately, this means full ejaculatory responsiveness on her part. It starts with the man's ability to control himself because if he can't, she's never going to have the chance to develop it. If he can control himself and continually meet her in open, full awareness, then her innate reflex shows him where and how to take her deeper into the frequency.

Guiding each other to meet in a point of pleasure builds a wave of energy - the *Shakti* wave - for the pair of lovers to move through their bodies. Expressing their appreciation of each other's efforts and their results strengthens the frequency. This creates another point of pleasure to build upon.

Refining the frequency develops through jointly embodying the attitude of the intention in the symbolic ritual.

This dance is the art of sexually weaving the finer sensual realms into physical reality. Some call it Tantra. It's one expression.

The increase in the sign born of the perception of pleasure is and isn't subtle. There are immediate visual and energetic effects as the signs of progress. The first visual sign is a more attractive appearance to your lover's face through his or her features refining into greater symmetry. Accompanying this is a change in the texture of the air surrounding him or her. The physical sign is simple. It's the increasing sensual deliciousness of the expanding sexual energy.

Keep creating energy, storing it in your body's peripheral awareness and directing it back into your lover. Sometimes eye contact is essential. Stay balanced in your dance. Do it 'til you're satisfied.

That may come to mean many hours later (perhaps six to eight, depending) you're a pair of wonder-filled, euphoric lovers cuddling down in your nest. You've morphed through the sensual celestial realms right there in the universal amphitheatre with plenty of profound lessons. Perhaps soaking up to thirty bath towels in gallons of woman's *amrita* (Sanskrit: nectar) in the process. Namaste! Time to integrate.

Women relate to sex in a ritualised format as a precious experience and personal shrines as having profound meaning. They inherently feel symbols without having to think about them like men do. What a bouquet of flowers does to a woman is evidence of this. It's because of what it means. A man shouldn't underestimate the value of creating a formal ceremony honouring their intimate connection. He limits himself if he does and everyone loses.

The intention of the ritual is all-important. It's the 'official *adhittana*' for the exercise. The three words it takes in English, 'intention-determination-resolution', to cover the meaning of this Pali word shouldn't be considered as equivalent definitions of projected desire. An *adhittana* is more properly a formula with three parts, just as the path to enlightenment has three parts: theory, practice and revelation.

This intention is written down on a slip of paper, then placed centrally on a shrine composed for the occasion. That anchors it into the unfolding of what's going to happen. The focused mental and physical actions of what follows determine its effectiveness. Purposely integrating it both during and after the ritual is 'the resolution of the equation', as in, 'the resulting state'. That takes it out of the realm of hypothesis, through a process into conclusion. The success of the endeavour requires conscious effort throughout.

Preparing the *adhittana* for the ritual is best done by the participants together with a lot of forethought. Freshly created ones work best, but sometimes one will have such significant results that it's useful to use it again as an experiment. In my experimentation spanning untold hundreds of occasions, the beginning and ending have taken on a uniform tone.

Those are 'Intending to maximise our sexual tantric connection... (so as to...) and integrate this into our daily living.' A basic sample *adhittana* could then be 'Intending to maximise our sexual tantric connection, trust in our guides to bring us into the highest experience possible, and integrate this into our daily living.'

I stipulate 'daily living' as Phra George impressed upon me the need to be both careful and precise with an *adhittana* if it was to come to pass and not potentially short-circuit itself or me. He once said to me, "'Life' is an abstraction but 'living' is a reality, just as 'people' is an abstraction but 'persons' is a reality."

171

The written *adhittana* isn't written in stone. Sometimes my sacred consort and I will add to it or rephrase it partway through if it occurs to us that to better manifest something such is needed. It's most certainly not worth fighting about. That's a sure way to blow everything.

On that note, a playful tone of co-endeavor throughout is of utmost importance as well. You're both there to celebrate the opportunity to become better persons through your loving! Your tantric ritual is sure to crash if you forget that.

Guys: if your sacred consort starts to get all angular in facial appearance, diminished in glow and inharmonious of voice, then you're off track. Returning to the emotional range of the 'divine abidings' is best done sooner than later. The secret is as long as she's happy and continuing to appear more attractive to you as the phenomena-instigating Noble Magician; then you're on the right track. It's that simple.

Let me remind you of Vajrayogini's nature. For the sake of brevity, here's her introduction from the start of Chapter 1:

> *Vajrayogini, the 'Diamond Yogini' is also called the 'Red Dakini'. She rules over a semi-wrathful, sexually superior form of finer-frequency beings. These are the* Dakinis *(Sanskrit: 'sky dancers'), a category of* Devas, *('the shining ones'). 'Uber-sexy Angels' doesn't quite cut it as a translation for* Dakinis, *but it starts to give you the idea. They can also be Hellions in a snit.*
>
> *Vajrayogini is the archetype or 'embodied sentient primordial force' of this semi-wrathful class. As such, she is potentially quite volatile and never to be underestimated in that. She's not always wrathful, just when she wants to be. Other times, when it suits her, this goddess is the most seductive, irresistible enchantress that you could ever imagine but didn't know enough to.*

Remember: diamonds can and do cut. Classically depicted, Vajrayogini has a few men's severed heads impaled on her staff and a long necklace of skulls around her neck. She has slightly elongated incisors, both upper and lower. Here is no defanged Virgin Mary. There's no question: she *is* carnivorous. She eats milquetoast men. She'll settle for nothing less than a Noble Magician or his equal.

Gentlemen: I've warned you. Stay impeccably noble on your part, and you'll never glimpse her eyeteeth. Happy at play, both tigers and minxes mercifully keep their claws tucked in. Ensure you enjoy her as a living, shining jewel.

Ladies: play fair, and you're worthy. I expect you know what I'm talking about. My teacher of red Tantra put it bluntly more than once, "It's the Dakini's responsibility to turn on the man." Everyone loses when you don't actively entice him.

She also liked a quote of Coco Chanel's, the iconic French designer. "Nature gives you the face you have at twenty. Life shapes the face you have at thirty. But at fifty you get the face you deserve."[1]

If you don't play fair as a habit, you'll look like it eventually, which is never becoming. Recovering a feminine shine isn't easy at any age. Youth is a gift of nature; old age is a work of art. To be a masterpiece requires wise attention. It's best to start young.

It takes maturity, aka 'wise attention', on the part of a yogini to handle a couple's sexual energy. So many women have to wait to incorporate Vajrayogini successfully later in life after paying a lot of attention for a lot of lessons in love. As well, cultural programming wilts their natural ability to flourish sensually, which should be every woman's birthright. Too often, their age is a prerequisite for the wisdom to maintain Her frequency. They morph younger into the full flush of puberty while entering access to absorption.

* * * * * * * *

---

[1] *Coco Chanel*, Isabella Alston, TAJ Books International, 2014

The shrine for the placement of the *adhittana* for the ritual can be elaborate or simple depending on personal tastes. I prefer the concept of a shrine rather than that of an altar. I advocate a 'Zen Pagan' approach to its construction.

A shrine is a symbolic 'home' for ideals or deities. It can be temporary or a permanent fixture. It should be in the same room as the main event. So, if creating one where your nest is going to be has to happen; then so be it. It can have a threshold for offerings, and the whole thing can be utilised as a piece of sacred geometry while playing house with one's icons.

Strictly speaking, an altar is a surface where one makes sacrifices to a god or gods in exchange for a favour. A red tantric ritual is a loving celebration of living and an act of co-creation by its participants. Self-sacrifice has its place in love, but just by definition, any other type of sacrifice takes somebody that clings to existence or something still desirable out of the living celebration. That doesn't seem very inclusively loving to me. Some say an altar is a designated surface for working magic and keeping the tools for such. Well then, enter the concept of 'the magical shrine'.

In keeping with the Zen Pagan approach, 'sacred geometry' in this context is more like Feng Shui. Feng Shui isn't just Chinese interior decorating; it's their science of 'placement with intention'.

A shrine is meant to empower you as you empower it first and foremost. You are the instigating tantric shamans creating a symbolic touchstone through sovereign decisions. You're not slaves to regurgitated ideas from writers who read books written by writers who read books, *ad infinitum.*

That said, some ideas do hold up through the test of time resonating as good ideas. In keeping with such after careful consideration, it's useful to have all four of the elements; earth, water, fire and air each represented by something placed with that intention on the shrine. More accurately, consider these 'elements' to be 'the primordial tendencies all matter exhibits'. Aether, the fifth element, is inherently represented by the symbols for the deities you've chosen to resonate with. Think of aether as that which carries your cell phone signal across space.

On my shrine, I place a symbol of the Buddha centrally located as an acknowledgement of the highest ideal that humanity can aspire to. As the Buddha discorporated over 2500 years ago, this doesn't mean he's going to incorporate for this occasion but that His Teaching holds court. Thus 'Zen Pagan' means polytheism with the noblest of ideals enshrined as an anchor.

On my shrines, there are no pictures of living beings unless they're specifically part of the intention of the ceremony. There are just representations of the archetypes we wish to accompany us or become extensions of. The latter means incorporating them through their purest qualities. We relate to them as guides.

There's always an image of a guardian or two to keep out unwanted entities. We always acknowledge these watch-beasts. All of these icons can be statues, pictures, objects, or personally done drawings, you name it: as long as the designation means something distinctly tangible to you. That's what's important.

If a visual representation limits complete identification with the deity one wishes to incorporate, omit it. In such a case, it's 'non-placement with intention'. Do still make offerings to her or him. Just be clear about why you're doing what you are to be successful.

Lit candles, pleasing incense and fresh flowers, if available, are always present for the ceremony. These attract beings from the finer realms to the location and help establish a pathway to their frequencies. Doorways work both ways.

The Anagarika Tibotuwawa once said, "Sandalwood is the only thing that wipes out the stench of human beings enough that the *Devas* will come down and hang around."

Just remember that what is pleasingly symbolic for you is what matters most. Respect takes many forms.

To show respect is an excellent way to start. All involved in the ritual should bow three times. I stipulate that the first bow is for the Buddha as the ultimate Teacher. The next one is for His Teaching.

The third is for the Community that practices His Teaching. Buddhists refer to these as 'the Triple Gem'.

First, at a corner of the shrine, I always offer a small vessel of water with the stated intention, "I offer this to the *petas* (Pali: hungry ghosts. They can only partake of what is offered to them as they are unable to take anything for themselves). May all beings have fresh water to drink." This act determines the intention of the shrine as lovingly inclusive.

Then, on previously placed offering dishes (fresh flower petals work well) at the front of the shrine, we offer any entheogen that we will consume to our guides as a respectful gesture. Cannabis we offer separately. I call each guide by name in turn. The last offering is for a major protective deity (We like the Tibetan *Mahakala*, '*Mahakala*' means 'Great Black') to watch over the proceedings. If necessary, to stretch the entheogen for all it's mixed with a little water and a drop of the solution is placed on each petal.

I offer no meat or alcohol so as to keep the etheric vibration elevated. They're traditional offerings in Tibetan ceremonies but just because a deity like *Mahakala* usually has meat and alcohol offered doesn't mean he or she will refuse other things. I prefer to keep out any shades of grey and stick with the light. I only offer entheogens, but some people like to offer dessert. They're all dessertarians.

The Thais maintain and I concur there's a difference between an ennobling Buddhist ceremony and a Brahmanical ceremony where meat and alcohol are considered necessary. An example of a Brahmanical ceremony in Thailand is the capturing of a loose entity who will become a property's guardian in a 'spirit house'. These are on every property, both domestic and commercial.

Monks aren't allowed to even be present for a 'spirit house entrapment' ritual as this is definitely black magic although all of the Thais do it and hardly think of it as such. Housewives sometimes make deals with the trapped spirit. Like, if it makes such and such happen, then she'll sacrifice so many chickens to it as a reward.

Back to the sunny side of the street. After the symbolic offering of the entheogen to the guides, which is always done first as a gesture of honour, the participants take it themselves. Keeping the conversation positive and focused or affirming their intimacy through physical contact they wait for it to take effect. Breathing or meditating together facilitates their mutual resonance. Lightness of tone is essential.

For some of the visual and energetic signs of access to finer realms refer to the relevant parts of Chapter 2.

I only prepare an *adhittana* when using an entheogen other than cannabis. This is just a personal choice. I always offer cannabis to at least one of my guides when smoking it and not engaging in a red tantric ritual. It always enhances the vibration of the event, as noticed by anyone involved.

How a god or goddess appears is very culturally specific. As stated in Chapter 2, my date with a sexual archetype is going to be very different than a Tibetan's date with a sexual archetype. In my cultural mindset, post-Marilyn Monroe being responsible for a generation of platinum blondes, my sexual goddess has long hair I can run my fingers through for both of our sensual delight. I anoint her groomed body with essential oils, so she is lusciously scented. She wears light makeup, pleasing jewellery, and alluring lingerie for starters.

As introduced in Chapter 1: Vajrayogini is the awakened female sexual access to the matrix of existence in Tibetan *Vajrayana* (Sanskrit: 'diamond vehicle'). 'The Shining Diamond who bestows sacred union', classically appears in their iconography as a naked, ravishing young maiden adorned with intricate silver and bone ornaments. These fully express her pure feminine essence. Her hips move in the manner of generating bliss, the urge to undulate unfettered. Her colour is ultraviolet fire. An aura of blazing flames of the same tone surrounds her, elucidating her fiery nature.[2]

---

[2] Images with all of these attributes as well as the following ones are readily available on the internet.

Her left foot pins a small prone yogi in servitude; he has no choice. Open-eyed, he knows what's happening and relaxes, firmly staying where she needs him to. The skin of a tiger girdles his waist, showing he's conquered the ego. His upright staff mirrors hers in appearance.

Her right foot flattens an equally tiny yogini *who looks exactly like her* on to her back. She gazes up, enraptured, at her radiant, powerful form dancing freely. Like him, her open eyes show she too is equally conscious of supporting her in motion by being a living extension for her to feel through. Their donation of love to her, a primordial reservoir of such, bigger than them both, feeds their joy of participating in the matrix of creation with divine purpose.

Also in this classical depiction, Vajrayogini has her head tossed back, drinking blood and bodily fluids from a skull cup with one hand. In her other hand, she holds a large skinning knife. All consuming, pure feminine sexual energy manifest, she derives her sustenance from the sentient heat that pulses through our veins.

The lotus platform beneath the couple she dances on arises from an underlying six-pointed star, the demonstrated equation of two equilateral triangles evenly interweaving balanced energies. Based on this calculation

> They embody "As above; so below."
> But this star must horizontal go
> So love can always freely flow
> And never should be turned on end
> Or else aggression will attend.

> Now a Euclidian expression
> of "Fearful it must stay."
> Limits humans' use
> of boundless DNA.

> Diamond realms were known
> To the Himalayan Bon
> Since long before an oil lamp shone
> In the ancient land of Babylon.

Empathy works to right this script
And trouble in the bud gets nipped.

All is condensed out of ultraviolet, lava-pink steam rising from a boiling skull pot of the meditator's body parts chopped up. This symbology shows from all he is, he's intending to support her, determined to sustain her; resolved to die for her if need be. Up through this hot, pulsating, biological effervescence leaps his thunderbolt of creative force, kindling her noble, refined existence.

Ennobling each other elevates a relationship and is key to sacred sex. Talking 'dirty' is a turn on for some people, but it's elevating to have a vocabulary that honours the body as the temple for Tantra. For instance, in Sanskrit, a penis is called a *lingam* which means 'wand of light'. The word for a vagina is *yoni* which means 'sacred space'. I offer these up for your consideration as there are no single-word equivalents so respectful in English.

Working with this form of Tantra is quite literally 'incorporation': the conscious embodiment of an archetype. Be it the very human Noble Magician, a finer frequency being, or thought of as the refinement of your own DNA's wavelength. They all can work, fortified through repeated application. Then the stored energy shines through every pore.

Remember, not everyone appreciates a shining light. In Buddhist lands, they love to say that when the young monks walk down the road, everyone stares at how brightly they glow. But when the old master walks by, nobody knows anyone's even been there.

Meanwhile, whoever looks upon you with eyes undusted knows without ever hearing your names, "She is Fire! He is Dance! Now she's Royal, elegant and free. And he? Her Noble Magus! They exist beyond the Unformed Block, caressing it in the rhythm of the Ages. They've descended from the Ones whose names aren't known to human tongue."

Sacred sex doesn't culminate in rituals but extends into daily living through embodying what you realised as mattering the most in your concerted efforts. In this way, a woman's erogenous zones extend past her body to include the way her lover helps takes care of the kitchen sink, the trash, the garden, and other mundanities. Expressing her appreciation keeps the Shakti wave rolling.

A man's cohesion of what matters so as to be able to withstand her semi-wrathful tests of his solidity is one benefit of him integrating the lessons presented in the ritual. Another benefit is his ability to refine the vibration for them both to abide in emotionally. These are extremely commendable achievements.

Bargaining while purchasing anything for magical purposes, or for a shrine, destroys its usefulness as a vessel for an etheric (as in aether) vibration. Helen taught me this before she sent me looking for an amulet case in the market beside the Temple of the Tooth. When I didn't haggle as I pulled out the money, the vendor immediately dropped the price. Knowing what I was up to, he wanted to be fair out of respect.

Phra George concurred on the matter regarding buying a Buddha *rupa* (statue, literally 'form' in Pali). It's general knowledge in the occult. If you don't like the price, just walk away.

After a ritual, discard respectfully anything used on the shrine that needs disposal. Whatever it is, it now deserves better than the household garbage. Burning, burying or composting are suitable ways. So is washing by a running drain. Always pour the water for the hungry ghosts on to a living plant. These acts give proper closure to the sacred cycle.

Caution: The oldest warning in the entheogen tantric playbook, especially regarding MDMA, is that *you need to be careful as you might just fall in love* with someone whom you perform union with while chemically influenced. 'Fall in love' means being willing to rewrite your life, even if that is an abstraction, so as to include that person. Such is not always appropriate. Be thankful for the ones that get away.

Chapter 16

The Whole Loving Package

This is a practice:

I've already lit the candles and offered the water. The shrine gleams in the soft firelight. On its threshold sits a line of six fresh flower petals. Each one holds a tiny drop of elixir, sacramental offerings to our honoured friends from Buddhist lands.

My Beloved Yogini kneels on scarlet towels in front of me as I sit in half-lotus. Enhancing her charms are the alluring panties and velvet shawl she wears. Her full, pouty lips, shimmering with gloss, part in a knowing smile. Maintaining eye contact, she removes one gold hoop earring before placing it on the shrine respectfully. It's time now for the panties, too.

While softly intoning Vajrayogini's thirty-two syllable love song, I anoint my Beloved from above to below with exotic oil which we have determined as always only Hers. Warm breasts swell in welcome as my fingers linger in their journey. The delicious, tantalising energy moves downward in union with our breathing. I gently tap the final syllables into place on the gateway to her sacred treasure. What makes the treasure sacred is that her precious love is freely given.

Slowly, the light percussive beats increase in tempo as primal energy fills her willing vessel. Electric fingers of thrilling sparks rush upward into her belly then down to her knees. They crest in a seductive invitation of throbbing desire, pulling the Goddess into her morphing sorceress.

Droplets of nectar moistening her sacred space give way to crashing gushes of *amrita* cascading over my clapping hand, drenching her belly, her thighs, towels, and walls. The Diamond One manifests. Gasping for breath, she lowers her quivering body onto her heels as the contracting rushes subside. I hold her *yoni* tenderly, maintaining this frequency in stillness.

The Holy Consort breathes deeply, requesting water. Dry crimson towels freshen our temple's silk carpet. Sensitively kissing each other, our anticipation pounds.

Purified coconut oil appears beside us. My Guiding Star fills her hands and motions me up onto my feet. Kneeling in front of me, she removes my *sarong* so she can worship through me. I lean back against the wall to relax and watch.

Starting her celebration of being, my gorgeous Dakini strokes me with one hand. I rise to fullness in her loving touch. With her other, she caresses my tender gems. Her teasing gaze shifts from his purple crown to my eyes and back again.

Smiling up at me, she plunges, engulfing me in her hot, wet mouth. I spring to attention as my *lingam* aches with desire in her dance of lips, teeth, tongue and hands. I breathe deeply into my wand of light as rushes of ecstasy fill me with strength.

With a toss of her head, insisting on being free from my grasp, she plunges, again and again, drawing my energy into her mouth and down into her glistening body. She pauses, drinking in my scent with a deep inspiration. Returning to our pleasure, the accelerating rhythm and sudden whimpers alert me to the fresh stream of *amrita* surging from between her legs. Now her divine current freely flows.

Crawling backwards onto the red towels spread over our wide, low bed, she beckons me to enter her. Kneeling in front of her, my radiant Goddess places one arched foot delicately on my chest, her elegant anklet dangling gracefully. Our eyes shine with joy. Applying oil and fresh aloe, I look down upon her gate of heaven, groomed to celestial perfection. She welcomes me with every beating breath to explore her feminine mysteries.

Waiting at her threshold, her luscious heat thrills me at our first contact. Pulsating, the electric attraction arcs between us. The erotic rhythm of our music urges us to undulate in the timeless dance our bodies understand as their reward for living.

Slowly penetrating her sweet, pink rose, I'm enveloped in exquisite hot wetness trembling with the invitation of completion. My Beloved's ultraviolet beauty fills my vision as her infinite sacred space grips me in rippling welcome.

Our breathing paces our expansion. Passionate yet patient, we know well this coursing river of desire roiling over fulfilment. We ride its every rise and fall, grateful for each other. Flooding our united bodies with waves of molten lava from her *yoni*, the Exalted One clenches me, over and over, in continuous orgasms. Taking us beyond our minds, through our bodies, into this moment of awareness we realise our part in donating human love into the matrix of creation.

Our unfettered lust refined through our joy of sacred participation places us among the gods who whisper in our ears their knowledge of the workings of the Ages. As our peripheries attend their sanctity, we feel their wisdom condense into the pulsing of our blood here in the centre of the universal amphitheatre. Conceptualised thought denies us access past this recognition of our becoming.

Fleeting as all perceptions are, the memories do endure of our journeys into the tantric expansion of holy union. Rejuvenated by the night's transmutations, full and spacious, we greet the dawn with hearts tender and strong.

Having entered the stream that flows towards the ultimate bliss of cessation, I know it will come in its own time. Meanwhile, the unfolding journey has its own rhythm, an exciting peace, and that's just fine.

The Buddha repeatedly stated that it was through the complete passing away of sensual and mental desires that a being finds total freedom from suffering. But he also gave directions to monks on how at death to access the sensual realms as well as the other more refined frequencies that make up the 'ocean of life and death', *samsara* in Pali.[1] *Samsara* alternately translates as 'cyclic phenomena'.

He even instructed a loving couple on how to be together again in the next life.[2] How romantic is that?

If a person had the potential to access Nibbana at death, yet only received instruction on how to reach the Brahma world through aligning their emotions for access to it, Sid considered, "there was still more left to do."[3] If he knew that a finer frequency was all the questioner could obtain, he kept the guidance to that.[4] He wasn't fixated just on Nibbana as the one-size-fits-all solution.

Arguably, the Buddha's greatest gift was teaching deserving persons how to develop the ability to achieve the best possible subsequent becoming (what happens next) for themselves that was blamelessly pleasurable and to grow from there. He graded pleasure as becoming "greater and more refined" as one climbs through the bands of frequencies that make up existence on all levels. He defined Nibbana, the cessation of perception of all of them, as the greatest pleasure there is.[5]

The Buddha wasn't anti-pleasure. Sid was *anti-attachment to pleasure* as that's a sure cause for misery, even here and now. Nonattachment is the foundation of his teaching.

And therein lies the great tantric challenge. Joy and sorrow are inseparable. Together they carve a deeper channel for understanding the nature of reality. Passionate loving and attachment to pleasure can be separated. Letting go is within everyone's reach when they just stop spinning.

When I landed in Vienna in 1994, George met me at the airport with a driver. He looked dapper in a two-piece suit, no tie. I'd discovered in 1988 when he'd shown up at my home in one right after he'd left the robes that, with or without the tie, this was his

---

[1] Majjhima Nikaya 120.6*ff.*
[2] Anguttara Nikaya 4.53
[3] Majjhima Nikaya 97.37
[4] *Ibid.*, 99.23*ff.*
[5] *Ibid.*, 59.7*ff.*

preferred manner of dress. It distinguished him as a British gentleman of his age.

George was always direct. While waiting for my luggage, he looked me in the eye and said, "Now that I've had more experience teaching Westerners in the West, I can tell you it isn't that you can't have sex at the next level. You just don't have to."

He knew that for years I was concerned that advancing my attainment levels would evaporate my lust. Much attuned to it as a primal generator, I found the prospect unnerving. Lust was a central identity reference point in my system.

Again a layman, George found out that an adoring woman he loved could elicit an erection in him via acupuncture but that his connection to sex as a source of pleasure was gone. Young, healthy and vivacious, looking at her naked all he could see was parts. "I see a foot as a foot. I see a knee as a knee and a leg as a leg, but I can't put them all together into a woman and get excited," he said, a little perplexed but not exasperated. For him, it made no difference.

My ability to further unravel the propulsions of the mind in Vipassana bent quite dramatically under lust's impact during my last retreat in Thailand six years before. Phra George had tried to use the energy to propel me further, as he would with any obsessive distraction such as chronic pain or noise, but it wasn't to be. I'd never had a wild ride like it before while spiralling through the rabbit hole. Sitting or walking in meditation, I soaked my sarongs in 'moon drops', pre-ejaculatory lubricating secretions, continually for days while my erection raged on, and on, and on.

One night was so filled with intense sexual energy that the walls dripped giant balls of colour as if I was on superlative acid. I had to have a new sperm test afterwards. Extreme changes in the two-year-old surgical scar showed my vasectomy had suddenly started reversing itself. It was a healing miracle I certainly didn't want. I was relieved to learn my tubes were still separated.

After that retreat in Bangkok, I returned to the hotel where my girlfriend had stayed while she attended the wat for those thirty days of retreat with me. Making love, we blew out the two separate circuit breaker boards in the room with a powerful electromagnetic pulse (EMP). The electrician was dumbfounded. We weren't telling.

Phra George watched me through the first years of that relationship. I brought her to Thailand my first visit back. George became her teacher with me for two six-month sojourns. It was at our house he taught a workshop one month after leaving the robes. She was never interested in incorporating sex into our spiritual practice, or accessing the matrix of existence through Samadhi, only in discorporating it.

Our relationship lasted for over five years, most of it as Vipassana hermits. We filled our functional sex life with love right to the end, but my sense of polarity towards her flattened with time. We parted well, as we knew we would, at the end of our long bicycle tour Down Under.

Still in touch by phone, she insisted that I should go to Vienna as she had the year before, to great benefit. Excelling in her solo practice and ever practical, she even suspended her menstrual cycle with an *adhittana* as it just didn't suit her anymore. She brought it back years later to see if she could.

In Vienna, deepening the experience of Nibbana to the next level proved elusive. The slippery nature of perception presented itself impressively one afternoon while I was practising alone in the very large, older apartment that was George's group's centre. Quintessentially European, it sat on the top floor of four flights of stairs.

Rising from my meditation cushion, I went to the window. Not being outside for a month, I'd removed my contact lens some weeks before. As my gaze took in a kilometre of a busy city street, every business sign extending into the distance was in crisp, clear focus. In disbelief, my mind started to form, "No... it can't be."

That was all it took. The all-too-familiar fuzziness gelled over as I watched in wonder and horror.

As a creature of modern society, I've had a variety of long and short-term sexual relationships since being a monk. My increased presence made sex a more intense experience, for both my lovers and me. I was more tactile-kinesthetic than before. Sex naturally evolved into a vivid play of energies as well as in the rhythm of friction. The enhanced ability to surf perceptions and link up recognitions turned it into an exercise all-encompassing of everything that makes me up as a human being. Sex became a dynamic form of meditation, feeding my growth in every direction.

All of this honing of attention has nurtured the long-term relationships in a resonance of purpose that's made them a joy and a refuge of mutually supportive, loving friendship.

Careful analysis of this variety of intimacy, free of the concern of making babies, has afforded me a sexual perspective unknowable in history. The structure of our present society is radically different than any other. That includes our personal growth through intimacy playing a whole new role than it ever has before. Our expectations in our relationships reflect this shift in importance.

An intimate partner enters our lives for a reason, a season or a lifetime. We can't always know which while with one. The Buddha's teaching of universal impermanence reminds us to love when we can and understand when we can't. And sometimes, you can only go so far together. You can't process another person's mental nutrition for them, just like you can't eat their food for them either.

My current relationship is the longest to date approaching 134 months and counting. We've always counted them. It's also the most intense, enduringly polarised, and deeply committed of them all. The entire pantheon of archetypes plays out between us. That's no hyperbole; we also have our unenviable moments. As this broad spectrum appears according to the circumstance, we learn how to both act and respond.

My total woman doesn't give me any space for complacency. Extremely feminine, she expresses as carved-in-stone reality what, to me, is only her emotional weather report of the moment. I've learned that sometimes when stuff happens, just to let time pass. Then love remains.

We're also age-appropriate which brings a textured harmony to our living together. Enjoying the same music is natural for us. She fusses over my greying temples and pays adoring attention to a new wrinkle. I hold her while she sleeps that little bit longer when she needs to.

I so respect a woman who takes good care of herself, and I appreciate that she also loves to take care of me. We seek out ways to make things easier for each other as we go about our day. All of this and more orchestrates our loving play and choreographs our dance of roles.

Just as music is an art whose medium is sound, so too, is the spiritual path a symphony whose medium is mind and form. Every culture and subculture defines music, creates it, and relates to it differently. So too, a spiritual path is defined by current interpretations of eternal universal laws applied to a culture's circumstances. This is why the Buddha's teaching of those laws of composition has proven to be panculturally applicable throughout history.

A big part of the Buddha's message is to choose carefully where to pay attention so as to compose a contemporary masterpiece celebrating purposeful construction in daily living. With proper attention, mind and form can spiral upward in a symphony of evolution.

For instance, I cherish the Little Girl in my woman even though at times I wish she'd grow up. I usually realise after several minutes that my approach of trying to lawyer her into changing her mood is all wrong because the storm just intensifies. When I'm smart, I whisk her up instead in a spontaneous display of light-hearted love. Then the skies clear, she crawls into my lap and in her musical, innocent voice tells me what I needed to hear in the first place. And funny, I do hear her. Fresh harmony reigns thanks to mindful attention. That's when I know I'm evolving.

Making the Little Girl feel safe allows for the Full Woman to come out and play. With so many facets, my sacred consort is the jewel in my lotus, and I polish her gratefully. I wouldn't want it any other way.

It helps to weather the emotional turbulence of a relationship to know when one is obsessing in insight knowledge number nine, *desire for deliverance*, with all of its myriad twists of "If I just get outta this all together, everything will be fine…". The symptoms of this stage, like all of the stages, always feel fresher and stronger than the last time the mind got stuck on the same annoying details of what imagined part of perfection is missing. Consciously establishing a new cycle of applying and sustaining thought on a pleasurable subject works wonders.

Like the last storm that just passed. Now my darling wants to write short stories. She says the first is going to be entitled 'How my New Boots Saved my Marriage'.

My baby is my path of passionate patience, my reward of understanding, and my test to make sure I got it right. I know not to try to rest on any victories, and it helps to pick my battles because something fresh is assuredly always right around the corner. Completely devoted to me, she's certainly committed to my enlightenment as well. Her immediacy demands it. Her love deserves it. She celebrates my becoming with me.

The basis for this celebration of my becoming is the fourth and last 'noble truth' of the Buddha's teaching that beings need to know. These four are:

> 1) Life is inseparable from suffering.
>
> 2) The cause of suffering is attaching.
>
> 3) To end suffering stop attaching.
>
> 4) There is a path of becoming which leads a person to number three, the end of suffering.

Number three is Nibbana in bare attention and clear comprehension in action.

The Buddha taught this fourth truth as 'the noble eightfold path'. Helen preferred to group it into 'remorseless conduct, concentration and understanding', as found in the *Visuddhimagga*, which the eight factors fold into. She'd laugh about how a threefold division is so much easier to remember than one with eight.

As a developmental cycle, these eight factors usually translate as right view, right intention, right speech, right action, right livelihood, right effort, right mindfulness, and right concentration.

Right also translates as simply as 'proper' (*samma*). 'Concentration' also translates as 'blissful absorption' (Samadhi). These alternate renderings help keep the lightness in enlightenment.

Men have always loved to count, and the ancient Indians were no exception. The Buddha used this as a teaching tool to group concepts. Phra George liked to point out that this famous eightfold path just gets one mention in the 'Book of Eights' in the Numerical Discourses (*Anguttara Nikaya*). The Numerical Discourses of the Pali canon totals 8,122 sections (by one count) and is just one of five massive collections of his words.

Although missing from the 'Book of Eights,' the noble eightfold path is listed many times in the 'Book of Tens'. That's because it results in right knowledge and right freedom. These two are essential tools for forging ahead in life. Together they make for clear comprehension.

Right knowledge is the basis for right freedom. There are two types of freedom: freedom from and freedom for. Part of right knowledge is knowing what to be free from. Right freedom is applying that knowledge to unique personal circumstances for more satisfying daily living.

Think of that as real freedom. It manifests in many ways. It's a great destination for a spiritual path to lead to and a great reason to celebrate.

The canon is full of the Buddha's warnings about the dangers of sensual desires. But of particular note is that at the end of his life, he said to his long-term, devoted attendant Ananda seventeen times in seventeen listed spots (and I paraphrase), "This is a delightful place. Anyone who develops and perfects the bases for certain supernormal powers can live out the aeon if he wants to. I've developed and perfected those bases, and I could live out the aeon if I wanted to."[6]

It was a repeated cue for Ananda to ask him to stick around. Ananda missed it every time. So the Buddha, who wasn't attached either way, decided enough was enough, and he'd discorporate within a few months. We know how that played out. One last gigantic rush...

The world is perceived through the senses, and Sid, the much-loved Good Friend, didn't have anything against hanging out delighting his own. But his life was already a symphony of accomplishments. His story would resound throughout history for everyone at all levels of ability of how to achieve a peak experience according to their own conditions. So he was satisfied: mission accomplished.

There's a lot of precise information about supernormal powers in the Pali canon.[7] The *Visuddhimagga* goes into great detail about developing them to the point of mastery.[8] It's too much information to be ignored, but selective focus for things that don't fit current culturally accepted ideas knows no bounds.

If you still scoff at the idea of mind affecting matter, think about the Krubar's footprint, the multi-coloured crystals in his bones, and extrapolate from there.

Or think of it in terms of this analogy: say an unprecedented huge EMP (electromagnetic pulse) from a massive solar flare knocked out all of the electrical equipment humanity depends on. This could potentially plunge us forward into a survivalist's Stone Age nightmare. How would stories of what a cell phone or a laptop could do sound a couple of thousand years down the road if

---

[6] Digha Nikaya 16, 3.3. A few translators disagree about the word 'aeon', as they can't accept the idea of such a 'great miracle', even though the meaning and usage are clear.
[7] Majjhima Nikaya 77.30*ff.*, for one example.
[8] *Visuddhimagga* IV, V, XII, XIII

mankind never again accomplished such technological mastery? Such was the mastery of mental abilities during the Age of Penetrating Attention that died out.

And so we can expect regeneration of form, the basis of legends and myths throughout time, would have been known in those days of incredible mental accomplishment.

The Buddha stayed in a tiny corner of the travelled world of his times, roughly only 370 miles by 185 miles.[9] He taught the laws of universal composition in that region for forty-five years. It's recorded that a number of his monks and nuns also developed supernormal powers. Some of the original monks simply vanished, like Rahula, his son, for example.

They were all wandering mendicants. No one knows how far they travelled. Many different adepts would have heard of Siddattha of the Gotama clan. Even just from merchants on any of the trade routes, including the sea lanes of the day. The commercially navigated Ganges flowed right through his turf. Interested persons could have found him if they wanted to.

If any adepts or his own monks or nuns wished to live out the aeon, and didn't already know how to, Sid would probably have obliged with the instructions. If the prerequisite concentration levels were already there and that person asked, why wouldn't he? He said he didn't hold any secrets back.[10] Wouldn't that include any ethical adepts who practised suprasexuality?

That means there might be persons walking around who learned how to regenerate from the Man himself. Maybe they like hanging out because the total human experience is a richly textured trip in this universe like no other.

If so, what, in celebration of the laws of the universe he taught them, do you think they do for kicks on a Saturday night?

---

[9] *The Historical Buddha*, H.W. Schumann, English translation by M.O'C. Walshe, 1989, p. 231 (reference: 600 kilometres x 300 kilometres). Motilal Banarsidass Publishers, India, 2004
[10] Digha Nikaya 16, 2.25

Chapter 17

Knowledge of Review:
The Path by Which I Came

Comprehension test: what is the sound of one hand clapping? You already know the answer to this if you've been paying attention.

What's the Golden Rule to renunciation? Don't give up anything you still want. Cancel that if it's physically addictive.

I was leaving again for India and went up to the Forest Hermitage to say goodbye to the Nyanaponika. It was 1983. He stood in his doorway as I sprung the question on him I'd brought with me. "Venerable sir, is it possible for a man to become an arahant [fully enlightened being] living with a woman?"

Surprised, he brightened and smiled. When an accomplished monk does this, you can expect he's already given the subject some thought. "Well, anything's possible. It's just how probable."

He then added a Burmese folktale and his personal commentary in the lightest of tones. He figured the odds were against it.

I expect he's right. In a long essay, he once quoted Frederich Nietzche, the German philosopher, 'All lust wants eternity'.[1] Yes... and it wants it now.

But, as I came to learn, what's a man from my culture to do? Be miserable in his isolated way of life? Who benefits from that?

Man is a pleasure-seeking animal. Nobody ever gave up a greater pleasure for what she or he considered to be a lesser pleasure. To play is necessary for sanity.

---

[1] *The Worn-out Skin: Reflections on the Uraga Sutta*, BPS, WHEEL 241/242, 1977

Undeniably, things are a little different now, twenty-five and a half centuries after Sid held court camping with his in-phase community in the warm countryside around the Ganges. Growing up on canned pink lemonade, wall to wall carpet, and Star Trek, I expect to be a different creature in phase with an entirely different world. Plugged in and online.

Back in Sri Lanka in 1986 things weren't the same as before either. The civil war was full on between the Singhalese army and the Tamil guerrillas. I couldn't get to my favourite half of the island; the army was pulling foreigners off the busses. Even the food tasted as if they were cooking their hatred into it. Naïve, simple people were easily led by clever aggressors who piled up atrocities on both sides. For many reasons, I made the difficult decision to leave the monkhood.

Being in a Theravadin country, I needed to do it properly. That would take a minimum of four monks to perform the act of the community. I wryly noted that this was the same number required for funerals as well. I asked around for any Thai monks to perform the disrobing ceremony so I could get my monk's ID from Thailand correctly filled in. A Sri Lankan monk told me there was a small contingent of them in a temple on the green outskirts of Colombo.

Descending from the bus, the first person I saw was a young Thai monk I knew from Wat Phra Buddha Bat Tak Pah. Then: two more and another. I couldn't believe it. Neither could they. Their delight bubbled over. They told the novices to cook a special lunch.

Amazed to find them there, I asked what they were doing. Their innocent grinning was almost mischievous, like school boys out on vacation. In a curious tone, one replied, "We're here to study Pali."

I laughed, and so did they. They didn't need any instruction from the Singhalese. They were already Pali scholars having graduated from the university inside of Wat Mahadhatu.

These monks, some a little older than me and some younger, would be in the robes for the rest of their lives. As such, they were there to establish connections with their Sri Lankan counterparts. Church politics, as it were.

Wat Phra Buddha Bat Tak Pah was an important temple as the fifth largest outside of Bangkok at that time. This was the other arm of the clergy. Their generation would be one more twist in the living rope of Asian men maintaining this ancient form of the Buddha's teaching in a changing world of technology and cultures.

Finally, they asked me if there was a reason for my visit. I told them I'd come for them to disrobe me. Several had been at my ordination. They stood stunned as if a bomb had dropped even though being a monk temporarily is part of Thai culture as a rite of passage to manhood. A man isn't an eligible bachelor until he's been one. I didn't fit that equation in their eyes.

After a moment's silence, they freaked, surrounding me in a flapping of orange robes.

"No-o-o-o! Tan A-rex, you don't want to do tha-at!" said one, elongating his vowels to show emotion as the Thais do in their own language as they don't use tones for that purpose.

"I know! Let's go for a tour!" piped up another.

"Here! Have my bowl! It's a very nice bowl!"

This one had been at my ordination. He eagerly displayed his large stainless-steel bowl. It's a favourite material among the young monks who grew up as novices although it makes no sound when struck.

"You know they made sure I had a great bowl when I ordained. It rings like a bell. No, thank you."

Yet another: "Ummm... let's have lunch then."

In true Thai fashion, they decided together at once to avoid the subject, shifting the conversation to lighter topics.

After lunch, I reminded them of my purpose. We went into the small library and sat on the carpeted floor in Thai temple posture, legs folded underneath us, so our feet didn't point at anyone disrespectfully. I sat in the centre with the oldest one as the other nine formed a circle around us.

The younger ones didn't know how to handle it. Soon enough, their nervous laughter gave way to total silence. Deadly serious, this older, dedicated monk who had been at my ordination so seemingly long ago faced me, looking me straight in the eye.

The Thais never do this as it's usually interpreted as an aggressive gesture. In this moment together, our gaze met evenly. We both knew I sat at a decisive fork in my road like no other would ever be.

"You sure?" he asked.

"Let's do it." I raised my hands in prayer salute.

Sharp in-breath: "Repeat three times," he said in English, "I'm not a monk anymore."

After I'd finished, he leaned forward. With his right hand, he swept the folded outer robe off of my left shoulder. That was it. I stepped outside of the circle to change into the civilian clothes an American friend had loaned me.

Keeping the mood light, we conversed in a mixture of Pali, English, and Thai as I dressed. I corrected one of them on his Pali which made us all laugh. Another suggested I keep my robes and bowl. We all knew he hoped their presence with me would pull me back. I reminded him that they were community property and not mine to take.

Stepping back into the centre, I sat back down in front of the lead monk for what I knew came next. First, he looked around at these men in the circle who he would know for the rest of his life before addressing me in English. "I'm going to say this in Thai because it's important and some of us don't speak English very well. Phra Lek? Please translate."

Again, his gaze met mine. As he spoke in paced Thai, the translation came from over my shoulder. "Now I'm supposed to give you a lecture to send you on your way in life as a layman. But I have nothing to say to you. You've done it. You know it. You have spent your fifteen months in robes better than most men spend fifteen years. Good luck."

This was a deep honour from one of the Krubar's committed monks, an honour that wasn't lost on me. I took it stoically then, but now my eyes fill as I write this almost three decades later.

Leaving the monkhood was like voluntarily accepting a lower income lifestyle to have time to smell the roses. My contemporary journey in the traditional lands of the wandering mendicant had transformed me in ways it might take the rest of my life to unravel. Helen and George, both extraordinary communicators, only existed for a brief moment of time in archetypal tenures of fortunate opportunity for me. If we hadn't been in phase culturally, their teaching would never have resonated.

While I was at the monastery in the north, a young Dutch yogi who was a friend of Helen's told the president of the Nepalese Ayurvedic Association about my degenerating spine. "Tell the monk to contact me," he said. "I have medicine for him."

For six months, I swallowed hand-rolled pills of Himalayan botanicals which looked like black and brown rabbit turds. Back in my home city four months later, x-rays showed everything had regrown except for one vertebra that had a compression fracture. A chiropractor first noticed it when I was fifteen.

When I was forty, x-rays showed the erosion had returned. Phoning Nepal, I discovered the Ayurvedic doctor was dead. His son, the fortieth generation in line practising the family's herbal art, told me the medicine didn't work as well for older persons. I had him send me a year's worth. I wrapped a potent nutritional cocktail around it. I became more pain-free than I'd been my whole adult life.

Just as we have nutritionally based bodies, we are chemically based doorways of perception. Think of minute amounts of hormones and how their balance changes us both mentally and physically. There's a window of opportunity that exists when influenced by the right combination of chemicals to have experiences that aren't possible without them.

If they can influence us, it's because our cells have receptor sites for them. That means our bodies produce something similar on their own. Wise attention to this phenomenon allows us to work with the laws of nature to expand our understanding of the universe. Not just for personal betterment, but for everybody's good.

A young man recently confided in me about his exciting explorations in polyamory with his girlfriend. "It's not fair to ask just one woman to be all things for you," he said.

I heard an echo of my own words from almost twenty-five years before coming back at me. Although still at the start of his journey, he agreed wholeheartedly with my mathematical formula about what to expect.

No, it's not fair to ask just one person to be all things for you. What is fair is to appreciate the gifts that person brings into your relationship which others can't. Patience with whatever part of imagined perfection is missing tends a person towards enlightenment. Part of enlightenment is accepting that living is "inherently insufficient as to give lasting pleasure" as Helen said so long ago. Some things, though, are non-negotiable.

Whether if you live with your lover or not, be prepared that the sexual polarity may flatten with time and exposure. Romantic love is conditional. Maintaining attraction to each other requires consistent personal effort. Taking the space necessary to rejuvenate yourself for the health of the relationship is a must. So is maintaining your physical health and appearance.

Complaining is death to polarity. Especially to each other about each other, but sometimes it's necessary for insight. After all, you both want to win which is why you teamed up in the first place.

I'm always coming up with imaginative new ways to tell my wife I adore her. Some stick around for a while; some don't. One that gained traction a few months ago and continues to amuse us is her latest royal title: "My One and Only Perpetual Everything."

A beneficial maxim within everyone's reach is "Love more; want less: be gratefully wiser!"

Ananda's pivotal role in the Buddha's story deserves reflection. The Buddha always had an attendant, but out of the eight named ones in the first twenty years,[2] none proved lastingly suitable. At a meeting where all of the monks readily volunteered, he picked quiet, unassuming Ananda, who held back. Asked why, Ananda said he knew the Buddha would choose whom he felt was best suited for the position. His easy-going, good nature, and the devotion he'd tirelessly prove earned him that honour.

Sid could've had his choice of brilliant conversationalists or another great magician to fly the realms with. Instead, he chose for constant companionship a person who brought appropriate qualities for the task which the others couldn't even though they wanted to. They were together for twenty-five years until the Buddha's end.

As you read in the last chapter regarding enjoying oneself, after dropping overt hints seventeen times looking for a certain, simple answer which never came, Sid knew his and Ananda's relationship had gone as far as it could. Being fully enlightened, of course he never expected it'd be satisfying in absolutely every way. But he valued their relationship to such a degree that he based his decision to continue living on Ananda's presence in conversation.[3]

Being fully enlightened means always being totally present. Being listened to by the person one is closest to isn't just a sign of their level of presence, if what you're saying is important. It's a basic need and as such, non-negotiable. The universe could be Sid's perpetual oyster, pleasure its perpetual pearl, but the game-changer was repeatedly not being understood by his chosen companion. How touchingly human.

---

[2] Nagasamala, Nagita, Upavana, Sunakkhata, Cunda, Sagata, Radha and Meghiya. *The Historical Buddha*, H.W. Schumann, English translation by M.O'C. Walshe, 1989, p. 128. Motilal Banarsidass Publishers, India, 2004
[3] Digha Nikaya 16, 3.4*ff*.

Woven together, this tapestry of stories, esoterica, and observations, along with the Theory and Practice section, is a manual with cultural context. What you do with it will determine a conclusion. The Buddha would sometimes finish a lesson with "Now it is time for you to do as you see fit."[4]

Sometimes, Phra George would end a lecture with "I can't give you my knowledge, I can only give you information. It's up to you to take that and turn it into knowledge."

May this book help you in a way that nothing else has.

Travelling up through India for the first time, I had a pair of very long ocean-going swim fins strapped to my backpack. I felt as silly as the Aussies looked with their surfboards who were also heading to Nepal. From Calcutta, I shipped the fins south to my new friend Helen with a letter asking her to please keep them for me until I returned. She replied to me at 'General Delivery, Kathmandu'.

In her letter, she reminded me that I asked her for Buddhism in twenty-one words or less at our first meeting, and now here they were. She wrote that the first six summed it up completely but since she had fifteen left she'd fill in the rest. For filling, she added *'Greed, anger and delusion are the roots of all karma.'* That took some study on my part. To end, she added the 'divine abidings' in Pali with the English bracketed beside them: *'Metta* (loving-kindness), *Karuna* (compassion), *Mudita* (sympathetic joy) *and Upekkha* (equanimity).'

The first six words she typed reverberate through time and space as the most sagely of injunctions any human could ultimately ever utter:

'Want nothing; fear nothing: be free!'

---

[4] Samyutta Nikaya 35.88, 35.243, 44.1, 54.9, 55.6

Theory and Practice A

Grasping the Big Picture

Referred to on pages 32 and 34

Nikolai Tesla, genius physicist and the inventor of alternating current (1856-1943), famously said in 1942, "If you want to find the secrets of the universe, think in terms of energy, frequency, and vibration."[1]

This irregular flux we call the universe consists only of networks of states acting as conditions for other sets of states to come about. It's all very specific. With the removal of any of the conditioning states as a factor, the resultant network of states changes as well. In Theravada, this law of nature is called the 'interdependent origination'. It forms the basis of existence, the same mechanism working moment to moment as well as life to life.

Nothing exists independently of other things. Everything that exists does so because other things exist. Nothing is permanent. Even anything you might consider to be a permanent 'you' is just a (tightly woven) network of states that hasn't been unknotted. A sense of self is the result of these states rolling over and conditioning each other too quickly to know them separately. As Bhikkhu Sumedha once said to me, "It's like the whirling brushes of a dynamo creating an electrical force."

The Buddha didn't teach an originating cause of the universe but instead spoke of multiple expansions and contractions of multiple world-systems.[2] As such, it's all just empty phenomena

---

[1] www.teslatech.info/ttstore/conftapes/teslatech/2010jul/2010p13.pdf. In conversation with Ralph Bergstresser.

[2] Anguttara Nikaya 10.29.2; *Visuddhimagga* XIII, 13f. *Gods and the Universe in Buddhist Perspective* by Francis Story is a very accessible treatment on Buddhist cosmology. 'Multiplicity of world-systems' p. 37f., BPS Wheel Publication

rolling on endlessly. This is why an experience outside of this state of flux - an experience of Nibbana - is crucial to know it accurately for what it is.

There are four ways to get there:[3]

1) Vipassana preceded by Samadhi.

2) Samadhi preceded by Vipassana.

3) Samadhi coupled with Vipassana.

4) Ratiocination around a single point until the logical mind breaks down, not finding a resting place inside its parameters.

1) *Vipassana preceded by Samadhi*. First, one develops the ability to change frequencies. This is called 'mundane absorption'. Then a person changes the object of awareness to one that leads out of frequency awareness altogether. This is called 'supramundane absorption'.

Taking the analogy used in Chapter 1 further; it's like developing the muscles in a weak arm so you can lift it to tune the radio using a dial. This takes less strength and dexterity than learning how to turn it off with, say, a small, stiff, flip switch which takes more of both, and so comes after. In this case, it's developing mental muscle and accuracy, so penetration of the moment with full concentration is easier.

Samadhi is so important it's the centrepiece in the Pali formula *Sila-Samadhi-Panna*: (developing) remorseless behaviour, (to develop) concentration, (to develop) understanding. This formula is the basis of the *Visuddhimagga*, 'The Path of Purification', written in Sri Lanka in the fifth century CE. It's one of two main commentaries considered as authoritative as the Pali canon in Theravada. An encyclopedic manual of the wandering ascetic monk's path as it existed up to that point in Lanka, it's complete with detailed instructions on developing supernormal powers as well as understanding the nature of reality.

180/181, 1972
[3] Anguttara Nikaya 4.170

As my Samadhi teacher said, it was written to try and stop the onslaught of the Buddhist Dark Ages. By then, care for the texts and preaching them came before practising their contents as official church policy.[4] Predictably, bitter political infighting between powerful monasteries had become the norm.[5] At the same time, a loss of supernormal abilities among the remaining ascetic monks was coming to pass. The future was anticipated to be a descent into chaos.

This ancient commentary is referred to many times throughout this book.[6]

Vipassana preceded by Samadhi is the traditional way for yogis, also known as 'the magician's path'. The practice of 'accessing the matrix of existence' can enable one to develop abilities with the mind to cause changes in the world around one, if so wished, before 'discorporating the matrix'. Or just for kicks afterwards. Such powers are called the benefits of developing concentration without necessarily developing understanding.

This first method is considered to be the long road to the point of emergence, but one is comforted by the blissful nature of the concentration. Hence, we have the translation of 'serenity' for Samadhi. What's the hurry anyway, if you're serene?

2) *Samadhi preceded by Vipassana*. Often, this is defined as 'bare Vipassana alone'. I heard this definition from both my Samadhi and Vipassana teachers as well as the Thai monk who was the meditation teacher in the monastery in the north of Thailand where I ordained. That's because at the moment of penetration there's fully concentrated absorption into the chosen object of awareness which is in motion. This results only in the cessation of the awareness of all frequencies. Access to supramundane absorption (Nibbana) just requires momentary concentration, *khanika-Samadhi* in Pali.

---

[4] *Visuddhimagga*, Introduction, p. xxix
[5] *Ibid.*, pp. xxviii-xxx
[6] *Visuddhimagga* (The Path of Purification) is available as a free download from the internet.

3) *Samadhi coupled with Vipassana.* These are developed together in tandem or, in collaboration in a stepwise fashion. The Thai meditation teacher in the northern monastery put it simply: "One changes the object of awareness back and forth, very quickly from one to the other," he said while wiggling two fingers to demonstrate back and forth.

4) *"Ratiocination around a single point until the logical mind breaks down, not finding a resting place inside its parameters."* was how my Samadhi teacher in Sri Lanka defined this one. My Vipassana teacher in Bangkok agreed with that when I spoke with him about this concept.

This is the way of the koan in Zen Buddhism. A koan is a nonsensical question which the logical mind can't answer. This pushes a person into an experience unreachable by reasoning. Stories of such are famous. In Zen, they call this 'sudden enlightenment'. Nothing might happen for twenty years of honing concentration through severe monastic discipline, but if it finally does, then it happens quite suddenly. The habit of discipline makes it easier to review the path by which one came to the point of emergence and deepen the understanding of the experience.

Among Theravadin scholars, there's confusion about this fourth method. Translators speak about 'agitation' of the mind or 'restlessness'. Others: 'excitation'. It's either about the nature of reality, the Buddha's teaching or some corruption of insight. They aren't certain as to whether this is under control or not. They contradict each other. Thus, academic discourse itself falls into the paradox it fails to explain.

Sustaining that applied thinking a little more, perhaps their logical minds will be on the verge of breaking down, not finding a resting place inside their parameters.

Theory and Practice B

Hindu Tantra and Assumptions

Referred to on pages 38, 154 (footnote), 216, 247

Hindu Tantra, as we know it, post-dates Theravada Buddhism by at least seven centuries. It works with an interpreted pantheon of archetypal roles that co-evolved with the societies of post-Buddhist India. This development preserved techniques rooted in pre-Buddhist antiquity of resonating with the forces of nature. The principle deities are Shiva, the solar lord of yoga, and Shakti, his sacred consort, who goes by different names in different regions and ages. Hinduism presumes the finer frequencies to be an eternal godhead that an equally eternal part of a person reabsorbs into, coined as 'becoming one with Brahma'.

Hindu cosmology is embroidered in the fashion that only something that has been around that long with so many influences can be. Seeing the weave of the fabric underneath that is difficult. Looking is best done with the magnifying glass of Pali Buddhist cosmology. The Buddha taught a lot about Vedic (pre-Hindu) cosmology and the pantheon of his day. He both interacted with and instructed these 'gods' as a fully realised being. Many sought him out but sometimes he'd just go for a visit.

Think of such deities as beings occupying archetypal stations on different molecular wavelengths similar to ours in structure. The First Council recorded some of their interactions with the Buddha. The monks portrayed them as being similar to worthy, powerful persons being the kings and nobilities of different realms for a period, in, for us, a once-upon-a-time style. A common honorific for Sidhattha in Pali is 'the teacher of gods and men'.[1]

---

[1] *Sattha deva manussana*

We can sophisticate this picture of 'gods' with quantum theories of multiple dimensions. The Buddha's cosmological explanations for the structure of our universe and the limited perceptions of beings, even in the finest of realms, line up with these.[2]

The mind and body respond to yogic practices properly applied even though based on incorrect theories. It's how far a theory unravels the universe adhering to logic and supported by empirical evidence that makes it the rational one to apply for best results.

For example, a person can reach a full absorption experience of Samadhi believing or expecting that some of what one is experiencing is a permanent state. That one is becoming unified with one's higher, immortal self or an eternal god. It's easy to get lost in the labyrinth of the mind chasing constructions to justify such an explanation. This is the nature of 'woolly thinking'.

Any experience, no matter how euphoric or otherwise, that happens in meditation needs to be examined according to the logical three characteristics of all phenomena. These are called the *tilakkhana* in Pali, sometimes translated as 'the three characteristics of existence':

1) The experience was impermanent (*anicca*) as it came about due to a specific network of states acting as specific conditions for it to happen. With the passing of those conditions it too passed. This fact is a self-evident truth.

2) That it has the characteristic of being inseparable from suffering (*dukkha*) if there's any clinging to it or craving for it again as being preferably pleasurable because it's proven it was impermanent as it's no longer happening. This too is self-evident.

3) With or without your, or anyone's, permission (*anatta*) the changing show goes on.

The self-evident conclusion from these three characteristics, as summed up in number three, is that there's nothing experienced in which something can be pointed to as being permanently ownable

---

[2] Digha Nikaya 1, 2.6

of that phenomenon or it could be ordered to stick around - be controlled - without needing a network of states to support that command. Nothing ownable means inherently there's no owner. No owner of any of it equals no self (*anatta*) or soul in any of it. Only a ceaseless, conditionable but not controllable, network of states acting as conditions for another network of states to arise, all quite specifically. This is the cosmological nature of emptiness.

Theory and Practice C

The Insight Knowledges

Referred to on pages 97, 134, 231, 234

There are the three parts of the path to enlightenment: theory, practice, and revelation. Most people try to leave out the practice, attempting to jump straight from theory to revelation.

Tell a Burman or a Thai the mechanics of how to practise Vipassana meditation, and they'll simply do so because that's "the way of the Buddha." Try that with a Westerner, and you can expect the response to be, "Why does it work?"

Phra George always said I gave people more information to work with than they needed but that was in cloistered retreat circumstances. I see it as my job to give you complete information. It's up to you to turn it into wisdom.

This section maps the rabbit hole of practice. Not that everyone sees the same scenery every time they go through it. The practice of Vipassana progresses through stages of purification of view about the nature of reality called 'the insight knowledges'.

Even though the journey through the insight knowledges is always a progression in the same sequence, different symptoms may show up at different times. Which ones you might end up hanging out in for a while depends on the depth of focus and whatever your particular craving or aversion may be at the time. Phra George likened it to climbing a ladder. You always hit every rung but what you see depends on which way your eyes are pointing and where you stop to rest.

The insight knowledges developed through to completion lead to an experience of Nibbana; the here and now free of definition. This experience apparently changes a person's destiny irrevocably. Repeating the experience helps hasten this effect. Other effects of the practice are seen in daily living. These usually manifest as, at the very least, an improvement in general mood and empathy even if the goal of Nibbana hasn't been realised.

The Thais and the Burmese differ on the distinct categories of what constitutes the final stages of mundane awareness. Edges blur in trying to do so. I'll leave it up to the intellectuals to split hairs about these stages. I'm just a storyteller.

The method I learned as a monk is called 'the Mahasi method' as it was developed by the Burmese monk, the Mahasi Sayadaw. The variation that I learned in Wat Mahadhatu is in the next section. Phra George said many times, "Don't blame the Mahasi for what I'm doing to you."

The sitting part of the practice emphasises focussing on the movement of the abdomen associated with the breathing as the primary object of awareness. One must focus without influencing it in any way. The movement of the abdomen is the gateway in this technique as it lies in the realms of both autonomic and voluntary movement.

A person must completely still the mind for a moment of observing it as an autonomic movement. Any thinking causes, at the very least, a distracting ripple effect on the diaphragm while watching it. Full momentary absorption into the motion, free of thought, drops the awareness into the space in between moments of defining.

Western medicine, which is full of holes, tells us it's impossible to observe your respiration without affecting it. A person's rate of breaths per minute goes on every medical chart. Every doctor, nurse, and paramedic is taught to hide from the patient when they're observing the patient's respiration rate so that the patient can't influence it.

Patients think that nurses are taking their pulse for thirty seconds. In fact, nurses take it for fifteen seconds, then multiply it by four. The other fifteen seconds they're clandestinely counting the patient's breathing. They multiply that by four as well.

To just watch and label the autonomic movement of the abdomen caused by the breathing takes practice. The practitioner passes through well-documented stages of trauma because the incessant renewal of personal reference points is seen to constantly interfere with and be the antithesis of just watching. If we have, say, 50,000 thoughts per day, to just pick a number, 30,000 are the same as the day before, like them or not.

The Vipassana classic about these stages is a very short book written in 1950 by the Mahasi Sayadaw entitled 'The Progress of Insight'. It was translated by the Nyanaponika in 1965. The book deals with the mental symptoms of each stage and what understanding has been gained by each one. It's available as a free download from the internet.

In my possession is a tattered, yellowed booklet, the text is twenty-one pages long, originally written in 1961 by Phra Tepsiddhimuni (then Phra Rajsiddhimuni). The commendable English translation by Thai volunteers in 1964 is entitled 'Manual for Checking Your Vipassana Kammathana Progress'. Kammathana in Pali means 'place of work'. Here, it refers to the insight knowledges as stages of development or 'places' within the mind. It's available for free on my website, SexDrugsEnlightenment.com.

The copy I have is undated but was reprinted for use by a Malaysian Buddhist association. It even lists all of the names of the donors who made the publication for free distribution possible, as is the quaint custom throughout Buddhist Asia. There were only a few of them lying forgotten on a bookshelf in Section Five. Phra George didn't consider it useful for students to occupy their minds with the insight knowledges as a map. He just wanted to push them through the stages to get to the point of emergence. Time is vital in a retreat and not to be wasted.

Phra Raj's (Phra Tep's) book lists more details of the physical symptoms and emotional reactions of each stage than the Mahasi's does. It's the perfect complement to 'The Progress of Insight'.

The insight knowledges are considered to be part of the seven purifications listed in the Pali canon[1] which form the basis for the

Visuddhimagga. This basis is reduced to the threefold formula *Sila-Samadhi-Panna*: (developing) remorseless behaviour, (for the purpose of developing) concentration, (for the purpose of developing) understanding. The insight knowledges are part of the concluding section on developing understanding.

The insight knowledges are part of the meditator's mundane consciousness. The symptoms of them can be induced without actually having reached them if one knows what they are. Craving for signs of progress through the sequence is natural but is counterproductive, only messing up the outcome.

This is why Vipassana is considered impossible to teach yourself. It's best to undertake it with the direction of a teacher who has been successful in her or his own practice and is familiar with the student's progress through close supervision. That way, the right instructions can be given at the appropriate times.

During a meditation report, the teacher will understand which stage a student has reached by different clues in the conversation. It may just be an offhand phrase as an aside which the meditator doesn't consider to be important or which he or she may interject as a piece of humour. The Thai meditation teacher at the monastery in the north once closed our afternoon conversation by telling me he had to check his retreat students' moods.

So, students are kept in the dark about their advancements through the stages. In his book 'Practical Insight Meditation', the Mahasi Sayadaw wrote: *'It is not good for a pupil who meditates under the guidance of a teacher to get acquainted with these stages before meditation begins.'*[2]

However, he did state in the conclusion of 'The Progress of Insight': *'Though in the beginning it was mentioned that this treatise has been written for those who have already obtained distinctive*

---

[1] Majjhima Nikaya 24.2ff.

[2] *Practical Insight Meditation: Basic and Progressive Stages*, p. 35. Buddhist Publication Society, Kandy, Sri Lanka, 1971

results in their practice, others may perhaps read it with advantage, too.'[3]

Okay, you've been warned. If you continue reading, consider yourself to be a consenting adult.

Let's follow a hypothetical meditator, male, merely for ease of pronoun usage, as he progresses through the enumerated sequence of insight knowledges.

1: *The analytical knowledge of mind and body.* While watching the rising and falling of the abdomen associated with the breathing, he labels the phenomena as "rising" or "falling" without interfering with it. He notices what is a body (form, a formation) and what is mind (that which labels).

2: *The knowledge by discerning conditionality.* Simply put; cause and effect. He sees the intention to label the action makes the labelling happen. He realises a single distracting thought precedes a whole spiral of thinking based on it.

Now he also sees how sometimes the rising or falling of the abdomen causes the labelling to happen. Other times, he sees how labelling precedes the rising or falling as the mind gets ahead of the action which then catches up with it. This is his first indication that he's not completely on top of the game. He knows he's supposed to just be watching in synchronisation with the action and not influencing it or getting distracted by other thoughts.

3: *The knowledge by comprehension.* He's been practising for a bit now. The body is getting a little sore as manifestations of the tension he carries around with him become apparent. They come and go, sometimes in an exaggerated, bizarre fashion. He sees that neither the body nor the mind is permanently one way or another, suffering is an inherent part of existence which shows up at times, and he has no authority over it to be otherwise.

The *ten defilements of insight* can arise at this point in either stages three or four. The Mahasi lists them as part of the fourth

---

[3] *The Progress of Insight: A Treatise on Buddhist Satipatthana Meditation*, p. 31. Buddhist Publication Society, Kandy, Sri Lanka, 1994

stage, calling them 'The Ten Corruptions of Insight'.[4] Phra Raj placed them in the third stage, as does the *Visuddhimagga*.[5]

Concentration develops ahead of mindfulness and the building of a finer frequency starts. Lights may be seen; mental powers can spontaneously begin to manifest, even euphoria or manic behaviour can result. This is the point in this sequence at which such phenomena can be the basis for wild assumptions about the nature of reality, i.e. taken as proof that the phenomenon is, say, a manifestation of a permanent god.

Such are the dangers of meditation experiences not examined according to the logical three characteristics of all phenomena, as explained in *Theory and Practice B*. For the sake of continuity, here's that passage again:

> '*Any experience, no matter how euphoric or otherwise, that happens in meditation needs to be examined according to the logical three characteristics of all phenomena. These are called the* tilakkhana *in Pali, sometimes translated as 'the three characteristics of existence.'*
>
> *1) The experience was impermanent* (anicca) *as it came about due to a specific network of states acting as specific conditions for it to happen. With the passing of those conditions it too passed. This fact is a self-evident truth.*
>
> *2) That it has the characteristic of being inseparable from suffering* (dukkha) *if there's any clinging to it or craving for it again as being preferably pleasurable because it's proven it was*

---

[4] *The Progress of Insight: A Treatise on Buddhist Satipatthana Meditation*, p. 13, Buddhist Publication Society, Kandy, Sri Lanka, 1994
[5] *Visuddhimagga* XX, 105*ff.*

*impermanent as it's no longer happening. This too
is self-evident.*

> *3) With or without your, or anyone's,
> permission* (anatta) *the changing show goes on.'*
> Again, self-evident.

Not examining the experience logically in this way can derail what should be knowledge by comprehension. If one wants to go down the fork in the road to have a concentrative absorption (Samadhi experience), then it's best to know that's where things are going. Then, in blissful, complete awareness, build it with applied and sustained thought.

Phra George told me about reaching this point in his first practice with Phra Tep (then called Phra Rajsiddhimuni) in London. He'd practised Samadhi and was familiar with the arising of spectacular phenomena but not with their relationship to the path of Vipassana. In his meditation report, he said to Phra Raj, "I saw a light like the most magnificent sunrise I could imagine. I was completely awestruck by it."

Phra Raj's response was short, "Did I tell you to watch a light or the movement of the abdomen?"

4: *The knowledge of arising and passing away.* While continuing to watch the movement of the abdomen associated with the breathing, our hypothetical meditator clearly notes the rising and falling. Distractions disappear quickly after a couple of acknowledgements. As he sees the distractions rise and fall as well, he understands this is the nature of both mental and bodily phenomena.

The *ten defilements of insight* can also happen during this stage. The risings and fallings of perceptions can link up into a continuum resulting in an increase in mentally generated phenomena. Knowing these increases as the signs of the fork in the road is crucial. All Samadhi experiences happen during these two phases of consciousness, stages three and four in the sequence.

5: *The knowledge of dissolution.* Our diligent meditator now sees more distinctly the ending of thoughts, and the ending of the rising or falling of the abdomen. He finds himself in the middle of many thoughts without seeing them start. He thinks he's lost focus. What's happening is that he's dropped through to a deeper level of noting. For the first time, he's seeing a subtler level of mental activity that's been running in the background the whole time.

6: *The knowledge of awareness of fearfulness.* Now he's become more aware that he's not in charge of these incessant thoughts. He sees that with or without his permission they continue, the slippery little devils. The reaction is fear. He knows it, but they just won't stop.

The gifted English translator of the *Visuddhimagga*, Bhikkhu Nanamoli, a contemporary of the Nyanaponika, labelled this one dramatically (hmmm, perhaps not) as *'knowledge of appearance as terror'*.[6]

7: *The knowledge of danger* or *the knowledge of misery.* It seems that now, "There is nothing but a bad situation…" (This phrase is in Phra Raj's booklet. Meditators laugh in recognition.) because of this incessant rising and falling of impermanent thoughts and formations. The novelty and the wonder of it all have worn off.

8: *The knowledge of disgust.* Now he's disgusted and weary with what he sees. With all of it for being so miserably uncontrollable but also, after a while, with himself for getting fearful and miserable because he realises it's always been like this anyway, so why the big deal about it now? He's bored with his reactions and everything he can think of. Again, Phra Raj's booklet makes one laugh, "Formerly only heard people said (sic) about being bored, but now one really knows what is boredom."

'Dispassion' or 'disenchantment' are alternate renderings for disgust but just don't express the emotional tone of it.

9: *The knowledge of desire for deliverance.* Now he just wants it all to stop. Ideally, he wants the experience of Nibbana as the

---

[6] *Visuddhimagga* XXI, 66

antidote for the ceaseless drama. All he can think about is escaping. In his more frustrated moments with the practice, he just wants to run away. "If I can just get outta here, everything will be fine..."

Or he might just give up, figuring that's he's not up to the task at this time, period; it being harder than he ever imagined. This is a tough point. Keeping him meditating puts the teacher's skill to the test.

The *Visuddhimagga* considers this insight knowledge and the next two to be one divided into three parts: onset, middle and culmination.[7] As such, the mind can reel between the symptoms of the three very quickly, ricocheting from one to the other.

10: *The knowledge of re-observation*. He didn't run away. Great! Now all that thinking and obsessing or dreaming as a means to escape the boring, painful reality of sitting there watching his abdomen move with the breathing has been seen as useless. He finally decides just to watch the movement as he was told to in the first place even though his body and mind are hurting badly. The instructions take on fresh clarity as he sees them as the path of deliverance. A tactile sense of undifferentiated solidity to the bodily sensations may arise because his concentration on the movement is good.

11: *The knowledge of equanimity about* (mental) *formations*. He's already been traumatised over and over by the incessant nature of his favourite dramas. He knows they all just lead back to the reality of him sitting there watching the abdomen move with the breathing. The only break he gets from these dramas is focussing and labelling the movement, so he sticks with it. The movement and the labelling of it are clear.

Other bodily sensations, which are usually painful, as well as other distracting thoughts, hold no attraction for his attention. When a thought arises, it doesn't turn into a deviating cycle of thinking. Instead, it's noted, and the rise or fall of the abdomen quickly returned to. The body buoys upright effortlessly.

---

[7] *Visuddhimagga* XXI, 79*ff.*

The Pali name for this knowledge, *'Sankharupekkha Nana'*, is usually translated as *'knowledge of equanimity about formations'*. *Sankhara* is usually translated as 'mental formations', and 'mental' is usually left out in this usage. Phra George concurred on my translation of *sankhara* as 'habitual tendencies' or just 'habits' for their part in what makes up a human being when he taught in my home back in the West. *See the start of Theory and Practice E, 'Inner Sanctum Secrets of Vipassana'.*

Burmese number 12: *Insight leading to emergence*. Here the Thais and the Burmese differ, affecting the rest of the sequence of stage divisions. The Thais consider the symptoms of the Burmese number twelve just to be part of the next insight knowledge. Nanamoli considered it a composite category, naming but not numbering it in the sequence of insight knowledges. That's because in the *Visuddhimagga insight leading to emergence* refers to three insight knowledges lumped together. Those are *equanimity about* (mental) *formations* with the next two, *conformity knowledge* and *change-of-lineage*.[8]

It's understandable that the Burmese consider this to deserve its own label as a knowledge because of some very distinctive symptoms. It's what the *Visuddhimagga* lists under *'equanimity about* (mental) *formations'* as 'the triple gateway to liberation'.[9] It's what I took to calling "the triple-sided doorway."

The three characteristics of all phenomena (*tilakkhana*) form the three sides of the doorway, so to speak, through which an experience of the supramundane – Nibbana – is accessed in Vipassana. This doorway leads to the outside of the looping cycles per second of the defining mind which perpetuates all continuums. Fully comprehending any one of these three characteristics will access Nibbana as they all frame one opening. Mundane awareness always bounces off of one of them as it discorporates across the threshold. It's a mental process that registers as a visceral experience.

---

[8] *Visuddhimagga* XXI, 83
[9] *Visuddhimagga* XXI, 66*ff*.

As for what's the feeling of bouncing off of the side of a doorway? That depends on what characteristic that final perception has. Often it bounces around all three repeatedly. It'd be nice if that just felt like relaxedly circling a drain, but because penetrative focus isn't sharp for starters, it's more like an imbalanced flailing against the current of one's own habitual propulsions.

The characteristic of *anicca* (impermanence) takes the form of the breath speeding up and then ceasing. The characteristic of *dukkha* (inseparability from suffering) takes the form of the breath feeling obstructed, then ceasing. The characteristic of *anatta* (not-self) takes the form of the breathing becoming steady: evenly spaced with wider gaps before ceasing. These are tactile sensations. I say 'visceral experience' as that's how it feels when one is paying attention and next, everything suddenly discorporates.

The sensation of any of these three starting or continuing is *insight leading to emergence*.

Thai 12 or Burmese 13: *Knowledge of adaption* or *conformity knowledge*. This is the perception of the ceasing of the sensation of any of those three characteristics. This is the last moment of mundane awareness. Phra Raj placed the symptoms of 'the triple gateway to liberation' in this stage.

13 or 14: *The knowledge of change-of-lineage* or *maturity knowledge*. This stage happens too quickly to be noticed separately from the next stage which is called *path knowledge* (14 or 15) and the one after that which is called *fruition knowledge* (15 or 16). It's discerned through logic and analogy as existing.

The *Visuddhimagga* has an excellent analogy that goes like this: a man needs to get to the other side of a river. There's a rope hanging from a tree branch that he can swing out over the river on to get to the other side. He takes a run, grabs the rope, swings out over the river, lets go of the rope and lands on the other side. After an initial wobble, the man steadies himself on his feet.[10]

---

[10] *Visuddhimagga* XXII, 6

In this analogy, this side of the river is mundane awareness. The contemplation of the rising and falling is the taking the run. *Conformity knowledge* is the grabbing of the rope, then swinging out on it over the river. The falling through the air after having let go of the rope is *change-of-lineage knowledge*. The other side of the river is Nibbana – the supramundane. Landing on it but not yet having a steady footing is *path knowledge*. Steadying himself is *fruition knowledge*.

The first moment of awareness of no phenomena is indeterminable from the next moment of it. These are divided into the two, *path knowledge* (14 or 15) and *fruition knowledge* (15 or 16), as the second moment of awareness is now considered to have Nibbana as an object of perception/recognition (*sannya*).[11] See the splitting of hairs? Welcome to the Buddhist world of analysis of consciousness which has been taken very seriously for the last 2500 years. As you'll read a bit into *Theory and Practice E*, this distinction is a very important point.

For our purposes, the first experience of this pair may subjectively just last as long as a finger snap. The pair might only be known in review. Thus, number 16 (or 17) is called *knowledge of review*. It can be as simple as the thought, "what happened?" One knows something just did which is unprecedented in all of the hours, days, weeks of watching the movement of the abdomen that have proceeded this moment. Or it can happen in the slow-motion walking where a person labels each step in as many as six parts and which forms the other part of this practice.

There are false Nibbanas. Momentary lapses of awareness, the flavours of which are well documented. The key is to be in *the knowledge of equanimity about* (mental) *formations* as the jumping-off point (ledge-of-knowing) and go through a visceral experience of one of the three characteristics immediately before the experience. All false Nibbanas fall into the category of the *ten defilements of insight*.

---

[11] 'Sannya' is one of the five components that make up a human being. I use a '/' to indicate that perception is inseparable from recognition. See T&P E.

Theory and Practice D

Grokking Nibbana

Referred to on pages 97, 130, 135

There's only one Nibbana but four levels of understanding the experience of it. Those who have attained these levels are called the 'community of noble ones' (*ariya-sangha*). Ideally, repeating the experience deepens the understanding.

These levels of understanding are permanently lessened levels of delusion about why clinging and craving, which are what perpetuate suffering, might seem like attractive ideas in the first place. Completely comprehending the ramifications of this perpetuation eradicates all tendencies to cling and crave, i.e. attach, which also generate a false sense of solid subjectivity.

This complete eradication of any tendency to attach comes with the fourth level of understanding Nibbana. It means then when the body dies there is no more becoming, the basis for continuation having been dissolved. Permanent Nibbana is the result, the final cessation of any suffering. It's considered to be the ultimate goal in orthodox Buddhism. Not everyone's wish, but hey, that's why there are menus in restaurants.

Buddhas and arahants share this fourth level of understanding Nibbana. Arahants are human beings who have completely comprehended the experience. The path to the experience was pointed out to them by a Buddha or through the teaching of one handed down.

Buddhas figure it out all by themselves without having anyone direct them to the three characteristics of life as being key to the endeavour. Nobody ever said anything to a Buddha like, "Pssst, look at it this way: it's all impermanent, no exceptions. Even that which experiences it all: no exceptions. Try to hang onto it, and it's going to hurt, no exceptions."

There are two types of Buddhas. *Pacceka-Buddhas* are 'silent Buddhas'. *Pacceka-Buddhas* arrive at the full conclusion which eradicates all tendencies to attach. But they didn't see the path through the insight knowledges by which they got there so they can't teach anybody else how to do the same.

Sammasam-Buddhas see how it happens for them which means they can teach. Also, as a result, they have supernormal powers beyond those developable by anyone else. Our historical Buddha, Siddhartha Gautama, was a *Sammasam-Buddha.* He said they only appear one at a time when there are no other *Sammasams* around.[1]

I'm well aware that acceptance of supernormal powers as a human possibility isn't in vogue these days. That doesn't mean they weren't once an actuality. Sid's teaching didn't spread so far or last this long based solely on his intellectual prowess impressing the masses and capturing their imaginations.

But I digress…

'All analogies eventually break down' is one of the laws of the universe but bear with me:

Imagine there's no music in the world made by humankind. Not even whistling. There's only an uttered cacophony of intentions and judgments based on wants and aversions passing for communication. Then a guy comes along who not only discovers how to whistle himself but teaches others how to whistle as well. Because he's the one that discovered it, he saw how to take it apart into notes and melodies, and can explain time signatures, etc., while the others only know how to follow his lead when he emerges with a tune.

His close buddies develop the understanding necessary to create songs as well. They learned their new whistling ability by example with explanations from the original guy himself, but it took

---

[1] Majjhima Nikaya 115.14

studying how he did it for them to figure it out. And some guys just 'get it' by themselves. They didn't see how they did so they can't explain it even though others can hear them whistling.

Those original tunes and the theory are recorded for future generations to study. It doesn't mean those songs are the only music or the theory can't be applied to other instruments as well as just whistling. The discoverer of whistling didn't imagine limiting its freedom of expression. It's just the way he and his friends joyfully found to bring music into existence in their particular situation.

So, an arahant has completely eradicated all lust to be reborn even in any of the finer frequencies of formations. She or he has no conceit about having accomplished this, nor any restlessness for the current experience to be anything other than whatever it is. There's not any confusion left either as to why this is the best way to be with all matters right from the start, the nature of all things already fully understood.

At the other end of the spectrum of having had the experience of Nibbana is the lowly *sotapanna*. *Sotapanna* means 'stream-enterer' as in, one who has entered the stream of becoming which leads to the final destination of fully understanding the nature of reality. One has stepped outside of the incessant defining at least once. As a result of this, one's mental flux will eventually completely discorporate. The current of this stream is supposedly irreversible.

This isn't provable to the stream-enterer. The Buddha said it will happen within seven lifetimes at the most in either the human realm or a finer frequency.[2] This is considered a major feat compared to the prospect of endless rounds of rebirth diving in and out of despair. Identification is possible with traits and events spread over many thousands of them before it seems like a story about someone else entirely.

Think about it: an experience that may subjectively last only as long as the blink of an eye can take up to five hundred years for the

---

[2] Samyutta Nikaya 13.1

effects to completely unfold. That is if one considers the possibility of, say, seven lifetimes of seventy odd years each. This makes the stream-enterer feel like not really that much has happened. 'Not provable' doesn't help either especially if she or he was banking on noticing a big difference.

'Not provable' means one requires confidence in the wisdom of the Buddha, who said so in these regards, if these matters are important to a person for him or her to start the mental training. That one's friends become nicer people for starters, like Phra George said, should be a good enough reason for some individuals.

The Buddha said not to have faith in something just because he said it to be so but to prove it to yourself.[3] '[W]ithin seven lifetimes' is one of those things that are simply beyond the range of vision of ordinary humans. The best definition of faith I've found in the Buddhist tradition comes from the *Visuddhimagga*. It likens faith to the confidence you have in your ability to swim when you set out in a flood.[4] This confidence comes naturally to the stream-enterer after the experience.

Rebirth in the lower realms of hells, animals or ghosts with unrelenting cravings has apparently been cut off at this point. The emotional matrix of attaching will never be so off-kilter as to lead to those extremes again. This also isn't provable to the stream-enterer but theoretically inferable.

Referring to this first level of understanding as lessened delusion about craving and clinging is generous. The only area this shows up in is a person believing that performing religious ceremonies or personal rituals will have a purifying effect on unprofitable actions or attitudes. Thinking such is possible is eradicated at this first level.

There is now no doubt about the method of practice that purifies one's view of the nature of reality as it's just happened.

---

[3] Anguttara Nikaya III.65
[4] *Visuddhimagga* XIV, 140

There is also no more belief in a transmigrating entity or permanent self as the experience itself has eliminated this mistake. Rebirth, through rebirth-linking factors, of this irregular flux we call consciousness, is entirely different than reincarnation. *The beginning of Theory and Practice E explains this.*

Even if the experience of Nibbana is not known for what it is at the time (this can happen, contrary to what many authorities may say), there is now an intuitive understanding, an understanding below conscious retrieval for the reason, of these truths.

The next level of understanding to that of the *sotapanna* is that of the *sakadagami*, the 'once-returner'. This second tier gets its title from the number of times one that has reached this level of understanding will be reborn in the human realm. The tendencies to feel lust and aversion have been weakened as a basis for rebirth, as well as in moment-to-moment reactions, by better comprehending their role in perpetuating misery.

After the *sakadagami*, the next level of understanding is that of the *anagami*, the 'non-returner', named so because of the lack of basis for rebirth in the human realm. This lack of basis comes about through eradicating all feelings of lust and aversion. One then instinctually understands how all lust and aversion are a basis for inseparability from suffering.

The non-returner will be reborn in what's called 'the fine-material realms', for completely understanding what happens as a result of craving and clinging. This means that even in the finer frequencies one experiences impermanence, suffering, and a sense of ultimately no control. If it weren't so, a non-returner wouldn't be able to unravel matters further while existing on one of these planes.

'Non-return' is still only a partial level of full enlightenment about the role of craving and clinging. One can still feel pride, agitation, even righteous indignation (anger), and desire rebirth in the finer frequencies of formations. The non-returner is still confused about the full consequences of craving and clinging. It means she or he can still react unprofitably from such a position of ignorance instead of always responding profitably in every circumstance. That is only the province of Buddhas and arahants.

These four levels are each divided into pairs. Each pair is composed of having an experience of Nibbana, an awareness outside of compounded phenomena, at a particular level of understanding, and the ability to repeat the experience at that level. This indicates that each level isn't just a more refined intellectual appreciation of logic, but that experiencing Nibbana at each level has a particular feel to it as well.

Warning: If you are seriously practicing Vipassana or intending to, skip the next paragraph. Heeding these warnings takes maturity but they're for your own sake.

The progress from one level to the next proceeds through the insight knowledges again, but at a deeper level of experience for each one. Now, though, they will start with (4) the knowledge of arising and passing away with its reflective symptoms instead of (1) the analytical knowledge of mind and body. It doesn't mean that (1) analysis of what constitutes the nature of body and mind, (2) their cause and effect, as well as (3) basic comprehension of the three characteristics of existence (*tilakkhana*) doesn't occur. Rather, it means they're intrinsically present as a baseline for response to any object of awareness as soon as registering it arises.

The difficulties of subjective awareness in each insight knowledge all feel fresh and more deeply so, but the practitioners have no doubt about the method of practice that sees them through.

Feel more enlightened now about enlightenment? Ideally, 'about': after all of this. There was a sign I liked very much in one Vipassana centre in Thailand that Phra George took me to where he respected the old Burmese teacher immensely:

'Talking about meditating and meditating are two different things.'

Theory and Practice E

Inner Sanctum Secrets of Vipassana

Referred to on pages 34, 97, 104, 135, 220, 222, 225, 258

First, a further clarifying word on what it is Vipassana practice works with. It was the essential realisation of the Buddha which, in its simplicity, eliminates all other speculations of what comprises a human being. It's within everyone's reach to grasp.

Many different times he taught that a human being is composed only of five bundles of various components.[1] The Pali word *khanda* translates as 'bundle', 'heap', 'pile', or 'mass' into English, to give you the drift although translators, ever the intellectuals, prefer 'aggregate'. The Buddha took this common term for material things and for the first time applied it as well to psychological processes to make his point.[2]

The point being that these five bundles are all impermanent. They cover everything that any person could consider themselves to be. Nowhere in them is found a permanent self, soul or transmigrating entity from one moment to the next. Chapter 2 stated,

> *'Even anything you might consider to be a permanent 'you' is just a tightly woven network of states that hasn't been unknotted. A sense of self is the result of these states rolling over and conditioning each other too quickly to be known*

---

[1] The Khandavagga, 'Book of Aggregates', of the Samyutta Nikaya contains over one hundred discourses dealing with the subject.
[2] *Five Piles of Bricks: The Khandas as Burden and Path*, Thanissaro Bhikkhu. Access to Insight, 2002

separately. As Bhikkhu Sumedha once said to me, "It's like the whirling brushes of a dynamo creating an electrical force."'

The first bundle, 1) formations (*rupa*) is the only physical component of what makes up a person.

The other four are mental components (*nama*). They are:

2) feelings (*vedana*). These are the basic ones: pleasant, unpleasant or neutral on the mental level, and pleasant or unpleasant on the physical level. Having a neutral physical feeling is impossible.

3) perceptions/recognitions (*sanna*). I use a '/' to indicate that in this mental faculty, perception is inseparable from recognition. As in, if you perceive a cowbell as a cowbell, you must recognise it as a cowbell from somewhere before, to use Phra George's usual example.

4) habitual tendencies, or just habits (*sankhara*).

5) mental objects (*vinnana*). What's on the mental screen.

None of these are permanent. Attaching to any of them is a sure recipe for disappointment when it changes, which is a guarantee, and since it changes, well, it just means that wasn't you in the first place.

Attaching to any of them is a rebirth-linking factor. The electrical force which was brushed up by it whirling around the other components maintains a quite specifically conditioned continuity to them all. This electrical force arcs the gap between lives, magnetised to a fresh physical existence according to habitual tendencies of perception. As well, the rebirth-linking factors perpetuate moment-to-moment continuity in this one. The mechanism is the same. And so, there is rebirth but no one that gets reincarnated. At death in Buddhas and arahants, this conglomerate of five components discorporates completely and finally.

The Mahasi method of Vipassana isolates the first bundle, formations (*rupa*), for observation although they can be considered to be like five fingers on a hand. By grabbing any one finger, the rest come along with it as they're all connected.

In this method, 'formations' primarily takes the form of the abdomen moving with the breathing in sitting or the feet in walking. Focussing completely on either as the object of attention allows the 'cycles per second' of awareness of it to be interrupted for a moment. Then there is a visceral experience of the space in between its own cyclic flux, and all of the other bundles. This is the cessation of all mundane awareness.

This now-experienced awareness of cessation can then be taken as an object of attention precisely because it has been experienced. That means awareness of it can be extended in length of time as the meditator ideally develops proficiency at maintaining full absorption into it. See the reason for splitting hairs as you read about in *Theory and Practice C*?

Before chronicling the mechanics of the practice, I'd like to make a point that is most significant about the Thai version of the Burmese method. The Thais added a building block to the Mahasi's technique that increases the effectiveness of it manyfold. This is the addition of *adhittana*, to use the Pali word.

Helen taught me that correctly it takes three words in English to cover the meaning of this all-important concept. Those three are 'intention-determination-resolution'. Phra George agreed that this translation is most appropriate. In English, this is left as 'intention' for practical purposes. Classically it's the first of the five masteries of Samadhi. Those are the masteries of intending, adverting (turning attention to), sustaining, emerging and review.[3] They form the basis of success with supernormal powers as well as *Nirodha Samapatti*, the 'attainment of cessation'.

In the Thai school of Vipassana, strengthening the ability to make an intention and see it through to completion was considered

---

[3] *Visuddhimagga* IV, 131

crucial for success. This starts innocuously enough with the slow-motion walking that forms half of the practice before extending to other parts of it.

For starters, a meditator stands erect, mentally labelling it, "standing, standing, standing," while feeling the whole body as an undifferentiated whole. She or he then states mentally and deliberately, "intending to move forward, intending to move forward, intending to move forward." While doing so, one feels the intention to move as an isolated urge. Then a slow step (half of a foot length) forward with the right foot.

Then, a step one and a half foot lengths with the left, before doing the same with the right, and on. This way, the distance between the toes and the heel is always around half of a foot length. These steps are labelled, "Right goes thus, left goes thus," as one lifts, moves, and places the respective foot focusing just on the sensation of it moving and the pressure of landing.

Phra George liked to say, "Become a foot."

A foreigner once asked Phra George, "Why do meditators always start with the right foot?"

"Simple," he replied. "Men of war always start on the left. Every army in the world marches 'left, right, left, right'."

After four metres (thirteen feet), one stops and again feels the body as an undifferentiated whole, labelling it, "standing, standing, standing." Then, while turning slowly around, labels that, "turning, turning, turning," feeling the body as a whole performing this change of axis. Then again, "standing, standing, standing," before stating, "intending to move forward, intending to move forward, intending to move forward," while freshly feeling that intention as an all-absorbing isolated urge to do so. Then one labels the movement, "right goes thus, left goes thus..." while becoming a foot.

Warning: The remainder of this chapter contains serious spoilers for the ultimate success of the Vipassana practitioner.

This is only the beginning of the graded entry in mindfulness and developing the power of intending something to happen into a force of its own. One makes the intention and sees it followed through on although the teacher doesn't explain this. It would be counterproductive to give the meditator something like this to think about. The details are kept simple for starters so that you don't just talk away to yourself while mouthing detailed labelling at a superficial level.

When the teacher thinks the student is ready, the labelling changes to, "lifting, moving, placing," in accordance with the movement of the feet. Eventually (perhaps a week later), between "standing, standing, standing," and "turning, turning, turning," "intending to turn, intending to turn, intending to turn," will be added. The "intending to turn," is also mentally recited with the intention of feeling the impetus to do so as an isolated distinct urge. Then once again, "standing, standing, standing," before, "intending to move forward…"

This way, another ability to make an intention, experience it followed through on, and then reinforced again, gets strengthened. Eventually (perhaps over three weeks), the slow-motion walking is broken down into a total of six parts for each step which are labelled as they occur. One new division is added at a time. The eventual six parts are: "lifting heel, lifting foot, moving foot, lowering foot, touching foot, pressing." One doesn't say, "pressing foot," so that a mesmerising rhythm isn't created. Instead, the abrupt halt helps keep the meditator present.

There needs to be a graded entry into this six-part division of mindful labelling, or it's meaningless. Too fast into this process and a meditator starts wandering off inattentively, a whole lot of mental chatter still going on below the level of conscious awareness. Everyone feels they're ready to progress to the next level of graded entry into mindfulness before they are. Phra George would invariably hold back on changing an experienced student's instructions to a more detailed labelling of walking meditation way past the eager student's taste. He was also invariably right in doing so.

The intentions to move forward and turn are always to be felt as fresh urges born of strong determination. It feels vacant of sensation at first, like a paralysed limb. We take intending in daily living for granted. We never feel the need to isolate the thought from the resultant action for any reason because of the repetitions we trained ourselves with as toddlers.

I remember once having a casual conversation with a dance teacher in which she tapped my next-to-last toe. She told me just to lift it while leaving the others down. I felt helpless; there was no connection established to do so, no matter how hard I focussed. She showed me that it was as easy for her as lifting just a ring finger was for me. It's all in the training.

The slow-motion walking is done for usually one hour as a 'gross object of awareness' before sitting to watch the abdomen move with the breathing solely as an autonomic function while labelling it. If, or rather when, the periods of walking and sitting would start feeling like a predictable rhythm, Phra George would mix them up. For instance: half an hour of walking and then two hours of sitting, or any other combination. He encouraged his students to get a cheap clock with several alarms which they could pre-set as well as to go off on the hour. These were readily available from the street vendors outside.

Get the intensity of the practice? There's no question about slowing right down into being wholly present in the process; there is no choice. As I wrote earlier, this isn't a challenge for everyone. Trauma *is* an inseparable part of the process.

This book isn't meant to teach Vipassana meditation or replace a competent Vipassana teacher. It's intended solely as contemporary commentary.

Everyone wishes to progress quickly and so they'd like to believe they're further through the insight knowledges than they usually are. As said in *Theory and Practice C*, this can lead to unconsciously inducing the symptoms of particular insight knowledges without actually being in them if one knows their signs.

Likewise, for the signs of *insight leading to emergence* that you may have read about in *Theory and Practice C*.

Too late for that now if you did and you're going to seriously practise Vipassana because now you know what signs to look for. You can still stop reading right here to not spoil your chances for ultimate success. Otherwise, the danger is in controlling the breathing into the pattern you're about to read as then you'll have read about it. In all fairness, once again, you've been warned.

The sitting part of the practice begins with the spine erect, back preferably unsupported in either half-lotus or easy posture (hero's), on a meditation bench, or a chair with the feet flat on the floor. Focussing on the rise and fall of the abdomen with the breathing, one mentally labels the movement accordingly: "rising, falling." If it takes its time rising, then the action is labelled, "rising, rising," as long as that's what it's doing. Likewise: "falling, falling," as long as it takes to complete that direction before reversing.

After some time (days or weeks), the rising and falling of the abdomen will smooth out into a natural rhythm. Then the teacher will change the student's labelling of the action to, "rising thus," and "falling thus."

The breathing then slows down. When this happens, then there's space between the end of the falling and the beginning of the rising, and vice versa. The student is instructed to fill in the gaps with directing the attention to the contact points of the bottom touching the cushion, floor, or chair. These are the 'sits bones' (ischial tuberosities), which are easy to remember as the two points that get sore on a new bicycle seat. If the student is sitting erect, they will be touching the horizontal surface.

First, the mind is to attend to one and then the other with the label, "sitting, sitting," if time allows. Sometimes the label is changed to, "touching, touching," instead. One only performs this noting if there is time before the abdomen starts to move again with the breathing. As soon as the abdomen starts to move, the student must label its action appropriately without interfering with its natural cycle, i.e., no inhibiting or inducing of it to move.

This secondary object of awareness, the awareness of touching the sitting surface, is critical for the student, so the mind doesn't wander. After a while, the breathing will slow even more as focus improves. Usually, the gap widens between the falling and the rising. When this happens, the student is instructed to direct the attention to the contact of the knees with the floor or the bottom of the feet with the floor as well as the sits bones. The labelling that accompanies these four points is, "touching, touching, touching, touching." Again, only if time allows before the movement of the abdomen, the primary object of awareness, begins.

It's possible that before the abdomen starts to rise or fall, the gap may allow for more time for noticing points of contact. If this happens, then the student is to again direct the attention to these four contact points in sequence, or, however many of them will fit into the gap between breaths.

The Burmese give a different sequence of contact points over the body to attend to, but Phra George didn't feel this was useful as it diverts the attention into a busy pattern of differentiation. Besides, such points as the elbows aren't contacting anything so it may become spatially confused mental imaging rather than a physically grounded sensation. Whether this was George's innovation or Phra Tep's, I'm not able to say although I expect it was Phra Tep's. Phra George and I were delighted by the appearance of bronze seated Buddha statues out of Burma with their pattern of touch points highlighted in little beads of brass.

Phra George would change the directions for walking and sitting once or sometimes twice per day. That depended on the meditation reports which were usually three times per day. These changes weren't always into more detailed labelling either. He'd also regress a student's labelling to help them through a difficult stage. Sometimes, this evoked stronger symptoms of an insight knowledge to arise. George wasn't interested in having the student hang out in them, but just in pushing her or him through them. Only for teaching a stream-enterer how to advance towards experiencing Nibbana at the next level or teaching one to teach did he drum in familiarity with them.

Eventually, due to repeating periods of walking and sitting meditation, the meditator reaches the final level of mundane awareness, *knowledge of equanimity about* (mental) *formations.* That could take weeks. It usually does. Once it's well established, the teacher gives a precise intention to be stated by the student at the beginning of the sitting period. This is the intention to have the experience of Nibbana.

It may even be augmented with instruction to label and feel all of the intentions to move, and their respective movements, between walking and sitting. Labels such as, "intending to lower the body...", "lowering, lowering...", "intending to sit...", "sitting, sitting...", "intending to fold the hands...", "folding, folding..." This way continuity isn't interrupted.

Phra George liked to give this new intention for the student to make as a euphuism. That way, the student didn't get excited or think too much. It would grow out of a conversation (meditation report) immediately preceding the next period of practice. George would be quite light but precise about it.

They were always seemingly tailor-made for the individual and usually were, although there were some I saw him give more than once. It could be as simple as, "intending to have a moment of truth," or "intending to know that which has not been known before." The purpose is to push the student past incessantly compounding mental phenomena and into a moment of cessation.

The ability to develop making *adhitthanas* into an effective force on their own was considered so important that, after a while, one was taught to be mindful with how one worded one's intentions going to the toilet. For instance, it was suggested a student state, "intending to go and see if the toilet is free," instead of just, "intending to go to the toilet," because if it wasn't free, then the student's intention was broken and the continuity interrupted. This is during sixteen hours or more per day of practice for weeks without speaking to anyone except the teacher, nor leaving the building.

One can then use this strengthened ability not only to attain Nibbana but also to extend the length of time of sitting in attainment. That can be from specified minutes up to hours. Eventually, even for twenty-four hours of *Nirodha Samapatti*, as mentioned in Chapter 9.

At Wat Mahadhatu, meditators who felt they had attained Nibbana were told to go and repeat the experience. This didn't always work for a variety of reasons. Either over-anticipation prevented it (trying too hard), the place was always distractingly noisy, or there was just too much excitement about the prospect. Always it boiled down to *equanimity about* (mental) *formations* needed to be better established as the prerequisite platform.

Often, landing in the knowledge of review is the first indicator that a moment of Nibbana has been experienced. The unprecedented "what happened?" and the resultant confusion can be the natural first reaction to what may just feel like a missing momentary frame to the movie. It may be just an absence of awareness of perceiving that which was being observed and then a continuation of it, except for the awareness that the absence of it had occurred. Happening repeatedly, it can feel like a strobe light of perception turning off and on. But the awareness of everything *is* the strobe light.

Phra George, by this point familiar with the student's progress through the insight knowledges, didn't let on that the sought-after experience may have happened. He would listen for the physical symptoms that marked the appearance of *insight leading to emergence* (the triple-sided doorway) at the end of mundane awareness.

He would also inquire thoroughly about how the next period of practice started. If the meditator started by exhibiting the physical and mental symptoms of the *knowledge of arising and passing away*, this was considered a big sign. After the experience, the process begins at this point, and the symptoms of the first three knowledges won't appear. This marks a permanent change in the mental life continuum.

If Phra George thought the meditator had been successful, the meditator would be asked to intend to have only one insight knowledge for a specific length of time. For instance, one might be told to, "Only have number six for one hour."

Even if one didn't know what was meant by this, the mind would have separated the stages accordingly, and amazingly enough, only the symptoms of the intended knowledge by number alone would appear for the set period. I don't know how many times I experienced this myself as it naturally became standard operating procedure in retreat. Phra George thought it to be equally amazing as well. That it was an actuality is irrefutable.

If the meditator hadn't been successful, then the intention (*adhitthana*) to experience just one stage wouldn't be successful either. Instead, the usual progress through the different knowledges would ensue as they usually did by then for the individual.

Monks with no credibility in a temple in another city twisted this phenomenon of stage separation into an imaginative fantasy of a technique. For twelve days, they'd instruct a meditator to intend to have one number in sequence each day and say the untranslated Pali name for that particular insight knowledge. Then, the person was told to stay awake for twenty-four hours of practice. If she or he nodded off, the monks then informed the person they'd "done it."

Sometimes the position of the hands while sitting in meditation would bring about a particular phenomenon that would be a sign. The preferred position in classical Vipassana circles is placing the right hand over the left, palms up, thumbs forty-five degrees to the palms with their ends touching in an upside down 'V'. Most teachers and practitioners never know why but just assume this form as it's traditional.

Sometimes, not always, immediately following a moment of cessation (Nibbana) while watching the abdomen move with the breathing, there will be an expansion of spatial sensation centred from the abdomen towards the hands. The erect position of the thumbs acts as a reference for this phenomenon. It's as if one's total awareness drops down to the abdomen, then after a quick wink, leaps forward with the sense of growing or flying towards the thumbs. At the same time, *knowledge of review* kicks in with "what the...?"

Phra George changed a component of the original technique in dealing with distractions which is of great advantage to the meditator. If remembering something, or imagining something else, the meditator doesn't need to label the distracting thought anything like "remembering" or "imagining", etc. Simply labelling any thought that arises as "thinking, thinking" cuts that thought whatever it is. Cutting through it by getting out no more than "thi..." or even adverting sooner is the game. By the time a meditator is labelling it by a characteristic, a deviated cycle of thinking has already started.

Labelling all of the distractions "thinking" works to interrupt any stimulus at any sense door. For example, a sensation of pain. Labelling it "feeling, feeling" in actuality minimally compounds the distraction as the evaluation of the interruption is already a thought. "Thi..." immediately allows the attention to return to the primary object of awareness a crucial moment sooner once the habit has been developed. Likewise, if something is heard, smelt, etc.

Phra George was surprised one day when I said the mundane insight knowledges were simply the weave of mundane awareness isolated into stages. He immediately agreed. "Usually, though," he said, "a person arrives at number nine [*desire for deliverance*] and changes the object of awareness for another one that holds their interest. There's no moving through it towards equanimity."

This sequence is the mechanics of subjective reaction: Something attracts one's attention and then when its fascination finishes the mind begins to drop it. A stage might only last a moment. As the looping, former thread of thought falls in the face of a new, attractive thought; a person has a twinge of not wanting to be stuck on the old one. One senses danger in missing out on the pleasure of variety, and disgust, or simply dispassion, with the last train of thought, follows. Desiring deliverance from the now-boring topic, the mind latches onto the new one. Then analysis of the new mental object starts a fresh cycle.

A stream-enterer naturally feels this fresh rise of attention as distinctly separate from that which went before. This distinction makes the weave of mundane awareness that much more intense a moment-to-moment experience. You could say presence naturally increases regarding the contents of the stream of consciousness. This develops the moments in between the moments into becoming fulcrum points of power.

It's always a person's 'body of habits' that carries their intentions through. Remember, habits are the fourth bundle (*sankharas*) of the five aggregates that make up a person. They condition everything we think of. To access Nibbana, a person needs to develop the habit of totally present mindfulness.

Vipassana practice, as I was taught it, is the mental training specifically for this.

Theory and Practice F

Formal Samadhi Practice

Referred to on pages 139, 141

This section details the mechanics of concentration practice with a little practical theory. You started learning basic theory in Chapter 1. It's both beyond the scope of this book and not its purpose to teach Samadhi past foot-in-the-door access to full absorption. For detailed analysis and further personal development, I recommend studying the *Visuddhimagga*.

The technique you're about to read has been distilled from many sources. From the *Anapanasati Sutta* (Mindfulness of Breathing discourse)[1] to my work with Helen and integrated with fundamentals of Thai forest practice. Belying my Vipassana roots, it's heavy on the mindfulness, but the emphasis is on concentration and building a finer mental frequency. The pleasurable 'sign born of perception' of such starting keeps the practitioner in either number three or four of the insight knowledges.

Chapter 1 stated,

> *'A person can teach themselves Samadhi to the first level of absorption if they have to as it's working with an increase in generated phenomena as the sign of progress. The 'sign born of perception' arises in many ways. For some, it may be light, for others sound, a tactile sensation or all three, plus taste or smell combined.'*

A Canadian member of a Hindu cult once told me that their particular technique gave a taste in the back of the throat they called, "the nectar of bliss." He started into access to absorption

---

[1] Majjhima Nikaya 118

while just describing it for me. An American woman I knew was told in Kashmir to listen for bells. That didn't work for her and wasn't about to. Don't limit yourself with expectations.

As Helen emphasised many times; it's all about creating energy, storing it and directing it. While with her, I regularly said that the experiences I was having were like being taken to the top of the mountain in a helicopter only to be dropped back down at the bottom and told to now walk the path she'd just shown me. This technique is the practice I developed to do so.

The beginner can compare this practice to just playing scales on an instrument without breaking into a tune. As such, it's preparation for walking through your day energised, alert, and in a better mood. Like developing strength and dexterity with any other skill, it depends on how much attention you put into it as to what you'll take from it. When you practice anything day after day, be it painting, singing or playing the violin, eventually, it'll come together for you.

In our age, people tend to focus quickly onto an object of awareness due to having agile minds from habitually processing information from many sources. They can rapidly apply thinking but tend to lose focus just as quickly due to an inability to sustain thought on the chosen object. We don't have years of mental discipline in a monastery developing such.

Although this technique may seem complex on an initial reading, it is, in fact, a very basic stitching together of physical awareness. Dynamic enough for short attention spans to quickly see results, it teases them into lengthening. *This is most important.*

Noise, the wind, an uncomfortable body; all distractions are thorns to developing a serene absorption. Eliminate them before starting. The best way to do that is to stop worrying about being distracted.

Remove any jewellery before starting so there's no sense of anchored containment. Loosen anything restricting your breathing. Pick a comfortable upright position, preferably with your spine unsupported, so there's less chance to drift. Rest one hand on top of the other. Be grateful for the opportunity to do this practice.

I suggest you read the following instructions out of this book or copy them so that you can have them with you until you memorise them or create something similar. Highlighting the mental labels in yellow or another colour for ease of reference works well. These instructions are for generating and working with the 'sign born of perception'. *Close your eyes when you're not reading.*

If you're male, as you breathe in, imagine you're breathing in, and down, and out your right-hand side. If you're female, as you breathe in, imagine you're breathing in, and down, and out your left-hand side. As you direct the breath in this fashion, mentally label it, "Breathing in, and down, and out the right- (left-) hand side."

Make at least three sweeps of attention in the above manner before switching over to breathing in, and down, and out the other side. Take your time with more repetitions if you'd like to fully establish the sensation. *Don't forget the labelling.*

Mentally label sweeping this other side, "Breathing in, and down, and out the left- (right-) hand side." *Energy flows where attention goes.* Memorise that last sentence.

Again, you can take your time with more repetitions to solidly establish a sense of moving the energy. You're using the breath as a vehicle for the attention. Forest monks call this practice, "Connecting up the winds in the body."

When you're ready, move your attention to the tip of the nose. Breathe in and out through the nose, labelling this, "Breathing in through the tip of the nose. Breathing out through the tip of the nose." Influencing the pattern of the breathing is part of Samadhi. Just be aware that you are when you are.

After at least three of these respirations, with labelling, move the attention with the breath from the tip of the nose up to the point between the eyebrows and back down to the tip of the nose.

Label this, "Breathing in through the tip of the nose up to the point between the eyebrows. Breathing out through the point between the eyebrows back down to the tip of the nose."

Also do that three times, at least. As well as all of the following directions except where indicated otherwise or if entering access to absorption. All mental labelling is to be done smoothly throughout the beginning, the middle, and the ending of each breath. This way, you can't talk to yourself about other things, including commentary on what you're doing. Changing locations of focus is best done crisply and with full attention.

Follow these labels: "Breathing in through the tip of the nose up to the point between the eyebrows. Breathing out through the point between the eyebrows."

See how that was a change of location?

"Breathing in through the point between the eyebrows. Breathing out through the point between the eyebrows."

"Breathing in through the point between the eyebrows up to the top of the head. Breathing out through the top of the head back down to the point between the eyebrows."

"Breathing in through the point between the eyebrows up to the top of the head. Breathing out through the top of the head."

Crisp changes of location with full attention make all the difference between success and failure in entering the major vortex centres. Labelling during the beginning, middle, and end of each breath is crucial for undistracted penetration.

"Breathing in through the top of the head. Breathing out through the top of the head."

Feel this imagined breathing coming straight in and down through the top of the head, and going straight up and out through the top of the head.

One starts with the side sweeps, then the tip of the nose, and up to accurately map the spatial awareness before starting with major energy vortex centres. This is all about coming into the body with focus. It has nothing to do with disassociating from it. To that

246

end, it's counterproductive to label the points of focus 'chakras' or other woolly ambiguities that pull in vain imaginings. It's best just to label it with a specific physical location in English that your mind can readily relate to. This assures that the energy vortex will eventually energise when your attention fully settles into it.

If any tension develops in the body while directing the attention, note it and release it. Then return to any centre where you strongly felt the attention penetrating it. Re-establish the connection with the labelled breathing before again extending the attention through the body. If a pleasurable phenomenon generates while breathing through an area, stay there longer. This return helps create and store energy represented by the strengthening of the sign.

Extend this 'sign born of perception' using the breath to carry it into the other areas in the following prescribed pattern. If possible, just absorb fully into it wherever it arises, and forget everything else I'm suggesting, except for analysing your experience afterwards in light of the three characteristics of all phenomena (*tilakkhana*). *You can find those in Theory and Practice B.*

Continue with these labels: "Breathing in and down to the centre of the head. Breathing up and out to the top of the head."

"Breathing in and down to the centre of the head. Breathing out through the centre of the head. Breathing in through the centre of the head."

Widen your mental peripheral vision. Feel the breathing coming in from every direction into the centre of the head and going out from the centre of the head into every direction.

"Breathing in through the centre of the head down to the centre of the throat. Breathing out through the centre of the throat up to the centre of the head."

"Breathing in and down to the centre of the throat. Breathing out through the centre of the throat."

Now, expand your range of focus to cover these three areas: the centre of the throat, the centre of the head, and the top of the head. Label this, "Breathing in through the unified three. Breathing out through the unified three."

Then: "Breathing in and down to the centre of the heart. Breathing out and up to the centre of the throat."

"Breathing in through the centre of the throat down to the centre of the heart. Breathing out through the centre of the heart."

"Breathing in through the centre of the heart. Breathing out through the centre of the heart."

Widen your mental peripheral vision. Feel the breathing coming from every direction into the centre of the heart and out from the centre of the heart into every direction.

"Breathing in through the centre of the heart down to the centre of the bottom of the solar plexus. Breathing out through the centre of the bottom of the solar plexus up to the heart."

"Breathing in through the centre of the heart down to the centre of the bottom of the solar plexus. Breathing out through the centre of the bottom of the solar plexus."

"Breathing in through the centre of the bottom of the solar plexus. Breathing out through the centre of the bottom of the solar plexus."

"Breathing in through the centre of the bottom of the solar plexus down to the centre of the pelvis. Breathing out through the centre of the pelvis up to the centre of the bottom of the solar plexus."

"Breathing in through the centre of the bottom of the solar plexus down to the centre of the pelvis. Breathing out through the centre of the pelvis."

"Breathing in through the centre of the pelvis. Breathing out through the centre of the pelvis."

"Breathing in through the centre of the pelvis down to the bottom of the pelvis. Breathing out through the bottom of the pelvis up to the centre of the pelvis."

"Breathing in through the centre of the pelvis down to the bottom of the pelvis. Breathing out through the bottom of the pelvis."

"Breathing in through the bottom of the pelvis. Breathing out through the bottom of the pelvis."

Feel this imagined breathing coming straight up and into the bottom of the pelvis, and going straight down and out from the bottom of the pelvis.

Now, squeeze your perineum tight. Contract the entire pelvic floor. This is called a *mula bhanda* (Sanskrit for 'root lock') in hatha yoga. Breathe in and out once or twice through the bottom of the pelvis, with labelling, while maintaining this contraction. Loosen the squeeze until it's only about two percent of the full contraction and maintain it at this level. When any tension arises anywhere else in the body, note it, and then release it, while maintaining this two percent hold. Continue breathing through the bottom of the pelvis with labelling.

Eventually, but don't be in any hurry to get there, loosen this 2% hold to a .2% hold and then a .02% hold. After applying some of the following directions, loosen the hold to .002% Maintain this .002% lock for the rest of the practice. *Don't forget it as this grounds the energy so it can build.*

Holding the lock to any degree, by .002% which is just the stored impetus to do so, activates the connection between mind and body. It becomes a natural response. It's the 'base' of balance. As such, it gets absorbed into the much stronger 'sign born of perception'. The strengthening of the sign occurs from successfully creating and storing the energy due to this activation. If or when the sign emerges, holding the lock is no longer consciously necessary as one then works with the sign.

Continue with: "Breathing in through the bottom of the pelvis up to the centre of the pelvis. Breathing out through the centre of the pelvis down to the bottom of the pelvis."

Use this label once only: "Breathing in through the bottom of the pelvis up to the centre of the pelvis and out through the centre of the pelvis."

Expand your range of focus to include both the centre of the pelvis and the bottom of the pelvis. Label this "Breathing in through the unified bottom two. Breathing out through the unified bottom two."

Use this label once only: "Breathing in through the unified bottom two up to the centre of the bottom of the solar plexus. Breathing out through the unified bottom three."

"Breathing in through the unified bottom three. Breathing out through the unified bottom three."

Use this label once only: "Breathing in through the unified bottom three up through the centre of the heart, the centre of the throat, the centre of the head and out through the top of the head."

"Breathing in through the top of the head down through all of the centres and out through the bottom of the pelvis."

Remember: if at any point in this any tension arises anywhere other than the .002% activated hold at the bottom of the pelvis, it's to be noted and released.

"Breathing in through the bottom of the pelvis up through all of the centres and out through the top of the head." Sweep the entire body up and down in this fashion repeatedly. Take your time to fully establish the sensation.

Return the attention to the bottom of the pelvis. Breathe in and up to the centre of the heart once, labelling this, "Breathing in through the bottom of the pelvis up to the centre of the heart."

"Breathing out through the centre of the heart. Breathing in through the centre of the heart."

Again, widen your mental peripheral vision. Feel the breathing coming from every direction into the centre of the heart and out from the centre of the heart into every direction.

Expand your range of focus to include the whole body while maintaining the centre of awareness at the heart. Label this, "Breathing in through the whole body. Breathing out through the whole body." Practice this repeatedly.

At this point, you'll have been sitting for at least a half an hour or probably more if you've been taking your time not to rush while attending to the different centres of focus. This *is* a practice. There isn't a destination other than a phenomenon, 'the sign born of perception', will arise in one of the areas you've been breathing through when you do it carefully. Take this phenomenon as the centre of awareness and extend it into the other areas using the breath as the vehicle.

When the mind wanders note it with a simple label like "thinking." Deal with these distractions the same as when you note any tension arising. Return to any centre where you strongly felt the attention penetrating it. Re-establish the connection with the labelled breathing before again extending the attention through the body. Eventually, at some point, as stated before, you'll be able to take this sign as the object of awareness itself and absorb fully into it via the breathing.

You may now give the breath a quality if you so wish. This quality can also become a spreadable sign. Whatever label has the most meaning to you will keep the quality increasing. "Calming the whole body breathing in. Calming the whole body breathing out." is simple.

"Feeling peace in the whole body breathing in. Feeling peace in the whole body breathing out." is another way of working with it. Experiment with what is most pertinent to you without distracting yourself with creative labelling just for the sake of it.

"Feeling energising bliss through the whole body breathing in, feeling energising bliss… breathing out." can work too. It just needs to be a desirable quality with labelling you can relate to.

"Healing the body breathing in. Healing the body breathing out." is a useful, practical application of a generated quality.

Focussing on any of the locations or a generated quality using the breath as a vehicle for the attention can lead to a full absorption of awareness to the first degree, called first *jhana* in Pali. It's accompanied by and due to five factors: applied thought, sustained thought, happiness, bliss, and one-pointedness.

To finish, it's beneficial to contain the awareness back into a central space for ease in post-sitting functioning. This helps eliminate any 'spaciness' in thinking or moving. Bring the attention into the centre of the heart. Label this, "Breathing in through the centre of the heart. Breathing out through the centre of the heart."

After an appropriate feeling amount of repetitions, express appreciation for having had this opportunity to practice. Slowly move out of position. Review what happened. Remember to breathe consciously. That will help integrate the entire experience.

A couple may find it enjoyable and useful to sit facing each other for the period of practice. Sometimes, it helps for one of them to narrate where and when to direct the attention, so both are in the same centre at the same time.

A couple can also create spreadable energy in their pelvises after loosening a root lock to .02% with a little sexually playful talk.

Sometimes great benefit can be had for a woman to hear from her lover something like, "Now imagine my *lingam* (Sanskrit for penis. Refer to Chapter 15) perfectly hard, hot, and electric pressed up against the bottom of your pelvis. Feel it penetrate as you breathe it in and up through the bottom of your pelvis. Squeeze it gently as it enters…"

Remember: profitable, playful fun takes many forms. This is about generating pleasurable phenomena; it helps to keep the 'light' in enlightenment.

A little advice: don't get frustrated. At first, a good level of focus can be maintained for a few seconds here, a few more there. All in all, in a half an hour or more of Samadhi practice you may achieve perhaps a grand total of three minutes of good concentration – if you're really on your game. No acrobat jumped up and danced the fandango on the tightrope for starters. That goes for Vipassana practice as well.

****

Developing the emotional frequencies of the gods (*Brahmavihara*) can be both a formal Samadhi practice and an informal generator or maintainer of energy at any time moving around the world. It's best to initiate it as 'loving-kindness' (*metta*). This quality is easy to relate to as the start of all-encompassing 'having consideration for others'. Some find it useful to end the above described sitting practice with it when bringing the attention back to the centre of the heart. The centre of the heart is where consideration begins.

Breathing in and out through the centre of the heart, and labelling it so, anchors the attention into a central vortex. It's easiest to approach access to absorption when the object of your consideration is someone you deeply respect or a friend you love, even a pet. If you're in a healthy, working relationship, it's wonderful to direct your attention towards your significant other. Realistically, though, sometimes you may be too annoyed with him or her for this to work.

Feeling this inspiring being while centred in your heart, you say to yourself something like, "Just as I want to be happy, may _____ be happy," or "Just as I want to be free from suffering, may _____ be free from suffering." See the two directions of intention? Experiment and go with whatever wording makes whichever direction come clearest as a concept for you for that being. The accompanying increase in energy is easy to gauge and is your indicator of success. Continuing to apply and sustain thinking along this line leads to the arising of the 'sign born of perception'.

It doesn't work just to repeat, "May I be happy." That leads to self-absorption, not blissful absorption. The old saying, "If you want to feel better, do something for somebody else," is entirely true, even if it's just wishing them happiness.

When the mind wanders, return to, "Breathing in through the centre of the heart. Breathing out through the centre of the heart."

and then again direct the attention to the person you've chosen to be the primary object of awareness. At this point, the breathing through a physical area of focus becomes the secondary object of awareness as a support.

The ancients said don't pick a person of the opposite sex as lust can result.[2] In our diverse world today, the broad range of personal proclivities renders that generalisation quaint. I say a contemporary-cultured adult can develop the maturity to differentiate between love and lust, no matter who is the object. After all, many of us have a lot more experience exercising the latter than the average ancient Asian did. Understanding the difference between love and lust, a person can use them both better as energy generators for having the extra clarity about their natures.

They also say the being whom you choose for inspiration has to be alive for the focus to reach access to absorption level.[3] I've always followed this suggestion as it certainly doesn't hurt to be prudent... sometimes.

As an exercise in emotional balance, a person starts with a much loved being, then transfers the generated feeling towards a neutral party. Eventually, this feeling of loving-kindness, or just plain friendliness, can be extended towards someone you're feeling hostile towards for any reason.

Compassion comes from seeing failure. The danger in this is it sliding into sadness. Sympathetic joy comes from seeing success. It's the "good on ya, mate!" of the Aussies. The danger in it is slipping into jealousy or envy.

Other beings are necessary as the objects of awareness for both compassion and sympathetic joy, just as they are for loving-kindness, for these emotions to be successful energy generators. These emotions are each a more refined frequency than loving-kindness, and a person can also use them as exercises in emotional

---

[2] *Visuddhimagga* IX, 6
[3] *Ibid.*, 7

balance. Sometimes more readily so than loving-kindness, depending on the circumstances.

Equanimity comes from seeing there's nothing personal in any of it, coming or going. Again, as discussed in Chapter 12, equanimity is the 'last resort option' for it to beneficially be a boundless source of energy. It neutralises resentment.

If your significant other is irritating you and loving-kindness is proving to be momentarily elusive, then he or she can still be useful as an object of any of these other three emotional responses. You may be feeling strongly about him or her anyway so it's best to direct the energy profitably if need be.

Although it isn't absolutely necessary, not leaning against something while meditating helps keep the attention from drifting. For this reason, sitting is also better than lying down. Sitting upright, unsupported comfortably for a short period may require a little stretching to condition the body for the task. A relaxing practice of restorative hatha yoga helps with this. Remember that word 'restorative' if you go looking for instruction and tell the teacher your intention.

As with meditation, how much regular time you put into yoga determines how much you'll get out of it. Never stretch to the point of pain. If you reach that point, back it off a bit or unwind a few degrees. Breathe through the stretch at the level it's comfortable. The next time, you may go a little further as your body will have registered it as favourable. Everyone is more flexible in the late afternoon than they are in the morning, so don't beat yourself up over the difference. Be kind to yourself and thank yourself for undertaking this physical support if you need it.

Helen mentioned more than once that Hindus open their energy vortexes from the bottom up; hence the idea of 'kundalini rising'. As she pointed out in those conversations, they can open in any order; there's no rule for such. That is my experience as well as that of many others.

She said, "Traditionally, Buddhists aim to open them from the top down as it keeps conduct in line."

I don't know where she got that, but it makes sense. That night in Wat Mahadhatu when my vasectomy tried to reverse itself because of the sexual energy exploding like never before, strange, all-consuming thoughts flipped through my head. Bizarre in retrospect, they all seemed like perfectly good ideas at the time. Good thing I knew better than to identify with every thought that popped up. I still do.

Years before that, always laughing when she did so, Helen also warned me repeatedly about a byproduct of practising Samadhi, "Be careful what you wish for. You might just get it!"

* * * * * * * *

However you may have arrived at this point in my exposition, there's a noble intention from sixteen centuries ago closing every chapter in the *Visuddhimagga* (The Path of Purification) that I amiably echo here for you:

[This was] '...composed for the purpose of gladdening good people'.

Woven together, this tapestry of stories, esoterica, and impressions, along with the Theory and Practice section, is a manual with cultural context. What *you* do with it will determine a conclusion. The Buddha would sometimes finish a lesson with "Now it is time for you to do as you see fit."[4]

Sometimes, Phra George would end a discourse with "I can't give you my knowledge, I can only give you information. It's up to you to take that and turn it into knowledge."

May this book help you to become fulfilled.

---

[4] Samyutta Nikaya 35.88, 35.243, 44.1, 54.9, 55.6

Glossary

This glossary is only of words that are used more than a few paragraphs after they're defined.

Adhittana (Pali) - 'Intention-determination-resolution'. A formula composed of these three parts but usually translated only as 'intention' for convenience.

Amrita (Sanskrit) - Nectar. In red Tantra, it refers to a woman's ejaculatory fluid.

Anagarika (Pali) - 'Homeless one'. An ancient title; most commonly used in Sri Lanka, for a Buddhist yogi with certain vows.

Bhikkhu (Pali) - 'Monk'.

Dakinis (Sanskrit) - 'Sky Dancers'. A sexually superior class of finer frequency beings. 'Uber-sexy Angels' doesn't quite cut it as a translation. They can also be Hellions in a snit. They're a category of Devas.

Devas (Sanskrit) - 'The shining ones'.

Entheogen - A 'substance that generates the divine within'.

Karma (Sanskrit) - Action and the consequences of action. It's the spiritual principle of cause and effect.

Koan (Japanese) - A nonsensical question which the logical mind can't answer. This pushes a person into an experience unreachable by reasoning. Helen Wilder's definition: "Ratiocination around a single point until the logical mind breaks down, not finding a resting place inside its parameters."

Lingam (Sanskrit) - 'Wand of light': a dignified term for a penis.

Merit - Profitable karma, cosmically bankable

Nibbana (Pali; Sanskrit: Nirvana) - The 'here and now free of definition'. Alternatively, the 'unformed'.[1] Literally: 'blown out' as in, the extinguishment of a flame. Note: No flame is a permanent thing, but rather, all flames are interdependently arisen phenomena, as is consciousness.

Pali - A Middle Indo-Aryan language. The word 'Pali' means 'text' in that language. One dialect was the everyday language of the ancient kingdom of Magadha where the Buddha lived, now the borderland between India and Nepal. Pali and Sanskrit were sister languages, having the same Aryan roots.

Phra (Thai. Pronounced with a hard 'P', breathy 'h') - 'Monk'.

Red Tantra - Active sexuality in a spiritual practice.

Samadhi (Pali and Sanskrit) - A type of meditation usually translated as 'serenity', 'tranquillity' or 'concentration' into English, also definable as 'accessing the matrix of existence'. Full absorptions in Samadhi are like changing the station on the radio to another frequency.

Sarong (Malay) - A rectangular cloth for wrapping the lower body.

Shakti (Sanskrit) - Primordial cosmic energy; the divine female principle personified as Shiva's consort.

Spiritual - 'Refining thoughts and feelings'. If that seems 'soulless', you're right! Please read the first two pages of *Theory and Practice E, 'Inner Sanctum Secrets of Vipassana'*.

Stream-enterer (*Sotapanna* in Pali) - One who has entered the stream of becoming which leads to the final destination of fully understanding the nature of reality. One enters this 'stream' by

---

[1] As found in *The Life of the Buddha* by Bhikkhu Nanamoli; *asankhata* as synonym for Nibbana, p. 223 (cited under Sources, p. 367, for Udana 8:1-3, 'utterances on Nibbana'), p. 256 (cited under Sources, p. 365, for Samyutta Nikaya 43:1-44, 'epithets of Nibbana'). Buddhist Publication Society, Kandy, Sri Lanka, 2015.

experiencing Nibbana at least once. As a result of this, one's mental flux will completely discorporate within seven lifetimes at the most. The current of this stream is supposedly irreversible.

Tantra (Sanskrit) - *Read Chapter 2.* (In 21 words) - Mundanely, it is mastering the comings and goings between interactive frequencies. Supramundanely, it is preparatory purification according to the human blueprint.

As such, Tantra is the art of living itself. It's the management of all we say and do to coordinate our passions with our intentions so that they correspond with the desired forces of the universe. It's recognising within ourselves those resonant qualities that are important. Then, it's striking a focussed chord of mindfulness with those desired forces to sort our identifications into alignment so that every part of daily living supports our becoming.

Tantrika (Sanskrit) - Practitioner of Tantra

Theravada (Pali) - 'Doctrine of the Elders'. Five hundred men, some of whom had been with the Buddha for forty-five years, held a council three months after his death. In this council, they committed to memory in verse form part of his teaching with the stories of how it came to be. 'Theravada' is what nineteenth century CE scholars termed the lineage from those monks at that First Council. Although a Pali word, its first known use was in 1882 according to the Merriam-Webster dictionary.

Tsok (Tibetan) - 'Feast offering': a type of ceremony that includes invocation.

Vipassana (Pali) - 'Inward vision': usually translated as 'insight meditation'. It's 'discorporating the matrix of existence', as in, the opposite of incorporating. It uses a different set of objects of awareness than Samadhi as the purpose of the practice is different. Instead of developing concentration for absorbing into one finer frequency, to the exclusion of coarser frequencies, a person develops mindfulness which is an inclusive form of focus.

Mindfulness sorts through the current impressions that flow through the sense doors moment to moment which create our everyday mundane coarse frequency of many working parts. As the mind naturally sifts through the mental and physical impressions that pop up, a person sees their reference points for self-identity. The opportunity arises to lose the ones that aren't profitable.

Completely developed, fully concentrated absorption into a Vipassana object of awareness drops a person's awareness in between the cycles per second, so to speak, of the coarse frequency they're already in. This is like finding the on/off switch on the radio instead of tuning into a different station. Then a person has an experience of no frequencies at all, i.e., Nibbana.

White Tantra - a non-sexual spiritual practice involving archetypes.

Yoni (Sanskrit) - 'Sacred space': a dignified term for a vagina.

Bibliography

A New Science of Life / by Rupert Sheldrake. Stone Hill Foundation Publishing Pvt. Limited (1981)

An Introduction to Buddhism: Teachings, History and Practices (2nd ed.) / by Peter Harvey. Cambridge University Press, UK (2013)

An Introduction to the Collected Works of C. G. Jung: Psyche as Spirit / by Clifford Mayes. Rowman and Littlefield, London (2016)

At the Eleventh Hour: The Biography of Swami Rama / by Pandit Rajmani Tigunait, PhD. Himalayan Institute Press (2004)

Coco Chanel / by Isabella Alston. TAJ Books International (2014)

Critical Terms for the Study of Buddhism / edited by Donald S. Lopez Jr. University of Chicago Press, Chicago (2005)

Critique of Pure Reason / by Immanuel Kant. Cambridge University Press (1998)

Five Piles of Bricks: The Khandas as Burden and Path / by Thanissaro Bhikkhu. Access to Insight (2002)

Hallucinogens: A Forensic Drug Handbook / by Richard R. Laing. Academic Press, London (2003)

Indo-European Language and Culture: An Introduction / by Benjamin W. Fortson. John Wiley & Sons, West Sussex, UK (2011)

Manual for Checking Your Vipassana Kammathana Progress / by Phra Rajsiddhimuni (1964)

Ordaining Reality in Brief: The Shortcut to Your Future / by Joseph E. Donlan. Universal Publishers, Boca Raton (2009)

Practical Insight Meditation: Basic and Progressive Stages / by Mahasi Sayadaw. Buddhist Publication Society, Kandy, Sri Lanka (1971)

Psychology and Alchemy / by C.G. Jung, translated by R.F.C. Hull. Princeton University Press (1968)

Psychomental Complex of the Tungus / by S.M. Shirokogoroff. Kegan Paul, Trench, Trubner & Co., London (1935)

Republic / by Plato, first published in 380 BCE

Root Canal Cover-Up / by George Meinig. Price Pottenger Nutrition Foundation, Lemon Grove, CA (2004)

Shamanism: Archaic Techniques of Ecstasy / by Mircea Eliade. Bollingen, Series LXXVI. Princeton University Press, New Jersey (1972)

Silent Messages / by Albert Mehrabian, Wadsworth, Belmont, CA (1971)

The Archetypes and the Collective Unconscious / by C.G.Jung, translated by R.F.C. Hull. Princeton University Press (1968)

The Beauty of the Primitive: Shamanism and the Western Imagination / by Andrei A. Znamenski. Oxford University Press (2007)

The Book of the Discipline (Vinaya-Pitaka), Vol. 5: Cullavagga (Classic Reprint) / I. B. Horner. Forgotten Books, London, UK (2015)

The Chatta Sanghayana Souvenir Album. Union Buddha Sasana Council Press, Yegu, Rangoon, Burma

The Concept of the Buddha: Its Evolution from Early Buddhism to the Trikaya Theory / by Guang Xing. Routledge, London (2004)

The Connected Discourses of the Buddha: A New Translation of the Samyutta Nikaya / by Bhikkhu Bodhi. Wisdom Publications, Boston (2000)

The Great Book of Hemp / by Rowan Robinson. Park Street Press, Rochester, Vermont (1995)

The Historical Buddha / by H.W. Schumann, English translation by M.O'C. Walshe, 1989. Motilal Banarsidass Publishers, India (2004)

The Life of the Buddha / by Bhikkhu Nanamoli. Buddhist Publication Society, Kandy, Sri Lanka (2015)

The Long Discourses of the Buddha: A Translation of the Digha Nikaya / by Maurice Walshe. Wisdom Publications, Boston (1996)

The Middle Length Discourses of the Buddha: A New Translation of the Majjhima Nikaya / original translation by Bhikkhu Nanamoli; translation edited and revised by Bhikkhu Bodhi. Wisdom Publications, Boston (1995)

The Numerical Discourses of the Buddha: A Translation of the Anguttara Nikaya / by Bhikkhu Bodhi. Wisdom Publications, Boston (2012)

The Progress of Insight: A Treatise on Buddhist Satipatthana Meditation / by Mahasi Sayadaw. Buddhist Publication Society, Kandy, Sri Lanka (1994)

The Scientific Basis of Integrative Medicine, Second Edition / by Leonard A. Wisneski and Lucy Anderson. CRC Press, Boca Raton, Florida (2009)

'The Stages of Life', published in *Modern Man in Search of a Soul* / by C.G. Jung. Harcourt, Brace & World, New York (1933)

The Worn-out Skin: Reflections on the Uraga Sutta / by Nyanaponika Thera. WHEEL 241/242, Buddhist Publication Society, Kandy, Sri Lanka (1977)

Udana: Exclamations / A Translation by Thanissaro Bhikkhu (2012)

Visuddhimagga: *The Path of Purification* / Translated by Bhikkhu Nanamoli. Buddhist Publication Society, Kandy, Sri Lanka (2011)

Wholeness and the Implicate Order / by David Bohm. Routledge, London (1980)

Suggested Reading

Gods and the Universe in Buddhist Perspective / by Francis Story). Buddhist Publication Society, Wheel 180/181 (1972)

The Heart of Buddhist Meditation / by Nyanoponika Thera. Buddhist Publication Society, Kandy, Sri Lanka (2012)

Note from the Author

If you enjoyed this book, please leave a brief review where you bought it.

Thank you for telling your friends.

Printed in Dunstable, United Kingdom

76948176R00153